How Faith Matures

How Faith Matures

C. Ellis Nelson

Westminster/John Knox Press
Louisville, Kentucky

Scripture quotations are from the Revised Standard Version of the Bible, copyrighted 1946, 1952, © 1971, 1973 by the Division of Christian Education of the National Council of the Churches of Christ in the U.S.A., and are used by permission.

Grateful acknowledgment is made to the following for the use of copyrighted material: Augsburg Fortress Publishers for a quotation from *Word and Faith* by Gerhard Ebeling, reprinted by permission from *Word and Faith* by Gerhard Ebeling © Fortress Press; *The Christian Century* for quotations from James A. Sanders, "The Bible as Canon," and William H. Willimon, "Growing up Christian in Greenville," copyright 1981/1980 Christian Century Foundation, reprinted by permission from the Dec. 2, 1981/June 4–11, 1980 issues of *The Christian Century;* ICS Publications for quotations from *The Collected Works of St. Teresa of Avila*, Volume I copyright 1976, Volume II copyright 1980 © translated by Kieran Kavanaugh and Otilio Rodriguez, ICS Publications, 2131 Lincoln Rd. N.E., Washington, D.C. 20002; Morehouse-Barlow Co. for a quotation from *A Faithful Church* by John Westerhoff and O. C. Edwards, copyright © 1981 Morehouse-Barlow Co.; W. W. Norton & Co. for a quotation from *Identity, Youth and Crisis* by Erik H. Erikson; Oxford University Press for a quotation from *A Christian America* by Robert T. Handy; Routledge, Chapman & Hall for a quotation from *Essays in the Sociology of Knowledge*, edited by Mary Douglas and published by Routledge & Kegan Paul; and Tavistock Publications for quotations from *Culture and Self*, edited by Anthony J. Marsella and others.

Book design by Gene Harris

First edition

Published by Westminster/John Knox Press
Louisville, Kentucky

PRINTED IN THE UNITED STATES OF AMERICA

9 8 7 6 5 4 3 2 1

Library of Congress Cataloging-in-Publication Data

Nelson, Carl Ellis, 1916–
    How faith matures / C. Ellis Nelson. — 1st ed.
        p.   cm.
    Bibliography: p.
    Includes indexes.
    ISBN 0-8042-0750-X

    1. Christian education—Philosophy. 2. Faith. 3. Individualism—Religious aspects—Christianity—Controversial literature.
I. Title
BV1464.N45   1989   89-31726
268'.01—dc20   CIP

Dedicated to my wife

Nancy Gribble Nelson

Contents

Preface

The occasion that prompted the writing of this book was the invitation of the faculty of Louisville Presbyterian Theological Seminary to give the Caldwell Lectures in the spring of 1983. I continue to appreciate this expression of confidence. My wife and I enjoyed the return to Louisville, where we had many friends, and to the seminary we served for seven years. We will always appreciate the hospitality of President and Mrs John Mulder, the faculty, and the staff of that fine seminary.

The thesis of the Caldwell Lectures, which is explained in the first chapter, required a fuller treatment than the original five lectures. Various teaching assignments and administrative duties prevented an early completion of the entire project. In retrospect I am rather pleased that publication was delayed. I have been able to rewrite the original lectures as I developed the other chapters. Fortunately, I have been helped by the students at the summer school of the Vancouver School of Theology, San Francisco Theological Seminary, the Graduate Theological Union, and Austin Presbyterian Theological Seminary. During the time I wrote this book I was invited to be the Theologian-in-Residence at the First Presbyterian Church of Houston, Texas. I was greatly helped by the lay people who responded to the ideas in Part Two, A Biblical Model of Experience. I appreciate the interest of the senior minister, John Lancaster, and of Joseph Rand, who was at that time the associate minister in charge of this program.

While working on this manuscript I had the privilege of participating in the National Faculty Seminar, a group made up of Dorothy Bass, Mary C. Boys, Don S. Browning, Walter Brueggemann, John A. Coleman, Bernard Cooke, Thomas F. Green, Karen Lebacqz, Sara P. Little, and Nelle G. Slater. Funded by the Lilly Endowment, and meeting three times a year for four years at Christian Theological Seminary, this group influenced my thinking on every aspect of this project. Because the seminar criticized several chapters of this book, the result is greatly improved; but the seminar members are not to be held accountable for the final product.

I also want to thank Jack Stotts, president of Austin Presbyterian Theological Seminary, for the encouragement and support that he and the seminary provided. The seminary supplied two student assistants, Sharon Sarles and Rose Gander, who checked the references and read the entire manuscript for errors. The seminary also provided one of its most experienced secretaries, Dorothy Andrews, who cheerfully and carefully typed the manuscript several times. The interest and competence of these people in the project has made the work much easier.

The writing would never have been completed if it had not been for the help of my wife, Nancy. She read and corrected every page and, from her vantage point as a church officer and teacher, pointed out what I might do to make the manuscript useful for congregations. Dedicating the book to her is the least I can do to make her contribution public.

C.E.N.

1

Introduction

This is an essay in practical theology. The question it attempts to answer is: How does faith in God become mature? The answer is "through religious experience," yet this answer is so brief and so broad it does not help ordinary Christians who sincerely desire to know how their faith in God can become more meaningful to themselves and more obviously related to the needs of the world in which they live. To be helpful the answer must explore the meaning of religious experience, must provide ways of judging the authenticity of such experience, and must suggest some practical means of relating personal religious experiences to the needs of people. The book is about these matters, with special reference to the way a congregation in its educational activity may focus attention on experience as the arena in which faith matures.

Practical theology may be distinguished from theology. The word "theology" means knowledge of God. It is a careful, systematic, critical examination of biblical, historical, philosophical, and often psychological data concerning beliefs about and ideas of God. Theology, although based on human experience, is several steps removed from experience, for its purpose is to explain general ideas about God and to defend such ideas from contrary positions. A person's formal theology has a bearing on practical affairs or it would have little value, but the two are not the same. Practical theology arises out of and attends to practical situations about which decisions must be made. This means that factors in the practical situation are equal to or sometimes superior to the theological beliefs which are brought to the situation. Perhaps a better term would be "operational" theology, for it concerns the bases on which we conduct our ministry in worship, preaching, education, counseling, and administration. Practical theology is our justification for what we say and do in human situations to which we must respond. How to do this thinking in which theology and situation play a role has recently come to the fore as a matter of considerable importance. There are different methods of or approaches to practical theology, depending on how one interprets our relation to God.[1] One's method of thinking about practical theology cannot easily be differentiated from theology, although each can be examined separately.

Without reviewing all the options, I would like to put the matter in sharper focus by explaining why practical theology cannot be the application of theological statements to life situations. Life situations that are the source of practical problems are seldom clear-cut. There are many factors involved in a human problem, and often we do not know the exact cause or what effect a specific remedial action will have. Take the simple problem of a little boy stealing a toy. There is no difficulty with the general moral commandment not to steal; the problem is why the child did it. Was it because he wanted the toy, wanted attention, was envious of the owner of the toy, was angry at his parents and knew this would be an easy way to strike back at them, was going through some deep psychological experience of need to take control of his environment, or was just testing his parents and peers as to how far he could go without getting caught? Dealing with this event would depend on the motivation for it—which is not easy to discern. If the practical problem involves groups of people in the congregation or community, the application of general truth becomes even more uncertain. The life situation has an authority of its own. It has to be examined and evaluated on its own grounds, just as an ethical or theological statement has to be judged in relation to the human situation out of which it comes.

Although there are many general theological statements in the Bible, they are embedded in narratives about human situations. The two go together. For example, take an important theological statement, such as "God is love" (1 John 4:8). This statement is found in a paragraph about how a congregation is to test whether prophets are teaching truth or error. The paragraph was probably written toward the end of the first century in order to correct the Gnostic idea that God was wisdom or power. If that passage is taken out of context and applied without discrimination to other human situations, then we have a serious problem. On other occasions Jesus—the example of God's love in this passage and in the Gospel of John (3:16)—said he came not to bring peace but a sword (Matt. 10:34–39) and even displayed bitter scorn toward the Pharisees (Matthew 23). We can explain this discrepancy by saying that the Gospel of Matthew was written for an evangelistic purpose, or that Jesus is showing how different his message is from that of certain sects in Judaism. But these or other explanations only prove the point that the situation of the people influences the theological message addressed to them.

Method

The method I use in this book has no special name. Although I believe it is in harmony with the way the Bible is written, it would be pretentious for me to call it a biblical method. It might be labeled a critical social method, because it takes seriously the cultural situation in which people in biblical times had religious experiences. This approach is necessary in order to extract an image of God that can be related to present human situations and thus produce some guidance as to how to look for and discern God's will for the present. Methods are related to beliefs; therefore I will outline my beliefs that led to the methods I have employed.

First, I believe the Bible to be a record of God's revelation to humankind, a record that shows God dealing with humans in the situation in which they lived. One must start with the cultural, social, and political environment of a people in order to obtain a map of their mentality. We are formed by our culture; it provides a worldview, attitudes and values, and—according to our particular case—a self-image.[2] In practical terms we must understand ourselves before we can understand people from another time and place. Self-knowledge must precede historical analysis; but, in fact, a study of history is essential for gaining a perspective on ourselves, so the two go on simultaneously. This topic is the subject of Part One, The Social Construction of Beliefs.

Second, I believe that God has a will for the world and that individuals are agents of that will. The biblical record from the beginning shows God's concern for a certain style of human life, and it also describes human behavior that is not in accord with God's expectation. God's efforts to bring about the kind of human life expected are accomplished when God's will is revealed to individuals for the welfare of the community. Exactly how this happens is not known; most accounts were written long after the event, and the writers were not concerned with an explanation of how it happened. They recorded the encounter with God and what God expected the receiver of the message to say or do. The method here is historical. We rely on biblical scholars to provide us with an analysis of the social conditions and an analysis of the meaning of the text. Until we have a working knowledge of the concrete situation in which the revelation from God took place, we cannot have a clear mental image of God. Unfortunately, Bible scholars do not always agree on their interpretation of the text or on the social situation to which it is addressed. But this is not a new condition. It was true in biblical times and was well illustrated during the life of Jesus. He had to contend with Pharisees, Sadducees, Zealots, and perhaps Essenes, all of whom had a different interpretation of the same sacred writings. Yet Jesus, knowing all these interpretations from his Jewish tradition, spoke with "authority" because he knew God's will for the world (see Matt. 7:28–29). These considerations are the focus of Part Two, A Biblical Model of Experience.

Third, I believe that the image of God we obtain from the Bible and from tradition must be related to specific human situations today. Notice that I said we apply an *image* of God. We cannot apply God to anything, for God is not dependent on human beings and is not under our control. But to stand aside from human events because we believe we are unimportant or are not capable of following God's will is contrary to biblical narratives. The problem is not to find a middle ground between assuming we know exactly what God wants and the other extreme of assuming we cannot do much to change or improve human conditions. Rather, the problem is how to explore the image of God that we have formulated through critical analysis both of our social self and of the human, biblical situation in which the will of God was revealed, and, with the help of that image, to try to understand God's will for contemporary events. The solution to this problem is the topic of Part Three, Experiential Religion, which describes how the congregation, especially in its educational activity, can be directed into a much more deliberate effort to be God's agent for God's will in the world.

Life Situations

Although I have separated the matter into three parts for discussion purposes, it is not easily separated in actual life situations. As indicated earlier, practical theology is our effort to respond to real-life situations, times when we must make a decision or must take action in some way. Both elements are significant. The life situation has a configuration of facts and forces all its own, which will never be repeated in exactly the same way. Rules and principles can be extracted from life situations; when applied to new situations, however, those rules often have to be interpreted or adjusted to fit. The need for decision or action distinguishes a life situation from all other situations in which we can simply voice an opinion or assume a posture according to what we think is appropriate. A decision or action puts something into motion to change or modify the situation in some way. Thus a decision demonstrates what we believe to be true and for which we are accountable. It is also an indication of what we think our corporate life ought to be like, since decisions always move life in one direction or another.

The only way we can understand how all three parts of this analysis fit together is to be involved in an event that forces us to make decisions we believe are in harmony with God's will. This requires congregational action in some form, for Christian beliefs are communicated through—and given practical meaning in—congregations. Individuals, of course, are the actors in life situations, but individual actions make no sense except as they relate to a drama in which there is a conflict of opinion about what ought to be done. For this reason, practical theology always starts with present life situations—that is what makes it practical. This does not mean, however, that the Bible is in a secondary position, it only means that the present situation is the place in which we show the meaning of our faith in God.

The logic of this approach to practical theology would lead us to conclude that we could deal only with events taking place in congregations. This would be a case-study method in which we examine one event after another to understand the way ideas and procedures actually work in a congregation. This approach has much to commend itself to us because it takes the present situation with utmost seriousness.

The Church of the Covenant

Fortunately, we have the story of a congregation that recently went through an experience which combined the three areas discussed in this book. The Church of the Covenant is the false name of a real Presbyterian congregation of about a thousand members in a town in Ohio. In 1984 this congregation, by a rather close margin, voted to become a "sanctuary" for political refugees from Central America. This act caused considerable surprise to the community and to the news media. The National Broadcasting Company did a television report, and several national news magazines reported on and reflected about this unusual situation. How could a conservative white middle-class congregation in mid-America vote to disobey the law?

While the Church of the Covenant was trying to decide about its response to political refugees from Central America, I was part of a national seminar of professors meeting regularly to discuss theology, ethics, and education. We became interested in how the elements of belief, tradition, social setting, ethnic sensitivity, education, leadership, and church government were involved when a congregation was faced with a significant decision. When we learned of the Church of the Covenant, we asked to study its situation during the thirteen months the sanctuary issue was before its members. We consulted all the official records, spent a full day in discussion with the ministers and lay leaders, and examined the reports of one of our representatives, who spent many days in the community. The report of the congregation during those thirteen months shows how intertwined all three areas are. The members' knowledge of themselves as white middle-class Protestants living in a stream of tradition that honors freedom (Part One) was in constant interaction with their knowledge of the Bible and a concern to do what God would have them to do under the circumstances (Part Two). The lay leader who started them on the road to becoming a sanctuary church used the story of the good Samaritan at an officers' retreat to set the stage for their thinking about responsibility (Part Two). All the weighing of evidence was done in the congregation, where the issue was discussed over a period of months in an adult class, in the official board, and later at the annual meeting of the congregation (Part Three). The "reality" in all of this was the individuals, their interpretation of themselves as Christians, the ministers and lay leaders with their sense of responsibility for refugees, and the congregation with its history and power to do what individuals could not do by themselves.

From our study of the Church of the Covenant we saw how an issue was raised and nourished, how the forces of American government policy clashed with a certain interpretation of the biblical record, how the Presbyterian governance in a congregation provided an orderly way for an official decision, and how individuals responded when they were required to speak and vote their convictions about what ought to be done in the name of Christ. A narrative account of the church's thirteen months of consideration has been published, along with a series of essays about different aspects of the story. Many unexpected decisions resulted when the reality of decision making forced people to search their souls and the scriptures for the correct response. For example, one leader had constantly opposed the idea of being a sanctuary church because it meant breaking the law, but when the refugees arrived he was the first person to step forward and offer them a job. An older man, greatly admired and of very conservative political opinions, rose up during the congregational meeting and supported the idea of sanctuary because the refugees were being politically oppressed. Some people quietly left the church, and a large number stayed away from the meeting during which the decision was made.[3]

The Use of Principles

A person who reads the account of the Church of the Covenant or who goes through a similar experience can appreciate the importance and limitations of such a case. The importance is the understanding we gain when we see how results evolve in a congregation over a period of time. A congregation, being a body of people in a particular time and place, with constant interaction among the members and their religious tradition, is under the compulsion of making a decision that will affect personal and church life. This is a complex matter, difficult to understand. In the case study we can see what motivates people, how they interpret the Bible, when their interpretation may cause them to be criticized by people they respect, how ministers and lay leaders function in conflict situations, which people in the congregation have influence and why, and the extent to which the congregation can rise above its social setting when stimulated to act according to religious beliefs.

From the discussion above, one can see how decision making about ongoing experience relates to an individual's faith. Although no one can be precise about the quality or strength of faith in another person, some of the people in the Church of the Covenant testified that the experience greatly strengthened their faith, others avoided the issue, and some people refused to let it open their faith to reexamination. One college student, who attended the annual meeting when the vote was taken, expressed astonishment at the congregation's show of interest in human need. Exactly what effect that observation will have on that student's understanding of Christianity in the future is unknown.

Cases are also wonderful for educational purposes, for they suggest significant "What if?" questions. What if the senior minister had preached on sanctuary during the thirteen months the issue was under consideration? (He did not.) Would it have changed the outcome? What if men had been involved in the small group that raised the issue in the congregation? (Two women were responsible.) Would the issue have changed its character? What if the congregation had not been at the same time deciding to relocate its church building? (The relocation plan created a conflict of opinion.) Did two major decisions occurring at the same time create too much anxiety?

Cases, however, have serious limitations for this study of how faith matures through experience. One limitation is our inability to apply one case to another. The case of the Church of the Covenant cannot be applied in a direct way even to itself, now that the sanctuary episode is over, for the congregation is not exactly the same. The ministers have left, some members have withdrawn, and everyone in the congregation now has a history of participation or nonparticipation and a voting record to explain. We certainly cannot apply this case to another congregation in a direct way, for leaders in other congregations would immediately point out that they are in a different location, are of a different size or denomination, and have a different understanding of their role in social issues.

What we can get from cases to help us in practical theology is a set of general principles that have to be interpreted to fit other cases. In the case of the Church of the Covenant, for example, we see that if the status quo of a congregation is going to be challenged, it will probably come from a small group of people with strong convictions who are willing to work and suffer for what they believe. Another principle that emerged is the need for a large group of adults to understand the issue on which a decision was to be made and an extended period of time in which to study the matter. These and other generalizations are transferable to other congregations.

In one sense, the Bible is mainly about life situations. What was revealed by God for those situations was carried along in the community of those who had faith in God. This is why it is difficult to systematize biblical teachings. What we can generalize from the Exodus era when nation-building was the paramount concern is not the same as what we can generalize from the book of Acts or from Paul's letters when the objective was the separation of the church from Jewish tradition. This condition, however, is what gives the Bible its power. The biblical account is usually about God's desire for a rather specific situation. Jesus' teachings in the Gospels referred to specific conditions that were well known, and his actions were about particular evils, such as the temple merchants' using religion for personal gain (Matt. 21:12–13). We, however, are able to extract general principles from the Bible, and these are the affirmations that we can relate to our situations today.

The process of relating general principles to the present is an extremely complex task that requires much study and discussion. An adult responsibility, it must be carried on over a period of time by people who share a common faith in God. It is largely educational in nature, because it involves thoughtful, prayerful, faithful adults who are seriously trying to find the will of God for their present problems. To that end they study their situation, the Bible, and their responsibilities in the area in which they have the opportunity to serve the Lord.

It is my hope that this book will be helpful to ministers, Christian educators, lay leaders, church school teachers, administrators, and parents who are directly involved in activities to help believers become more mature in their faith.

Thesis

In summary, a person's faith matures when life experiences are interpreted in the light of the Christian tradition in order to understand and do the will of God amid ongoing events in which that person is involved. Because a congregation is part of the body of Christ, it is the place where individuals receive guidance, as they work out the meaning of their experiences, and support as they attempt to follow the leading of God's Spirit.

PART ONE

The Social Construction of Beliefs

We must first examine the social and historical factors that have shaped our religious outlook. Before we can begin to compare our life situation with that through which the biblical revelation has come, we need to become conscious of what we believe and why we believe it. A thorough analysis would require that we understand our history, including our government and economic condition, the social class in which we live and work, the ideas about life, death, and destiny that form our minds, and the congregation in which we worship and serve. We cannot, however, understand how these elements constructed our beliefs without comparison to the biblical record, and to life in other times and places, and in contrast to people who have a different religious outlook. This means a process of present-to-past or of present-to-others-not-like-ourselves going on all the time. We struggle to understand what we believe and why.

Since a thorough analysis is beyond the scope of this book, Part One explores only the secular individualism that dominates our outlook and illustrates how society constructs our beliefs (chapter 2). This is followed by a discussion, in chapter 3, of how various elements from society—including religion—permeate our being so that our self, unless critically examined, will reflect what it has absorbed. The process of absorption and evaluation goes on continuously in the community of believers, resulting sometimes in conflicting beliefs, but the biblical record affirms that God's will can be discerned beyond such conflicts.

2

Our Age
of Secular Individualism

The seventeenth century is often called the Age of Reason because scientists during that century established reason as an independent method of studying our physical universe. In the eighteenth century philosophers began to think of the social, political, and moral implications of the discoveries and ideas of the previous centuries. The eighteenth-century Enlightenment started afresh and set forth new conceptions of what human life was and could be. Its major ideas were (1) the doctrine of progress—the notion that humankind was developing and improving; (2) the autonomy of the individual; (3) the necessity of a social order producing justice for all; (4) the preeminence of reason; and (5) the rights of individuals to happiness.

The United States came into being as a nation when the ideas of the Enlightenment were influencing statesmen and intellectual leaders throughout Western Europe. Thomas Jefferson, deeply influenced by the Enlightenment, incorporated its radical individualism in the brief philosophical section of the Declaration of Independence (1776). The part so often quoted reads: "We hold these Truths to be self-evident, that all Men are created equal, that they are endowed by their Creator with certain unalienable Rights, that among these are Life, Liberty, and the Pursuit of Happiness." The Declaration goes on to say that governments are formed by people in order to secure these "Rights." If a government "becomes destructive of these Ends," the people have a "Right" to abolish it and institute a new government.

Individual rights were so precious to the framers of the Constitution that they insisted the document be amended as soon as it was ratified in order that a list of specific individual rights be protected. Known as the Bill of Rights (1791), the list includes freedom of speech, press, assembly, and petition, freedom from unwarranted search and seizure, trial by jury, and many other particular rights that cannot be taken away by the government.

These documents give almost absolute protection to the individual. Because these were political documents written to support a revolution, they may have exaggerated the scope of individual rights. Certainly the writers did not apply them to all people at that time: some, like Thomas Jefferson, owned slaves; Indians were driven off their land; women were not allowed to vote. Later these rights were extended to all citizens, including slaves, but it took a civil war to accomplish that purpose. Today our political and social life is almost obsessed with individual rights. The Supreme Court is flooded with cases appealing to the Bill of Rights to legitimize almost any behavior that does not physically harm other people.[1]

Individualism Compounded

These brief comments about some of the ideas that produced the political order of the United States illustrate how social values become hardened into law. In times of revolution ideas and ideals prevail, and if successful they shape a government. In times of tranquillity the government shapes the people through the law courts, public schools, mass media, and the sheer weight of wide acceptance of values that formed the laws in the first place. The close connection between the radical individualism in the Constitution and the almost universal agreement about the rights of the individuals is enough to establish American culture as having a high regard for individuals and allowing them to "pursue happiness." But there are four other factors in American history that reinforce, supplement, or enhance the value given to individuals: (1) science, (2) immigration, (3) the expanding western frontier, and (4) education.

The scientific development of the seventeenth century that prompted the Enlightenment has continued on its relentless way, making more and more discoveries in every field of human knowledge. Two remarkable characteristics of science are its relative independence from history and from society. A scientist does not need to know the history of science to function as a scientist; scientists need to know only what has been tried in recent times. They often discount earlier attempts to solve problems because new knowledge has changed important factors in previous experiments. Also, many scientists are not concerned about society or the effects of their work on society. The lure of learning and the thrill of discovery overcome any hesitation about the results of their work. When the first atomic bomb was exploded on July 16, 1945, for example, scientists were stationed at a distance to observe this historic event. J. Robert Oppenheimer, who had directed the development of the atomic bomb, was asked if the explosion would set off a chain reaction and thus engulf the whole world. He was unable to give assurance that such a chain reaction would not occur!

Although nowadays a team of scientists is usually formed to work on problems, the mental image remains of one person finally solving a puzzle: Jonas Salk finding a vaccine against polio, Albert Einstein developing the theory of special relativity, James Watson and Francis H. C. Crick producing an analysis of the DNA molecule.

The United States is a nation of immigrants. Early colonists, although from different Western European countries and with different religions, were white Protestants. This first wave of immigrants formed the ideals of the nation, gave it stability, and shaped its legal and educational institutions. The next wave of people to come to this country was the slaves. By 1776 there were half a million, and by 1860 the number had increased to about 3 million. The population of the United States in 1860 was slightly under 32 million people, so one out of every ten was a person who had been uprooted from his or her culture and thrust into a new one. The third major population wave came from central and southern Europe between 1850 and 1930. During that time about 37 million people left the home of their birth to settle in the United States.[2] The flow of immigrants continued, with about 9 million people coming into the United States from 1941 to 1975: Jews after World War II, Vietnamese in the 1970s, Cubans after the rise of Fidel Castro, and a long history of Latin Americans crossing the Rio Grande with or without proper documents.

Except for the slaves, all these immigrants came to the United States because they wanted something they did not have at home. When we stop for a few minutes to consider how precious are our birthplace and the native language in which we learned to express our thoughts and wishes, it is something of a psychological miracle that people would uproot themselves and go to a foreign country with a different language and only the possibility of a better future.

People who immigrate have a special mentality. Although they may have followed relatives and friends, they had to make a decision to leave a psychologically secure situation for an uncertain future. When they arrived in the new country, they had to learn a new language, geography, government, and, above all, how to get a job in an alien environment. These decisions, activities, and new learning require enormous self-confidence. Immigrant mentality emphasizes the idea of a "new beginning." It glorifies individual accomplishments and has a high regard for individuals who take charge of their own lives. It is a situation in which one thing reinforces the other: the political documents—originally written against tyranny—become an independent statement of the rights of individuals, and this situation of political freedom attracts many people to America who in turn support the political documents in order to have individual freedoms.

An overview of American individualism would not be complete without at least the recognition of how the frontier situation emphasized individual initiative. It is easy to forget the frontier now that the United States is surveyed and settled. However, from the time of the first colonists in Virginia in 1607 until about the time of the entrance of Arizona as a state in 1912, there was a western frontier to which people could go. The ever-expanding West offered jobs, land, and the opportunity to dig a mine, build a lumber mill, or engage in other entrepreneurial activities. Several western states offered free land to families who would move in and settle down. Some historians have judged this frontier situation to be a decisive factor in the makeup of American character.[3] The strong sense of individual accomplishment against hardship was reflected in the World War II slogan of the Seabees: "The difficult we do at once; the impossible takes a little longer." The legacy of strong-willed individuals up against barriers to a better life has become so deeply ingrained in our thinking that we tend to state our worthwhile objectives as a "war" against crime, drugs, poverty, or pollution; such language resonates with our deepest feelings about how to conduct our life.

Education should also be noted as an important factor in creating American individualism. For immigrants, for members of the poorer classes, or for racial groups, free education is the way to advancement. Public schools and the egalitarian idea of society make it possible for almost anyone to realize his or her ambitions. As society in the United States became more technical, education provided more access to power, position, and wealth. Although some people attain their status by inheritance, most people obtain recognition by what they do with their education. Education is therefore a valuable personal asset; it can free individuals from a lower class or from family control. Thus education has been a major support for the kind of individualism that has emerged in the United States.

Secularization and Religion

American individualism has special characteristics because of its political base in revolutionary documents that became law, the long-term compounding effect of science, the surge of immigration, and the ever-expanding western frontier, all of which were augmented by an educational system that rewarded individuals. As a young nation preoccupied with securing its land and establishing a social order by founding and developing institutions, the United States may have been less influenced during the eighteenth century by the trend toward a secular interpretation of life than other Western nations shaped by Christianity and the Enlightenment. However, by the end of World

War I, the United States was in the front rank of industrialized nations and moved rapidly to the fore in scientific research. The explosion of the first atomic bomb in 1945 and a visit to the moon in 1969 are but two achievements in many scientific and technical areas in which the United States has made extraordinary gains during the second half of the twentieth century. During this time secularizing influences have blended with the long-term movement toward individualization to produce a special mental outlook that has formed our character and influenced our religion.

On the surface, the idea of the secular means just what the dictionary says: pertaining to the worldly or temporal rather than the spiritual or eternal.[4] A secular person defers to the facts and forces of the world rather than referring to or expecting guidance and help from a sacred realm. By definition the secular is posed against the sacred—or, in ordinary terms, religion. Problems emerge when the secular is assumed to be a movement—secularism—that will someday make religion obsolete. This judgment was made by such intellectuals of the Enlightenment as Sigmund Freud and Karl Marx. Freud considered religion an "illusion," not just a mistake. To him illusions were powerful human desires that people wanted fulfilled. Religious needs come from one's childhood, he asserted, and religious beliefs represent ways of meeting those needs. Thus the notion of God as a cosmic father taking care of believers is merely a childhood need expressed in religious terms. Religion, to Freud, was a hindrance to becoming a mature person. Rooted entirely in the secular, he wanted a society built on an application of reason to the problems of life.[5] Marx, likewise a secular person, believed that religion stood in the way of achieving a just social order.[6] Others have accepted the Enlightenment view that social conditions can become more just and personal life more fulfilling through the use of reason than through faith in God.[7]

There are so many problems with this Enlightenment view of secularization that the term has almost lost meaning among social scientists who have carefully considered the matter.[8] The following four positions, held by some of our best scholars on this matter, show how the term "secularization" has become inadequate for describing the relation of the seen to an unseen world.

1. Some make the case that biblical religion started the secular process by relating religion to nature and to human affairs. Part of the instruction to the first humans was to "subdue" the earth and to have "dominion over the fish of the sea and over the birds of the air and over every living thing that moves upon the earth" (Gen. 1:28).[9] Talcott Parsons takes this general point of view by affirming that our modern industrial society has been greatly influenced by Christianity. He contends that religion has not been secularized but rather has been effective in bringing ethics to bear on the structure of society. The

Reformation, especially in its Calvinistic version, emphasized individual responsibility to "Christianize" the social order; it charged congregations with the task of monitoring individuals' moral behavior and maintaining a surveillance of local governments and businesses. As these ideas became dominant in the past 450 years, Parsons notes, democracy in various forms has emerged as the preferred political order, egalitarianism has become important in social relations, and individual responsibility for one's own life has become the norm.[10]

2. Others make the case that because religion is so much a part of human life, secularization may have affected the formal aspects of religion, such as church attendance, but not the human quest for the sacred, which lies beyond reason. Andrew M. Greeley has popularized the notion that humankind has fundamental religious needs that have not changed over time. Religion, to Greeley, provides a sense of belonging, a system of meaning for the problems and paradoxes of life, and, through worship, a feeling of being at one with the unseen world. Although changes are constantly taking place in the relation between culture and religion, secularization as understood in the Enlightenment is simply an illustration of a particular set of circumstances, not a new process that will render religion useless.[11]

In reviewing the relation of religion to the social sciences during the past 150 years, Robert N. Bellah concludes that the secularization theory is wrong: "It is my feeling that religion, instead of becoming increasingly peripheral and vestigial, is again moving into the center of our cultural preoccupations." He predicts that as social scientists attempt to grasp more of the total life of human beings they will more clearly see the role of religion in life. Contrariwise, as religious leaders seek help in understanding the modern world, they will accept more of what the social scientists have to offer. The result will be not a new religion or a new synthesis of knowledge but a "reintegration of our culture, a new possibility of the unity of consciousness."[12] From different perspectives these writers seem to agree that religion offers an interpretation of life that is cogent on its own terms and comprehensive enough to include the use of reason and science as developed during the Enlightenment.

3. Other students of the relation of society to religion are not confident that the secularization theory is a useful way to understand the relationship. Much depends on the interpretation of religion and society and—above all—on the presuppositions one brings to the task of understanding the relationship. Mary Douglas, for example, brings a profound skepticism about the ability to predict exactly what will happen in the dynamic interaction of society and religion. Many of the situations we see today—such as the revival of traditional religion, the way traditional religion in Poland and South America has inspired

political revolt, the resurgence of Islam and its expansion in Africa—
were unexpected.

Douglas also criticizes the subliminal assumptions many scholars
bring to their analysis. For example, she questions the assumption that
religion is good for human life: much religion, she writes, is "emotionally restrictive, bigoted, fanatical, or psychotic." She questions the
widely accepted notion that modern people are different from people
in tribal cultures or in previous historical eras. There are some rather
dramatic differences in the way modern people live in comparison to
illiterate people, but does that take the awe and mystery out of life? If
religion is related to awe and mystery, then moderns are no further
along than ancient people were. We may know more at present about
the physical universe, but each discovery just opens up more questions
and provides no answers about why there is a world or where the
universe is destined to go. Again, some scholars unwittingly assume
that our modern times are the norm by which other cultures ought to
be judged, without realizing that we too are conditioned by the nature
of the society in which we live.

Douglas argues against the thesis that secularization has "quenched
the sources of religious feeling and undermined religious authority."
She does not believe that the effects of science, the modern individual's freedom of choice, the depersonalizing quality of bureaucracy, or
an increased distance from nature has any *proven* relation to religion.
In clearing this ground she is in somewhat the same position as those
who believe secularization has not had a significant effect on religion.
However, as a social scientist she does not affirm any religious beliefs
but asks that researchers pay careful attention to the exact nature of
pre-modern people before they make comparisons. Her work would
lead one to believe that the issue is not really whether secularization
has a negative effect on religion but what forms of religion are helpful
for the welfare of society.[13]

4. Another group of social scientists accepts the rationalizing of
modern life and recognizes that religion, especially in its institutional
form, is often closely related to social class interest. Religion on these
terms can be studied and analyzed, as can any other human endeavor,
in relation to the culture in which it exists. This group, however, does
not accept the idea that human beings are like other forms of life, those
which live without any special meaning. Rather, they are inclined to the
view that religion is rooted in self-consciousness. Persons can transcend themselves, thus creating a religious perspective that is greater
and more important than the self's own concerns.

Peter Berger starts his search for the supernatural with human life.
He contends that an anthropological approach will reveal *signals of
transcendence* (Berger's emphasis). Such signals include, first, the
human propensity for order. This trait is not just a need for social

regulation in order to provide food, shelter, and safety more efficiently; it is an effort to create a psychology of reassurance. Berger
compares this condition of reassurance to a mother comforting a child.
Second, play is considered a signal of transcendence because it takes
place in a casual relation to time and has no obvious utilitarian outcome. It helps people get outside themselves and obtain a perspective
on their more serious obligations. Third, hope is a human characteristic that challenges a person's imagination about what *ought to be* in
contrast to what *is.* Fourth, outrage against evil is another common
human trait that arouses people from their ordinary existence. There
are some things so hideous that almost everyone says they should not
be allowed. Fifth, humor is a spontaneous, unpremeditated response
when we see the tragic, the incongruous, or the limitations of life.[14]

Thomas Luckmann, who shares some of Berger's opinions, judges
that organized religion in Western industrial nations is in decline.
Secularization has moved the influence of churches to the margin of
modern life. Luckmann notes, however, that this is not the case in the
United States, where church membership is high and participation is
vigorous. He accounts for this situation by saying that religion in
America has been secularized and therefore privatized: that is, American religion supports secular values of success, individual achievement, and capitalism as an economic system. This does not mean that
religion is slowly being abandoned. On the contrary, Luckmann believes that religion is rooted in "the individual human potential for
transcendence." People have transcended their biological nature and
in groups have constructed meaning for life and death. This is a "religious" activity, and it will always be a part of human activity. From this
common experience various particular religions have arisen and have
become a part of the history of the people.[15]

Secularized Religion

The above discussion of secularization and religion was taken from
the work of sociologists and anthropologists as they responded to the
Enlightenment view that reason, when applied to human life, would
cause religion to wither away. These responses show little support for
that view today except from those who are already predisposed to
atheism. This does not imply, however, that Christianity or any other
religion is sheltered from the effects of secularization. In fact, the
writers assume that secularization has made modern life indifferent to
religion. They look for the roots of religion in human life in order to
explain why religion has not withered away. Although this is an important and interesting project, it is not my reason for using their analysis.
Rather, I want to elaborate their notion that religion has been changed
by modernity.

The idea of religion's becoming secular is difficult to grasp. By definition religion refers to God or to what one considers sacred. How then can it be secular? The answer seems to be that American churches, with some exceptions, have over the past few centuries become primarily the mediators of cultural values. They did so partly as a response to the new social conditions produced by industrialization in the nineteenth century and the rapid development of science and technology in the twentieth century. And they did so partly because of historical events. Alasdair MacIntyre believes that industrialization with its attending conditions has produced secularization. He has documented the long-term decline in church attendance in England to show how a secular society loses interest in religion. This is a general condition in all Western European nations. Why then, in America, is interest in religion so high—as shown by church attendance and by Gallup poll reports that almost all Americans believe in God? The answer, according to MacIntyre, is that "American religion has survived an industrial society only at the cost of itself becoming secular."[16]

By "becoming secular" MacIntyre means that the church has served several useful purposes from the days of the first colonists up to modern times, helping immigrants accommodate themselves to a new situation. This became more important during the period of great immigration. Immigrants needed a place where they could speak and act according to their ethnic heritage while they were being assimilated into a society with a different language and customs. The churches filled that need, and the social habit of church attendance became strongly established. Also, egalitarianism as an ideal characteristic of human associations was affirmed early in American history, partly in response to the rigid class distinctions the colonists knew in Europe and partly in response to Christian beliefs about equality before God. The ideal that all people possess equal rank was deeply rooted in people's minds and in our political documents before the industrial revolution came to America. Thus a hardening of class distinctions between workers, owners, and professional people did not take place.

Immigrants were attracted, in part, by the promise of an egalitarian society. When they arrived, they supported that ideal in order to achieve. Increasingly during the twentieth century, black citizens challenged the notion of "separate but equal," which was both the legal justification for separate public schools and the idea that justified segregation in society. Appealing to the Declaration of Independence and the Bill of Rights, blacks in the 1950s broke public school segregation through Supreme Court decisions. In the 1960s they changed social segregation through passive resistance. Complete integration has not yet been achieved; but the media, mass entertainment, public education (including higher education), and political offices are now staffed by a large number of black people. This emergence of blacks from their second-class status and the current struggle of ethnic groups for proper respect is based on an appeal to egalitarian values.

Churches were deeply involved in helping immigrants to understand America and to gain their rights. Black churches are still a major— perhaps the only—place where black people are at home with themselves, and the place where they have organized to gain their civil rights. One could interpret this historical situation as a normal way for the church to serve its members. The church, by this interpretation, was secular only in the sense that it related to the social conditions of its time. I judge, however, that in performing this role for its members the church became more and more an organization for providing a religious rationale for American cultural values. Such a judgment can be illustrated, not proved. Before the Civil War some churches and religious groups such as the Quakers opposed slavery and worked diligently to free the slaves; but almost all southern churches supported the custom, and many northern churches provided passive support by their neutrality. Seldom in the entire history of the United States have churches espoused the rights of Native Americans. In recent years, though, Native American churches have begun to support the civil rights of their members, thus illustrating again the phenomenon of a church's effectiveness when it becomes a champion of cultural values. If the churches succeed in helping Native Americans— as for almost two hundred years they have helped scores of immigrant groups and, most recently, black people—it subtly but effectively fixes the mission of the church as an organization for enabling individuals to achieve their rights.

Reason and Religion

The Enlightenment changed the situation of religion in the Western world. Before the eighteenth century most Western European nations had an established religion; indeed, most of the American Colonies had an official religion. This does not mean that all people were believers or that moral standards were higher than today. It does mean that a religious atmosphere surrounded the daily activities of the community and that a religious explanation of life, death, and destiny was offered through the churches, law courts, schools, and other social institutions. As the ideas of the Enlightenment spread to various nations, the exact form in which secularization took place differed according to the hospitality of the established religion, the particular intellectual leaders who took up the cause, the temperament of the people for change, the nature of the school system, and other historical facts. In America secularization proceeded slowly. A new country, it had many problems to be solved in a democratic political structure, the first of its kind in history. Moreover, the physical isolation of America from Europe made exchange of scientists and other intellectuals difficult. It was not until after the Civil War that Americans began to go to Europe for postgraduate education. And Americans did not have a research university founded on the German model until Johns Hopkins University was established in 1876.

My comments thus far seem to suggest that the Enlightenment was triggered mainly by science, with resulting changes in culture due to industrialization. But philosophers were deeply involved also, and every aspect of human life was scrutinized from a rational perspective. Probably the most disturbing intellectual development was the critical analysis of history and historical documents, including the Bible. Gerhard Ebeling illustrates the problem by pointing out that if a seventeenth-century theological faculty were to consider the matter of "Man and the Cosmos," they would assemble the timeless truth about both from historical documents where truth could only be unchanging truth. He continues, "Never in the whole history of theology up to modern times was there such a thing as taking a historical view of a theological problem."[17]

Now, most all theologians take the historical view. This means, in part, that there is little consensus about the meaning of history. There are only facts that can be connected with an interpretive story. And the documents we have are so rooted in time and place that they cannot be used until the context in which they were written is analyzed. Needless to say, this rational approach to history and documents, when applied to Bible study, drastically altered the authority of the Bible and opened up endless speculation about every one of its books. Moreover, the God of the Bible, rather than being accepted, rejected, or ignored as in former times, was now open to interpretation according to whatever interest the interpreter had in mind. When the evolutionary theory of history was strong in America, for example, it was applied to the Bible and—in the case of Harry Emerson Fosdick—was popularized to show that God was a tribal deity before becoming universalized and Christianized.[18] More recently, a Marxist interpretation of history has been applied to the early books of the Bible to show that the promised land was not invaded by Israelites under Moses, as described in the book of Exodus, but was conquered by a peasants' revolt seeking economic justice.[19]

It may be helpful to get a sense of how this particular matter was played out in one denomination. Dr. Charles A. Briggs went to Germany in 1866 for advanced study. When he returned, he began a long teaching career at Union Theological Seminary in New York. In his inaugural address of 1876 he announced his desire to use higher critical methods of Bible study. He did so to such an extent in his teaching and writing that he has been judged to be the most determined scholar of his generation to bring about a critical study of the Bible.[20] Briggs was so effective in this regard that he was charged with heresy by the Presbyterian church in which he was a minister. In 1893 he defended himself before the Presbytery of New York with a careful analysis of each charge, including his belief that the second half of the book of Isaiah was not written by the author of the first half.[21] Presbyterians in the latter part of the nineteenth century were typical of members of other major denominations—they had not been exposed to or influenced by the use of critical reason in Bible studies. However, the critical method of Bible study spread throughout the United States. By the 1920s these views were taught or discussed in all major universities and divinity schools. And by the 1950s, when the *Interpreter's Bible Commentary* was published, the critical method was accepted and widely used. Moreover, the Presbyterians in their *Faith and Life* church school curriculum published in the early 1950s used critical methods of Bible study, including the Second Isaiah thesis for which Briggs was tried.

The purpose of describing these soundings fifty years apart is not to suggest that Bible study became secular. The Methodist commentary and the Presbyterian publications just noted are designed to encourage faith. They do not challenge basic Christian beliefs. What we note from the two soundings is the way the critical study of the Bible has been accepted. Today even lay people who do not consult commentaries have an informal understanding of the historical method. They assume that polygamy in the Old Testament was related to social conditions of that time and that slavery as practiced in biblical times is unacceptable to us. The issue is how far one can go in using one's reason to assess books in the Bible without letting reason judge God. Or, now that reason has relativized history by providing several cogent interpretations of the past, how does one find the true interpretation? This question is at the center of our inquiry, and answers will be proposed in subsequent chapters.[22]

Secularized Education

Although enough has been written to indicate why we have secular individualism in America, there is another development in the social-political realm that greatly influenced the present secularity. It is the political doctrine of freedom of religion, which resulted in removing religion from public schools.

The First Amendment to the Constitution reads in part, "Congress shall make no law respecting an establishment of religion, or prohibiting the free exercise thereof." This amendment was the solution to a vexing problem. The political leaders of that time were reacting to several conditions, one of which was their knowledge of the abuse or misuse of political power by European state churches. Our political leaders wanted freedom to choose their religion; hence the language of the amendment. The other condition was political. Almost all the original states had, at their beginning, an established religion. Since these religions were different, there was little possibility of an agreement for any one of their religions to become a national religion. Making the nation neutral in regard to religion solved those problems. The religious environment at that time was a Protestant Christianity broad enough to encompass deism on one side and theism on the other. Christians' disagreements were within this broad Protestantism, and religion was assumed to be good for the nation by providing a common moral basis for law and society. George Washington's inaugural addresses clearly make this point. Thomas Jefferson, one of the most liberal of the founders, wanted religion taught in the University of Virginia, which he founded. His concern for religion and morals may be better illustrated during his presidency: in 1803, while "overwhelmed with other business" (the Louisiana Purchase, for example), he edited the Gospel accounts of the life of Jesus for the Indians because they did not have the teachings of Jesus in their culture. To Jefferson, morals came from religion, and morals were absolutely necessary for the new democracy to endure.[23]

Note the meaning of the separation of church and state two hundred years later. America is now a leading industrial nation, a superpower in the world, and the home of several hundred different religious groups. These developments have reinforced the neutrality of the state. Today, religious affiliation cannot be a condition of employment or of educational opportunity in public schools. In fact, the principle of an individual's civil rights to employment regardless of religious beliefs was, until recently, so strongly held that even church-sponsored day schools were expected to select teachers without regard to their religious beliefs. The Supreme Court has now ruled that church-sponsored day schools are an exception and have the right to select teachers with the religious beliefs that the schools want taught. And who could imagine any recent president of the United States "overwhelmed with other business" yet taking time from affairs of state to prepare a book on the life of Jesus because he was convinced a segment of the population did not have proper instruction in morals?

Public Schools

The secular state, neutral toward religion, may be one of the finest developments in government. Churches are free to make a case for their beliefs without fear of or favor from civil power. The civil authorities are free from the rival claims of religious groups. But the price America paid for this arrangement is public education without religion.

The price was probably not considered when the First Amendment was ratified. At that time free public schools hardly existed. The schools were sponsored by churches, teachers, or towns; with few exceptions, religion was taught as truth about life. Bible reading, prayers, and, in most cases, worship were part of the daily routine. However, when the states began to make laws requiring towns to provide free public schools, the issue of teaching religion came to the fore. Horace Mann, secretary to the newly established Massachusetts State Board of Education (1837), was one of the most influential leaders of the public or common school movement. Through his editorials in the *Common School Journal,* he shared ideas and considerable enthusiasm for a state system of schools. He took the separation of church and state in public education seriously by doing all he could to eliminate the influence of churches or the teaching of sectarian beliefs. Furthermore, he supported the teaching of a broad Protestant religion and morals in the schools and strongly urged churches to teach their doctrines in the Sunday schools, which were expanding rapidly at that time. However, religion did not disappear from the public schools. McGuffey's *Readers,* first published in 1836, were theological in nature, containing prayers, moral lessons, and some selections from the Bible. From 1836 to 1850, 7 million copies of McGuffey's *Readers* were sold, and by 1890 the book was the basic reader in thirty-seven states.An estimated 120 million copies were sold from 1836 to 1920. Considering the population of the United States during that time, it is probably correct to call McGuffey the "schoolmaster of the nation."[24]

Opening the public school day with prayer, reading from the Bible, and Bible instruction began to wane during the early part of the twentieth century. During that time sporadic efforts were made by Protestant leaders and interested public school officials to find a way to teach religion on an elective basis as a part of the regular school program. These efforts were regularized in Gary, Indiana, in the 1914–15 school year, when students were released early from public school to attend church-sponsored religious instruction. This movement—labeled "week-day church schools"—spread rapidly, indicating the desire of many people to have their children instructed in religion. By this time it was clear to almost everyone that the public schools could not teach religion as a part of their program. From that date until the Supreme Court ruled in the *Abington* v. *Schempp* case (1963) that the reading of the Bible in public schools was unconstitutional because such practice placed the schools in a position of officially practicing religion, there was constant turmoil among religious groups about the proper role of religion in public education. Many administrative arrangements were tried, but all failed the test of the First Amendment. Religious holidays such as Christmas and Easter, if recognized in such a way as to expose children to the beliefs behind the celebration, were the subjects of legal battles. When the Supreme Court ruled in *Engel* v. *Vitale* (1962) that public schools could no longer use prayers to open the school day, all aspects of religion were eliminated from public schools. The schools were completely de-religionized except, as Justice Tom C. Clark wrote in the Schempp case, "Nothing we have said here indicates that such study of the Bible or of religion, when presented objectively as a part of a secular program of education, may not be effected consistently with the First Amendment." Only secular study of religion would be allowed.

The de-religionization of the public schools was completed with the Supreme Court rulings in the early 1960s. But those legal decisions do not adequately reveal the secular nature of the schools. Prayer and Bible reading did not take place in all schools, and even when practiced, they occupied only a few minutes; these elements were more of a recognition of religion than a concern for its value. To get the spirit of the contemporary public school, one would need to analyze the required textbooks on which students are examined. Paul Vitz has done so and has found that there is a consistent bias against religion in many of the social studies textbooks. For example, in twenty-five of the forty major textbooks used for grades one through four, there is no reference to or illustration of American religious activity in any form. In ten high school American history textbooks religion is seldom mentioned, and no explanation of the contribution of religious faith to the health, education, or moral standards of America is presented. In twenty-three readers for grades three through six, there are articles on many subjects, including magic, but none on religion.[25] Now that this bias against religion has been revealed, textbook publishers will probably make some revisions—but only within the guidelines of religion as "a secular program of education."

Higher Education

Higher education in America has responded to the same secularizing influences as the public schools. If we took a sounding of the nature of higher education in America before the Civil War, we would find— especially in the Colonial era—that most colleges were founded by religious groups, as Harvard was in 1638, to educate ministers and civic leaders. The education provided reflected the religion of the sponsoring churches. It was not until after the Civil War that western states began to found and develop universities. This movement was given considerable encouragement by the Morrill Act, passed by Congress in 1862, which provided a grant to each state of 30,000 acres of land for each congressman from that state. The grant was to be used to establish a college in which agricultural and mechanical arts and military science were to be taught, or to establish such departments in an existing university. In 1890 Congress provided annual grants from the federal government to support these land-grant colleges, thus securing a system of large state college or university departments with federal funds.

In contrast to public schools, state universities may teach religion, and private universities have taught it as a special department for a long time. Enrollment in such courses is not large in comparison to the total university enrollment. However, professors of religion have an excellent record of scholarship. Being free of church control and yet challenged by research from other fields, college professors of religion have produced excellent studies of the Bible and have been at the forefront of scholarship in ethics, sociology, religion, philosophy, and related subjects. But departments of religion have had almost no effect on the ethos of the university. It is the judgment of Robert Bellah that "university professors are among the least religious people in American society."[26] Louis Dupré, a professor of religion at Yale, has said that intellectuals no longer argue for atheism, because that position is assumed. Serious and sensitive intellectuals are now trying to find a "humanism beyond atheism."[27] These judgments from professors in two of our finest universities might be properly merged into this general statement: American higher education, especially in its universities, is secular.

Our Religious Situation

The preceding discussion is a broad and sweeping analysis of the particular way secularization has affected American culture, with a special reference to its effects on religion. I have assumed that secularization would not cause religion to wither away, but it has profoundly changed the nature of religion. Religion within American culture is regarded as *Time* magazine treats it: a topic, like sports, for those who are interested, located toward the back of the magazine. American religion has become (1) optional and (2) private.

Optional Nature

The optional nature of religion in American life is not new. Since the early days of the Republic, segments of the population have not identified with any religious group; and some individuals have freely displayed their atheism or agnosticism. But such resistance of a person or group to conform to accepted beliefs was the exception which showed there was a dominant religion at that time. The option was to believe or not believe the prevailing religion in the community. Today the option of what to believe or not to believe is more complex, for there is no dominant religion. From the national culture displayed on television and in the mass media, one is aware of many religions. Popular or well-known people, especially entertainers and actors, often advertise their choice of religion, belief in reincarnation, or whatever has attracted their attention. People without a religious background are tempted to follow suit to obtain whatever advantage is promised. Those with a religious background are in a better position to select a church, but they still have to choose within a denomination the kind of religion that suits their needs. For example, within a thirty-minute drive of where I lived a few years ago, I could select within my Presbyterian denomination a church that was charismatic (speaking in tongues was approved), liberal (it sponsored many social programs, including the county office for nuclear disarmament), conservative (it sponsored missionaries and various evangelistic groups), concerned for homosexuals (one minister was openly gay), conventional (it followed the denominational program), racial (mainly but not exclusively black), or ethnic (mainly but not exclusively Oriental). Moreover, there were variations within the liberal, conservative, and conventional congregations. A second liberal church, for instance, had a youth program that consisted entirely of money-raising projects, such as car washes, in order that the group could go skiing after Christmas.

Having to select one's religion can produce the view that religion is more important to the individual than to society. Religion is considered an element in life in which a person may be interested—something like music, art, or sports. It is self-fulfilling to certain people, and respected because the person involved is serious about it. This view, of course, is not accepted by all religious people, but it is the dominant one and tends to shape the nature of all religions. If religion is restricted to self-respect, then religion has lost its power to be an ethical element in society; its value becomes limited to the psychological health of individuals.

This condition, however, is not without merit. Today there are few external pressures to believe in God or follow certain religious practices. Being religious is not necessary for success in any line of work as long as one adheres to the accepted morality of other people doing the same kind of work. It is no longer necessary to join a church for social approval. This may be a desirable state of affairs; if people must choose, they may think about the nature of religion. Such a situation could open up a valuable inquiry rather than just a mindless acceptance of conventional religious beliefs.

Private Nature

If the optional status of religion in America is fused with privacy, then we have a kind of faith that needs an analysis such as I shall do in later chapters. At this point let us look at what private religion means.

One aspect of privacy may be considered in a favorable light: namely, the power of faith to integrate a person's whole being and thus provide both a sense of authority for how to live and some clarity about how to decide ethical issues. Such inner confidence helps a person resist external authority, such as ecclesiastical power, preformulated doctrines, or rigid forms of worship. This kind of faith, essential for the thesis of this book, will be discussed in more detail in later chapters.

The type of privacy into which American religion has drifted is more likely to be one of self-fulfillment: authority is not in God, who comes into a person's life with a mission; it is rooted in a person's psychological needs. Although these needs may not be conscious desires, they exert enough pressure to make people choose a religion that feeds them. The search is not for truth about God but for religious beliefs and practices that help people cope with inner difficulties or provide a way to make sense out of the variety of events taking place around them. Seeing many options, including a half dozen or more on television, people select what fits their needs. Under these circumstances religion is secular in that it is used for self-fulfillment. It is not considered valid for making judgments about public policies and is not necessarily valuable for other people, nor is it expected to show up in art forms for general appreciation. Private religion has authority only in the congregations or churches that sponsor it. Don Browning, a professor of pastoral care, has suggested that ministers, to the extent that they have adopted nondirective styles of counseling and demeanor in their work, may have contributed to this privatization in religion. Nondirective counseling refers ethical issues back to the counselees on the assumption that they must decide what is true for themselves.[28]

Louis Dupré believes that we are in an unprecedented situation. The sacred "has lost the power to integrate directly the rest of life." "Religion," he continues, "is rapidly becoming desacralized." By this he means that few people have religious experience with a transcendent reality. Rather, the typical religious experience today "is marked more by personal reflection and deliberate choice than by direct experience."[29] This idea of religion's becoming sacred only to oneself is startling, but not too farfetched if we understand how religious authority has shifted, from a conception of God who reveals God's will for the world, to individuals who are concerned primarily for themselves.

Robert N. Bellah and colleagues have written an excellent study about how American individualism has grown out of the biblical conception of the individual that informed the minds of the early American colonists. The Puritans were obsessed with founding a Christian community in the new country. To them the individual was the basic unit in society responsible to God for creating and maintaining a community in which everyone would "delight in each other." The criterion of success, according to Bellah, was the quality of the community, not individual wealth or power.[30]

About two hundred years after the founding of the Massachusetts Bay Colony (1630), Alexis de Tocqueville visited America and wrote one of the most penetrating analyses ever made of American character and culture. He was one of the first to identify "individualism" as a major characteristic of Americans. But his appraisal of the kind of individualism emerging out of American history contained a warning. He was concerned that such individualism "might eventually isolate Americans one from another and thereby undermine the conditions of freedom."[31] In other words, if democracy became only a process by which individuals obtained rights, then anything is approved that can be achieved by majority vote. But American democracy was built on substantial social values, such as a concern for fairness, a regard for the rights of others, and the willingness to use one's own time and abilities for the welfare of the community. These social values are the necessary characteristics of our culture before a democratic political order can provide individual rights.

Bellah's study identified two types of American self-centered individualism. One is described as "utilitarian" and can be traced to Benjamin Franklin; the other, described as "expressive," is traced to Walt Whitman. Each type is illustrated by interviews concerning attitudes toward love and marriage, citizenship, religion, and other significant areas. Sheila Larson, a nurse, reports a belief in God although she cannot remember the last time she went to church. She claims that her faith is so meaningful she has labeled it "Sheilaism." Her description: "It's just try to love yourself and be gentle with yourself. You know, I guess, take care of each other. I think He would want us to take care of each other."[32] There is some gracious sentiment in Sheilaism, but it has no purpose other than a deification of her self-image.

Robert Wuthnow has just published a sociological analysis of changes in American Protestantism during the last half of this century. One of the important changes he documents is a shift away from the corporate aspect of religion. Until recent times Protestants had considerable loyalty to their denomination and a sense of accountability to a congregation. In the place of this loyalty has emerged the idea of the congregation as an assembly of like-minded individuals seeking personal satisfactions.[33]

Countermovements

The foregoing description leaves us with an American culture that encourages private religious life. When the Gallup pollsters ask people if they believe in God, almost all respondents say yes. This is a socially approved reply. The survey method used by Gallup does not allow for questions about the kind of God the respondents believe in, so we have no idea what their religion means. Although the percentage of Americans who are church members is lower than the percentage who believe in God, the number is very high. This reflects the values Americans place on the work of the church in helping people find meaning for their lives, adjust to society, and obtain their civil rights.

This description of private religion does not do justice to the revival-fundamentalist stream in American history. Except for a small liberal segment of the population, the Protestant churches of the nineteenth century were conservative. Revival movements came from conservative theology and in turn helped secure this theology as orthodox. McGuffey's *Readers*, as already indicated, provided a popular version of this Protestant stance. By the turn of the century, however, what is today called "American liberalism" was beginning to assert itself, a movement based on critical methods of Bible study and a strong sense of social justice for workers as industrialization began to dominate the economy. This liberal theology with its attendant social concerns challenged the dominant orthodox Christianity.[34] Beginning in 1910 a conservative group published a set of leaflets entitled "The Fundamentals" in an effort to assert a set of essential doctrines as a standard for correct Christian beliefs.[35] The word "fundamentalism" became the accepted term to describe those who insisted on this set of doctrines as a way to resist the spread of liberalism. For the first half of this century, fundamentalism was mainly on the defensive; but as liberal theology began to lose its cogency in the latter part of this century, fundamentalism has become more offensive. A movement as well as a theology, fundamentalism is found in all major denominations and is characteristic of many sect groups. I mention it here because its theistic theology is opposed to any secular interpretation of life.

The reader may wonder why I do not cite the growing strength of fundamentalism as an indication of how this form of Christianity may overcome the secular individualism I have been describing. One reason is that fundamentalism—although resistant to liberalism—has accepted much of American individualism. This is a subtle matter, for the gospel is person-centered (especially the Gospel of John). It is easy in an evangelistic form of fundamentalism to fuse the biblical idea of individual accountability before God with the political freedom of the individual. The result may be a privatization of religion. This has value, of course, in producing moral citizens, but it removes the obligations Christians have for creating and maintaining a society that is fair for all people.

The second reason fundamentalism cannot be thought of as an antidote to modern American culture is its inflexible doctrines, especially its insistence on verbal inerrancy of the Bible. This belief, more than the other theological statements of fundamentalism, makes it doctrine-centered: authority is anchored in the doctrinal statement rather than in the experience with God described by that statement. In fact, however, the Bible contains contradictions that need to be reconciled, and some of its teachings make sense only in the historical context in which they are found. Reason is so well established in modern life that it cannot be abandoned in our religious life, even though religion is primarily about nonrational matters.

3

Our Religious Experience

This kind of practical theology requires that we understand our-selves before we can properly appropriate the experiences of other people from other times. Strictly speaking, that task is impossible because we can never extract ourselves from our cultural setting, achieve a complete and correct description of what we are, and—with this purified self-understanding—make objective judgments about the meaning of the biblical narratives. On the other hand, if we fail to understand ourselves before we go to the biblical or historical text, we are almost certain of reading into those accounts whatever we want to find. So, to prevent gross misinterpretations and to be open to the leading of God's Spirit, we must identify and constantly monitor our worldview, attitudes, values, and beliefs as we search the past to learn about God.

Social Selfhood

Chapter 2 contained a brief survey of how we have developed the secular individualism in America that has caused religion to become optional or to be related to one's private life. This does not mean that all religious persons have accepted this position for their beliefs; it means only that this is the socially approved interpretation of the place of religion as referred to by the mass media, by political leaders, and by the Supreme Court.

Core Values

Society is held together by core values to which all subscribe. In an extreme case, such as a primitive tribe that has had very little contact with other cultures, almost everyone has similar beliefs about things seen and unseen. Thus the core of social values would be almost as large as the whole body of beliefs. Such a society is very stable, because there are no alternative interpretations of life and no threats to the established way of government. Teenagers do not say to their parents that they are going to leave home for a different life-style, for they do not know that other options exist.

Our Western nations have many options in almost every sphere. Teenagers can believe or not believe in God, can shape a life-style different from that of their parents, and, in fact, are expected to "find themselves"—including suitable vocations. But these options in beliefs, life-style, and vocation are all within a society with a core of values to which the majority subscribe. American core values include the rule of law, high regard for family life, equal rights for all people and both genders, concern for public health, medical and financial aid for the needy, and a government "of the people, by the people, and for the people."

Group Values

The core values to which almost all people subscribe are surrounded by values to which groups give special allegiance. Social groups—by reason of their ties to one another—interpret the core values and create special values that express their specific social situation. To be knowledgeable about ourselves we must also understand the special circumstances of the group of people among whom we have come of age. The major social factors include (1) racial or ethnic group, (2) economic circumstances of the family and friends, (3) educational attainment, including the schools attended, (4) occupation of parents, and (5) special experiences such as travel, stimulation of social environment, or engagement in public projects. Out of these conditions social groups develop and maintain their own values.

For example, here is a profile of the members of many of our mainline Protestant churches: they are white; the adults make their living as professionals and managers of various enterprises or as owners of small businesses; most have a college education; they travel away from home with some frequency; they read daily papers and some books. Such church groups emphasize church education, planned congregational activities, budgets and audits, individual initiative, and appropriateness of church architecture, furnishings, and style of worship. These people are in continuity with American society. They work in and manage church affairs according to the same values they use in their business and other human enterprises, and they give of themselves and their funds to support this version of the American way of life. Although the church is important, it is only one of the associations in which they find satisfaction.

By way of contrast, consider a congregation of Mexican Americans.

Being Protestant—when most of their ethnic group is Catholic—causes them to accentuate their distinctive Protestant beliefs. Most of the congregation make their living as laborers; they are barely able to meet their family expenses, and few have savings accounts or life insurance. Graduation from high school is considered adequate education. There is almost no discretionary travel and very little entertainment, other than television and movies. Such church groups may emphasize secular education because it is the way to get ahead in the world, but they may be rather casual about church education. Children are encouraged to attend congregational worship because the service is partly in Spanish and thus glorifies their ethnic origin. Pastors are given deference both because they are educated and because the members' tradition accords great respect for ministers. Such a church's congregational programs are not always well organized, and not many of its lay people take initiative to lead groups or start new programs. However, the congregation may exhibit great concern for its members, especially in crisis situations. To them the church is a gathering of believers who are withdrawing from the world for a while to share their love for God and for each other. The fellowship of the congregation may be more important to them than other human associations.

Although it is impossible to describe the many variations and combinations of core and group values, these two contrasting church groups open our minds to the countless possibilities. But these contrasting sketches also indicate how a congregation reflects the social conditions that form its members. The congregation, in turn, reinforces and enhances these social factors. Just as the folk saying "Birds of a feather flock together" is true, so is its reverse: "Birds in a flock develop the same kind of feathers."

Personal Appropriation

Thus far I have been following the assumption that society as reality outside ourselves shapes our self-understanding. Moreover, I have assumed that religion is a part of the culture that presses itself on us. If we consider religion a social fact rather than something people have accepted as their faith, then religion is whatever society says it is.

By starting with society, we recognize that we are born into a living tradition—one that has historical roots and strong momentum, and that will continue after we are gone. I am not speaking here of a particular political or economic order. The order can change rather abruptly in war or under serious economic dislocation, but the characteristics of people change slowly. Rather, I am speaking of the social values that characterize people in a living tradition—including their religion. Although the process by which this works is well known, it is not always taken seriously.[1]

From the moment of birth a person is surrounded with words and symbols that communicate the meaning of birth and of all other events that take place. The newborn baby does not yet know that pink has been designated for baby girls and blue for baby boys, but the blanket color is symptomatic of the way culture operates. Cultural interpretation is ready at hand for all the common experiences of life. Young children are constantly being told the name of everything and, at the same time, what they should think about or how they should respond to the object being named. For example, if the event "sunset" is seen and named, children also may be told to appreciate the sunset for its vast display of constantly changing color. When the child is old enough to ask why the sun goes down, adults explain the solar system to the best of their ability. Mary Douglas states the process in these words:

> Anything whatsoever that is perceived at all must pass by perceptual controls. In the sifting process something is admitted, something rejected and something supplemented to make the event cognizable. The process is largely cultural. A cultural bias puts moral problems under a particular light. Once shaped, the individual choices come catalogued according to the structuring of consciousness, which is far from being a private affair.[2]

"The structure of consciousness" does not mean that a person is a prisoner in a cultural cage; as persons undergo diverse experiences—especially in interaction with other cultures—they can change the interpretations of life that were supplied to them when they were children. It does mean, however, that the cultural explanation of life and nature we carry in our minds is as close to us as the language we learned as a child. Just as we normally use our mother tongue to explain our thoughts, so, too, we spontaneously revert to our culturally supplied interpretations of life unless we pause to examine them.

Elsewhere I have outlined how culture forms this structured consciousness by providing an explanation of our physical world and by giving us a set of values to help us make decisions and take action. Children internalize this consciousness by their developing perceptive system, by their conscience that labels certain behavior right or wrong, and by the self-image that emerges from their interaction with the human environment. This internalization is well established by the time a child enters first grade. Unless the milieu is changed drastically, as in a move to another culture, children will have their socioeconomic interpretation of life fairly well fixed by the time they become adolescents.[3]

This ready-made social interpretation of the world seems simple and well understood. But not until the "unargued assumptions" of our culture are challenged do we realize how deep within our being is our cultural interpretation of experience. Let us take, for example, the general but insistent pressure that urges a person to strive for independence or dependence. From babyhood we Americans are coached to develop our life as an independent person. Such is not the case, however, in Japan. There, according to George DeVos in a recent study of how the self develops in Japanese culture, mothers encourage in their children a state of dependency: "These [dependency] needs color intimate social relationships for many Japanese throughout their life cycle. They continue to color the subsequent relationships established outside the primary family."[4]

DeVos points out that Japanese parents consider themselves as mentors to the young. They teach correct behavior, for example, by showing deference to each other and by demonstrating how one is to act toward others; similarly, a Japanese mother sensitizes her children as to how their actions will affect other people. There is a certain amount of passivity in all this which the Japanese consider appropriate. Much of this concern for a stable social order is traced to Confucianism, including the notion that human nature is basically good and only needs to be trained. American individualism, in contrast, is rooted in the view that human nature is basically sinful and needs to be changed. Moreover, in the West our individualism leads us to think that children's behavior is the result of their wills, and we often label as a "contest of wills" the interactions between children and parents. The Japanese mother, however, simply assumes that small children are immature and should not be held responsible for their actions. These mothers give themselves so wholly to their children that Japanese schoolteachers sometimes complain of being unable to differentiate between the work of the mother and the child in homework papers.

The Japanese tend to form friendships with individuals in their own age group. This leads to close association with a group in the work situation, and persons in the work-related group do many things together. "It is very difficult, however," writes DeVos, "for Japanese to develop friendships that are not related either to shared educational experiences or to later experiences within a particular company or organization. . . . Conversely, Japanese are implicitly afraid of rejection by their group."[5]

The social self of the Japanese produces a certain psychological situation that becomes a part of the educational enterprise, just as it does in America. DeVos points out that in an American science class the teacher gives assignments and references to his or her best knowledge of the subject. The teacher then elicits ideas and responses but does not attempt to bring about a consensus or conclusion. There is an understanding that individuals may have diverse thoughts about what is observed. In a Japanese class the situation is reversed: the teacher starts with a discussion of the pupils' ideas. More than half the class time is taken up with the students' defending or changing their position. The teacher gently but persistently asks leading questions until the students form a consensus about the subject or about the meaning of what they have observed.[6]

Just as the culturally conditioned self of the Japanese makes for a certain educational procedure, so does it underlie all Japanese associations in the church, industry, and government. The same, of course, is true of all cultures; one's psychological makeup is structured by ready-made cultural explanations. Part Three of this book will discuss how this relates to the life of congregations, but at this point I want only to note that as a practical matter Americans are born and raised in a tradition that includes some attitudes about—or practice of— religion. Religion is a part of the ongoing stream into which a person is taught to swim, not something added later to children's inheritance. If parents decide that when children reach the age of six and start public school they should then go to Sunday school because it teaches "right and wrong" along with religion, such parents fail to understand that their children's conscience has already been formed. A set of unargued assumptions or a "structure of consciousness" governing each child's thoughts and actions has already been socially transmitted. Unless that set of assumptions and the related judgments of conscience are challenged by some other group, by a dramatic change in circumstances, by a personal struggle for emancipation during adolescence or later on, or by some combination of these things, the ready-at-hand social soul will become the personal self.

These comments about the factors that shape one's view of oneself are based on the observation that most people in a social group will reflect and reinforce the values of that group. There are always a few people, of course, who will resist or flaunt the dominant group values. In modern Japanese culture as just described, certainly some people do not have the typical psychological makeup. Because of personal experience they have become aware of their past conditioning and are resistant to it, or they conform to it just enough to live in reasonable harmony with their associates.[7] Even in primitive societies there are a few people who do not accept all of the attitudes and values of the tribe.[8] Although these exceptions are important, they serve more to prove the rule than to support the idea that individuals are independent of the social group in which they live.

Religious Selfhood

Religion is so much a part of American life that a person cannot grow up in this society without some knowledge of its existence. Whatever role religion plays in the life of parents and others associated with the rearing of children will be the social inheritance of the children. Inherited attitudes can range from rejection or indifference to wholehearted support of a particular religion. The issue is whether people (1) will understand that their inherited religion is a mixture of social values and religious beliefs and (2) will work to identify the truth about God in the religion they have acquired. Both processes are difficult. The rest of this chapter is related to the first point, and the chapters in Part Two explore the kind of religious experience that leads to truth about God.

Mixture

The easiest way to understand how we inherit religion mixed with social values is to look at some contemporary examples. One described in considerable detail by Nancy T. Ammerman is Southside Gospel Church, a fundamentalist congregation in New England made up of about three hundred people who are employed as teachers, clerks, factory or service workers, and managers. The members consider themselves separate from the world, especially from the lax morals they see about them. They have a strong faith in God's guidance in everyday matters as well as in the destiny of the world. Salvation, the goal of each member, is also the main motivation for bringing children in buses to the Sunday school. The Bible is used to find solutions to all problems about life and death, including whatever personal problems the parishioners may have. Clearly, a child growing up in this environment will have a rather unified view of religion in society. How much of this view is inspired by American social influences, however, is open to speculation. We can see a great deal of respect for law and order, for authority, for individual responsibility, and for disciplining oneself in order to succeed as a Christian and in one's vocation.[9]

A different story is told by Mary Newgeon Hawkes in her study of Apostles Church, a congregation of the United Church of Christ. This congregation of fourteen hundred members has three ministers and a part-time director of Christian education. In contrast to the fundamentalist parishioners, the members of Apostles Church are often unclear about their beliefs. Hawkes writes, "There is little sense that in baptism, through the communion service, and through commitment to Jesus Christ, Christians are proclaiming who they are, why they are here, and what they need to be doing." Furthermore, Hawkes observes, the members have little awareness of why someone joins a church; they "do not understand the importance of festivals in their lives or verbalize as to their meaning." Christian education has a low status in this congregation, whereas the much smaller fundamentalist church is considering starting a day school so that members' children will not have to attend public schools.[10]

The Apostles Church works at serving the needs of its members, especially the older ones, and there are various groups to which members can belong. This 250-year-old church is proud of its traditions and buildings. Made up primarily of professional and managerial people with diverse backgrounds and many different needs, the congregation organizationally is one, but its members are not unified in spirit or in program.[11] One might say that this is a fairly typical old, large, mainline Protestant congregation. The members have an allegiance to memories of their past religious experiences but lack clarity about the meaning of faith in the present. Many of these people are trying to understand the mixture of modern culture and Protestant faith they see and feel in themselves. The congregation is both a place to examine these forces and a place to act them out.

Interpretation

With the help of a little imagination, these two ethnographic studies of congregations illustrate how cultural-religious tradition communicates an interpretation of the Bible (past) and society (present). The fundamentalist church has an interpretive schema that places the Bible first and attempts to bring society into line with that view. Its view of the Bible is conditioned by both social setting and personal character-istics; with that aside, the interpretive schema does not allow much deviation. The liberal congregation places society first and then attempts to make sense out of the Bible, creating a rather loose system in which a variety of interpretive patterns resides.

In these and other congregations some interpretive schema is presented to the people and supported by preaching, teaching, and worship. What individuals do with the interpretive schema is another matter. Many will accept it as their own; some will accept it provisionally or amend part of it; and, surprisingly, there are members who support the work of the congregation because they judge it good even though they personally do not accept the church's theological position. This personal response, though extremely important, is not our concern at this point. Here I want to note three reasons why this socially formed self is important for our understanding of religion and therefore should be of central concern to congregations.

First, the factors in our social environment help set our interests and focus our energy on problems we want to solve. For example, Sir Isaac Newton (1642–1727)—one of the greatest mathematicians of the seventeenth century—assumed the Bible to be God's revelation of a world chronology. This notion reflected the medieval assumption that the books of Daniel and Revelation contained a timetable of future events. Working from that socially accepted notion, Newton spent most of his last years in mathematical and astronomical studies, trying to describe what was going to happen in the future.[12] As the medieval worldview disintegrated and critical reason was applied to history, as well as to the Bible, people learned that all historical documents are written by human beings and must be understood as responses to the context in which they were composed.[13] Thus if one finds a description of future events in Newton's books, the conclusions one may draw are related to the conception of God held by the people for whom those books were written.

Similarly today, people who accept a highly competitive capitalist economic theory from certain strands of American society will, unless challenged, find in the Bible passages to support this view. The same can be said for those who are socialists. People who are for or against abortion use both the Bible and tradition to support their contentions. Does this mean the Bible will support almost any position? No, it means that we who go to the Bible for help must first attempt to understand our prejudice so we can be open to what the text means.

Second, the society in which we live provides criteria by which we judge truth. Sir Isaac Newton, as pointed out above, assumed the Bible to be outside of reason but felt that reason could decipher its meaning. By the time of Thomas Jefferson, however, reason had become to some people superior to the text, so Jefferson excised the miraculous from the Gospels when he edited them for the American Indians. Today not many Christians accept either the idea that the Bible contains a calendar of coming events or the idea that reason should override the truths contained in the biblical stories.

American culture provides a variety of criteria for selecting truth according to our educational and professional background. One set of criteria with widespread acceptance is from psychology. The specific types of psychological criteria vary greatly; what they have in common is an assumption that whatever helps an individual to become a "self-actualizing" person, provides support, or cures someone of undesirable traits is good and true. Given this screen through which all of life is judged, the Bible is accepted when it illustrates or explains some psychological truth. For example, although Abraham Maslow uses the lives of some saints to illustrate his idea of "peak-experience" as a goal for creative living, he deliberately secularizes these biographies so the inspiration can apply to all people, whether they believe in God or not.[14] Another set of criteria may come from business, where success in measurable terms is the basis for making judgments. According to these criteria, the story of Jesus is true simply because Christianity is so widespread and influential.

Third, society provides the arena in which religious faith may be practiced. Puritan New England, for example, was considered a Christian commonwealth; Sacvan Bercovitch's careful study of Puritan theocracy shows the extent to which Cotton Mather considered New England to be "the holiest country in the world."[15] Those, like Anne Hutchinson, who did not agree with the theology held by the rulers of this society were banished.[16]

At the beginning of the national period, society approved religious practice as a separate but powerful element that supported morals needed for national resolve and cohesion. Today, as indicated in chapter 2, religion is optional and private. The government pays no attention to religious practices unless they challenge government policies. It was news, therefore, when individuals motivated by their religious beliefs protested the war in Vietnam. And if congregations become sanctuaries for political refugees from Central America, they may find FBI agents infiltrating church meetings in order to gather evidence for the government's case against them.[17]

Community of Believers

Thus far, I have attempted to show that we are born into a stream of tradition that contains values and worldviews coming from secular and religious sources. As children we absorb whatever self that the society around us has defined, and as adolescents and adults we accept, modify, or reject this prefabricated social self. For ordinary Christians the agency for blending and communicating a proper social self-image is the community of believers. I use this term because it is broader than the word "church." It includes residential religious communities, the kind of people who are disaffected with their denomination but are seriously seeking a congenial group of believers in retreat centers or elsewhere, and stable groups that gather in homes for Bible study and a simple celebration of the sacraments.[18]

Because the community of believers by its very nature will develop what it considers to be important, will provide criteria for judging what is right, and will suggest the arena in which religion is to be exercised, it is crucial that these matters be given critical attention. Our master guide for such critical appraisal is the Bible, for it is the account of the people who were called to be God's witnesses in and to the world.

The Bible is a book about experiences people had with God. Rather than a history, it is a logbook of events happening to people living a tradition. It was written *by* believers *for* people who were members of the community that shared the beliefs, and most of its books testify to what faith in God meant in specific historical situations.

The reason we cannot call the Bible a history is that it does not attempt to give a unified, sequential account of the life of the people of God. Much is left out. Even John, commenting on his own experiences with Jesus, said that he omitted many things (John 21:25). What we have is bits of history, narratives, songs, parables, poems, wise sayings, Gospels (a new genre of literature), philosophy, political intrigue, laws, customs, sermons, heroic stories, descriptions of festivals and fasts, procedures for settling disputes, and other writings that characterized the life of the community for about two thousand years.

There are sections where the account gives us a sense of knowing rather accurately what went on, as in the reign of David. At other times the account says that guidance from God almost died out among the people (1 Sam. 3:1). And there are some passages—especially in the New Testament—where we have an almost daily journal of intensive activity of the Spirit in the lives of believers (Acts 1—4). What is important in the biblical narrative is God's concern for the world God created and the way God intervenes to guide, correct, forgive, and encourage those who respond to God's initiative.

The narratives of the people of God have many large chronological gaps. The book of Exodus, for example, reports a gap of 430 years between the story of Joseph in Egypt and the beginning of the conquest of the promised land (Ex. 12:40). But each historical era is described in terms of previous historical eras so that the effect is cumulative. This does not mean that each historical era is a stage higher in religious and moral development than the previous one. Rather, the story is more about a struggle between God's will and human disobedience. Sin appears in every era; in the New Testament we have as graphic a description of sin as we have in the Old Testament. What is "new" in the New Testament is God's effort through the life and sacrifice of Jesus Christ to do something more decisive and dramatic about sin and to show us in human form the meaning of faith in God. The revelation in Jesus Christ, however, is meaningful only in relationship to God's previous revelations in the Old Testament; the "new" is thus in continuity and harmony with the "old."

Recently a group of Bible scholars developed a way to study and use scripture that is significantly different from the ways that had emerged in the previous two hundred years of critical Bible study. Known as the "canonical" school, these scholars start with the idea that the Bible is a book composed by and for a community of believers. The scriptures are intended for a religious purpose—worship and instruction—and must be interpreted in relation to that purpose. In practical terms, critical studies dealing with the date of origin, the composition of a book, the historical context, the literary form, and so on are important; but they are secondary to the crucial question as to why each book is in the canon—the accepted books of the Bible. James A. Sanders's answer to that question is "repetition": "What is in the canon got there because somebody repeated something, starting a process of recitation that has never ceased. Nothing anybody said or sang could have made it into canon unless someone else repeated it or copied it, and then another and another did the same."[19]

This answer has profound meaning. At once we are aware that many things happened to God's people, but some things are not known to us—either because an account was lost or because the people involved did not judge it important. What we have in the Bible is what God's people thought important and what, in their experience, was helpful. This means that the community of those who had faith in God recited to one another what some of their people claimed to be an experience with God. The community then judged the adequacy and authenticity of that claimed experience. This probably happened informally in conversations as well as in confrontations with false prophets. Moreover, we know through the discovery of the Judaean scrolls that other writings were available to the Jewish people that were not accepted for the canon. Sanders writes, "The canonical process was basically one of *selectivity and repetition* with interpretation."[20] The criterion for selection was the usefulness of a text for the community's worship or for instruction, and over a period of time the accounts that were certified as being authentic became the canon. What is important for us is the process whereby people of faith judged what was authentic, on the basis of their faith experience and the knowledge of God which that experience had brought them.

These are descriptive statements, not arguments. There are no arguments in the Bible for the existence of God; it is not a philosophical book, for God's existence is assumed. The Bible is the book of a community of people who already had faith in God. That community needed the record because it identified who they were; it also had practical value as a textbook for training the young and as a record of how the community's understanding of God changed with changing circumstances. The books of the Bible were used by believers for what, today, we would call educational purposes,[21] and the heart of that educational purpose was experience. The experiences people had with God became enshrined in story, song, and sayings and were approved by believers because they illuminated their experiences with God. Sanders puts it tersely: "Canon and community must be thought of as belonging together both in antiquity and today."[22] As the past community of believers judged the truth about God which we have in the canonical books of the Bible, so must the present community of believers judge today.

Paul D. Hanson recently published a remarkable study of the Bible as a history of God's community. Starting with the Exodus, he presents a community that responded to God's initiative to form a people— since earlier attempts to influence all of humankind had failed (Gen. 1—11). For each succeeding historical period he does three things: (1) he briefly outlines the historical facts; (2) he identifies the biblical narratives that illustrate the response of Israel to the social and political conditions its people faced at that time; and then (3) he discusses the way the community sought righteousness, exhibited compassion, and worshiped. The forms of righteousness, compassion, and worship changed as the social and political situation changed, but these matters are central throughout the Bible.[23] What is important for us is the

illustration of how the community of believers in biblical times functioned as the agency for keeping alive the traditions from the past and
interpreting them for the present. Both processes were public—out in
the open where everyone could participate—for that is the place where
truth about God is located.

Conflicting Claims

In each historic period in the Bible there are differences of opinion
about what God wanted, about how to live, and about what position
the community should take in regard to social and political issues.
These differences came about because groups interpreted the past
differently or because traditions from the past offered various answers
to the questions of the present. For example, Hanson charts the
streams of tradition from about 500 B.C.E. to 50 B.C. He notes a vision-
ary, apocalyptic, sapiential, royal, and priestly tradition from which
emerged the Essenes, Pharisees, and Sadducees found in the New
Testament.[24] Much of Jesus' disputation was with these groups as they
struggled to relate their interpretation of the Bible to the problems of
Israel. The church formed after Jesus' death contained groups with
conflicting claims. The most important conflict was between the group
around Paul who believed that the gospel was for everyone, and those
"from Judea" who contended that "unless you are circumcised according to the custom of Moses, you cannot be saved" (Acts 15:1). This
conflict was resolved by the church assembly with a compromise agreement favoring the Paul-Peter view that the gospel was for Gentiles as
well as for Jews (Acts 15:13–21).

This condition of conflicting claims to truth has continued into
modern times. Some of the differences between Christian groups are
minor, no more important than the variation one would find in any
human association. Others—such as those between Protestants,
Roman Catholics, Eastern Orthodox, and other groups such as the
Quakers or residential communities such as the Bruderhof—are significant and will not be erased or diminished in the near future. Moreover, *within* each of these branches of the Christian religion there are
sometimes differences almost as significant as between the branches
themselves.

Beyond Pluralism

Given the conflicting claims by various communities of believers
reported in the Bible or observed in our contemporary world, how can
we find the truth about God and God's will for our lives? The question
in this form is almost unanswerable, because the community itself
becomes the final authority.

From the standpoint of the sociology of belief, the process can be described in general terms. Beliefs are social in nature; that is, they are what a group of people considers true. In this sense beliefs exist apart from individuals, although the beliefs reside in the individuals who make up the group. As a result, individuals are committed to the group's beliefs. Over time, conditions change or events happen that challenge the belief system of a community. This presents the problem of validation: How does one reconcile beliefs with new conditions? Communities do this (1) by denying facts, as the current American Nazi Party denies that the Holocaust happened. Communities may also justify their beliefs (2) by interpreting facts to suit the ideology of the group, as do doomsday cults when they select certain facts (such as increased crime, nuclear explosions, exploitation of natural resources, or threats of war) as proofs of their belief that the world is soon coming to an end. Finally, communities may validate their beliefs (3) by associating the issue before them with some policy or situation that is disliked, so the problem becomes the fault of some other group—since some Protestants do not want to give up Christmas celebrations in public schools, for example, they blame secular humanists for opposing such celebrations.[25]

The above strategies are used by communities with a strong unified belief system not open to very much change. Many religious communities can and do change some of their beliefs over a period of time and continue without disruptive consequences. For example, most Protestant denominations in the South before the Civil War supported and, in some cases, defended slavery, but after Reconstruction years they changed their beliefs on this matter. Today large numbers of Roman Catholic lay people in the United States practice types of birth control not approved by official doctrine, yet they do not leave the church. Also, denominations facing new demands, such as the ordination of women, manage to change their beliefs on this subject without long-term dissatisfaction of the members.

The process by which all this happens is fascinating and important, but it is not our main consideration at this point. The matter before us is the self-justification process a community may use to maintain its beliefs. There are various Christian traditions: Orthodoxy with Russian, Greek, or other national traditions; Roman Catholicism with many orders emphasizing different theologies; and, of course, Protestantism with its scores of denominations.

Does this mean that religious communities engage in a form of circular reasoning and experiencing? The process seems to go as follows: a religious community sets forth a belief system with the attending elements of worship and correct moral behavior; it then interprets life experiences according to its belief system so that believers experience what they have been conditioned to experience. From the standpoint of social analysis this description is correct. To the extent that a community is formed around religious beliefs and attempts to hold itself together by *human means,* to that extent it validates its historical tradition as described without seeking elsewhere for guidance. Where is truth in this social process? How can we make judgments about the claims of a religious community?

God-directed Process

If one turns to the Bible for guidance as to how experience with God may be different from what the community has decided each member should experience, one finds considerable help in answering the question of truth.

First we must note that the Bible is written from what Israel interpreted as God's perspective. From a literary point of view this theocentric stance provides a majesty that is appropriate to its contents. But how could the writers be so positive about God? The answer seems to lie in the long period of time over which the written record was assayed by the community before the record was certified as authentic. From the community's experiences with God they were able to get a perspective on themselves so that they could see themselves as God saw them.

This God-perspective on human affairs does not mean that the biblical writers claimed to know all about God. On the contrary, they did not speculate about God, nor did they solve the problem of why there is evil if God is good. They affirmed that God discloses God's self to humans from time to time in a special way, and that what was disclosed was God's will for the people involved in the events in which the disclosure took place. It was their experience with God that gave them a God-orientation. The God-orientation in turn helped them transcend their own immediate situation to get a clearer idea of what God desired for the world.

This biblical way of getting a hold on religious experience is of first importance today. We tend to write our theology on the basis of the experience we have within a religious community. Thus we may have Roman Catholic, Presbyterian, Quaker, or Southern Baptist theology without proper regard for the whole world. Sometimes we have the inclination to write theology from praxis—that is, from the practical dilemmas of those who are poor or who have little political power. If we do this, we are in danger of absolutizing our experience within its immediate context rather than understanding that God has a concern for all sorts and conditions of people everywhere. God is free to be and do what God desires. A biblical way of expressing this notion is in the words "For my thoughts are not your thoughts, neither are your ways my ways, says the LORD" (Isa. 55:8).

All this presents us with a logical contradiction. God is separate, and different, and has unique thoughts and ways of being in the world, yet human beings are capable to some extent of seeing the world as God does. The Bible makes no effort to resolve this contradiction. We are required to do something we cannot achieve! But the requirement is of critical importance, for it forces us to break out of our parochial interests and realize that our beliefs must relate to all people. By that leap of imagination our minds can escape the circular reasoning inherent in religious communities.[26]

Second, the biblical story from the very beginning shows a conflict between what God wanted and what Israel wanted. This conflict was seen in the national sense of mission. God wanted a nation that would be an object lesson to the world, a showpiece to other nations as to what God desired for all nations. This was part of the promise to Abraham and to Moses as a part of the Covenant (see Gen. 12:3 and Ex. 19:6). But the people did not always share that vision. They had an agenda of their own, later demanding a king, in order to "be like all the nations" (1 Sam. 8:20). This request displeased the prophet Samuel. The Lord did not like it either, for it symbolized Israel's rejection of the Lord; yet it was allowed (1 Sam. 8:7).

Another conflict that surfaced immediately at the establishment of the nation and ran on for a thousand years was idolatry. The first and second commandments explicitly prohibit the worshiping of idols (Ex. 20:3–4). Yet in a short time Aaron, the designated leader in Moses' absence, helped the people create a golden calf and proclaimed a feast day to honor their new god (Ex. 32). In Elijah's time the worship of idols had become so widespread that the king, Ahab, erected an altar for his wife to Baal, a Canaanite god who controlled rain. The account, typically written from God's viewpoint, judged Ahab as having done "more to provoke the LORD, the God of Israel, to anger than all the kings of Israel who were before him" (1 Kings 16:33; see also Hos. 11:2).

Amos used brilliant, vitriolic language to say that from God's viewpoint feasts and solemn assemblies and offerings were despised because they failed to fulfill the mission of justice for the world (Amos 5:21–24). God's controversy with Israel is summed up by Micah in the passage where he says the Lord will not be pleased with any kind or amount of sacrifice—not even one's own child. The only thing God wants is for the people "to do justice, and to love kindness, and to walk humbly with your God" (Micah 6:6–8). The worship of idols continued in New Testament times. Paul had to contend with the problem among the people in Corinth (1 Cor. 10:14) and Athens (Acts 17:16).

Idol worship is associated in our minds with primitive people and with the gods of stone and wood we see in *National Geographic* magazine. Since such idols are not apparent in our "civilized" countries, we dismiss them as no longer competitors to God. We would do better to use the word "idolatry," for idolatry means anything to which we give the attention, respect, and trust due to God. Idolatry in this sense is everywhere in our modern society. Individuals can easily give attention and deference to such things as science, military superiority, or the goal of personal success.

Religious communities are especially vulnerable to idolization of their past. The temptation is almost irresistible; after all, past experience is what formed the community and gave it a belief system that has endured. Through the social validation process the believers are convinced that their interpretation of life is true, and thus the past becomes an idol worshiped by the present generation. The danger of this form of idolatry was illustrated in a dramatic way when Jesus confronted the Sadducees. The Sadducees believed there was no resurrection from the dead, so they approached Jesus with a question designed to prove that point. A man died, they said, and according to the law of Moses the widow married her husband's brother in order to raise children in his name. This happened seven times. Now, the Sadducees demanded, "In the resurrection, therefore, to which of the seven will she be wife?" Jesus' answer shows how the Sadducees misunderstood God: "You are wrong, because you know neither the scriptures nor the power of God. . . . He is not God of the dead, but of the living" (Matt. 22:23–32). This is a stunning reply to a conservative religious community. But Jesus in his person and in his teaching was the incarnation of what he said—the God of the living. God is related to what is going on now. The mental image of God is brought to us from past experiences, but God is free to be and do what God desires so that the present may be different from the past. To idolize the past or anything else is to desensitize us to God in the present.

Third, the biblical record describes Israel and the Christian church as communities made up of individuals who were often sinful and centered on their own interests rather than on the concerns of God. After the creation, including the Adam and Eve story, the Bible's first story of human activity is about sin due to pride (Genesis 3). There is hardly a page of the Bible—certainly no long sections—where human beings do not disobey God's commands or ignore God's leading. The most spectacular story in the Old Testament is probably David's sin against Bathsheba and Uriah (2 Sam. 11—12:24). The results of that act of adultery and murder continued in the family of David through his son Absalom. What is important to us is the frankness with which the scripture describes the shortcomings of the greatest king Israel ever had. The New Testament is equally clear on the weaknesses of Peter and the other apostles and on the sinfulness of some of the members of the first Christian congregations (Acts 5:1–11). However, in spite of sin and the self-interest of these and other characters in the biblical drama, God's will is done and God's grace is demonstrated.[27]

Acquired Religious Experience

Our religious experience is first acquired from the environment in which we are reared. As children we were not mentally capable or personally experienced enough to sort out religious beliefs from our social inheritance, so we entered adolescence with a social-religious outlook already formed from those around us. Unless some countervailing force entered our lives, we continued in the course already set and found groups of people who articulated and reinforced what we already believed.

If we have experienced the Christian religion, we have acquired a tradition in which the Bible is central. From that source we learn that the community of believers has always contained groups with conflicting claims to truth about God. Yet over a period of time the community was able to sort out truth from falsehood, because God kept revealing what ought to be done or said in particular circumstances. Thus the social context is taken seriously as the place to understand God's will, and all groups with conflicting claims to truth are subjected to God's present revelation. The way to truth about God is through the experience we acquire from the religious tradition in which we were raised. But religious truth is experiential, so we must now turn to Part Two of this book and examine the biblical way of describing personal religious experience.

PART TWO

A Biblical Model
of Experience

In the biblical record, which portrays human concerns contrary to God's will, the general term "sin" covers selfishness, idolatry, secularism, and compromise associated with religious leaders' efforts to protect their position or to help rulers control the masses. God's will is experienced by all sorts of people who are deeply involved in concrete life situations. Their faith becomes mature as they struggle to understand what God wants and what specific things they should do to influence the community of believers to change their ways of thinking and acting.

I use theophanies as models of experience because they are sharply focused, intense accounts of God's presence. The exact nature of each theophany is different because the life situation is different, but there is a pattern to help us understand religious experience. The pattern is (1) a situation in which God's will needs to be known (chapter 5), (2) a person or group who has become engaged with the Spirit of God (chapter 6), and (3) a charge, mission, or work assignment about what must be done for the welfare of the community of believers (chapter 7). Following this model does not guarantee that a person or group has the authentic "word of the Lord," but it does eliminate claims of religious experience that do no more than glorify or enrich the individual making the claim. Chapter 8 concludes this part by broadening the biblical inquiry to formulate a general understanding of mature faith.

4

Why Is Experience Necessary?

Chapters 2 and 3 pointed out that the meaning of life comes to us through society and through the community of faith to which we belong. As a result, the substance of our religion—that is, what we believe—is a mixture of religious tradition (biblical narratives, theological statements, worship experiences) with whatever society values. Exactly what kind of mix comes our way depends on our individual history. Some people with only a nominal relation to a church will probably have a set of beliefs that reflects the social class in which they live. Others who grow up in a strict religious sect may have accepted a set of beliefs and practices that puts them at odds with their society. In between these positions are many variations.

In practical terms, the congregation is the place where Christians sort out true from false conceptions of God. This sorting process is not easy; conflicts come from society whenever a community of believers interprets life in a different way. Furthermore, conflicts develop within the congregation about how they are to respond to their differences with society and about the interpretation of their religious tradition. Being a loyal and active member of a congregation, then, does not guarantee that the search for truth about God will be simple. In fact, we share all these conflicts within ourselves while we participate in congregational life, so we are not objective as is a jury listening to rival claims. We are more like individuals in a legislature struggling with each other about what is good for the whole community. The difference between the church and the legislature is that we are seeking the will of God for our lives, and our convictions may not change even though a majority votes against our proposals. This constancy comes about because we believe that God's will is communicated to believers through individuals; if we feel that we have the truth about a situation and that the majority does not, we resist compromise.

How can we get beyond the conflicts we find in the community of believers and in the schools of thought that form about the meaning of God's presence? The biblical answer is a revelation from the Lord or, in more modest language, an experience of God's presence by which believers develop confidence in their group's convictions.

Formula

The biblical formula shows the mix of social and religious beliefs carried along in a community or nation. As conditions change, God's will becomes known to individuals who influence the community. Sometimes the presence of God leads the people to a new life, as was the case when the new Israelite nation was formed, according to the Exodus narrative. There God's characteristics were already deeply embedded in the people's minds and in Moses' understanding. That is why the voice to Moses said: "I am . . . the God of Abraham, the God of Isaac, and the God of Jacob" (Ex. 3:6). This statement, repeated many times in the Old Testament, is also used in the New Testament as a means of identifying God through events of the past. The formula reminds the hearers that God is in current events just as God was present in the past (see Mark 12:26 for an example). Sometimes the word of the Lord offers reassurance; sometimes it condemns injustice. But in all cases the presence of God brings something new.

God's Initiative

Why does God continue to break into and assert leadership of the community that has faith in God? Why was one revelation of God's will not sufficient to set humankind on the road to happiness? Or, in more specific terms, why were not God's covenants with Noah, Abraham, the nation at Mount Sinai, and David kept? Why was it necessary in the New Covenant for the Holy Spirit to continue shaping the congregations?

Sin

The answer to these questions is sin. Humankind, from the first story of Adam and Eve to the end of the Bible, has displayed a willfulness of its own. Things have not changed during the history of the church. In every era we find leaders who attempt to usurp the place of God, personal weaknesses that lower the vitality of the church, misguided long-term projects such as the Crusades, religious wars, and prejudice against other religions that sometimes results in persecution and denial of basic human rights to non-Christians.

There is, of course, a good side to the life and mission of the church that can be documented in each historical era. But my purpose is not to evaluate the Christian faith or the Jewish religion out of which it emerged. Rather, as indicated, my question is, Why does humankind not learn from history? Why cannot the "word of the Lord" to one generation be carried over to the next generation? The answer seems to be that human beings in each generation have to struggle with the same basic temptations of the previous one. These basic temptations include the standard ones of lying, stealing, exploiting people for selfish benefits, misuse of time and money, and such matters—all of which are addressed in the Ten Commandments and are present every day of our lives. Even Jesus was tempted at the beginning of his ministry to build a kingdom by false means (Matt. 4:1–11). So sin comes first in any list of why we need the presence of God in our lives.

Secularism

Secularism—in the sense of placing our trust in the political and economic powers of the world to produce a satisfactory life, rather than in God—is a human condition into which each generation tends to slide. I indicated earlier that I think secular individualism is now the main characteristic of American selfhood and therefore the principal competitor to Christian faith. Individualism is so persistently communicated throughout our political and capitalistic system that it has even distorted the individualism of the gospel to mean salvation for one's self rather than salvation in order to be a servant of God's will in the world.

We could classify secularism as a form of sin, but that would not do justice to the subtlety of the condition. Sin is usually thought of as something so wrong that we can recognize it and feel guilty when we do it. But secularism is a matter of judgment about the degree to which we place our trust in something that does not have power to bring true satisfaction. Chapter 2, "Secular Individualism," pointed out that the biblical account of creation urged people to have dominion over what was created and to use it for their benefit (Gen. 1:26–28). That is a reliance on the secular, but in terms of obtaining food and shelter. Secularism as a matter of how we live our life came into the biblical account in a more prominent way with King David. He, like Saul, started out as a charismatic leader, but during his reign he used military and diplomatic power in rational and subtle ways to establish Israel as a power in the Middle East. Thus David's successor, Solomon, could secure the kingdom by diplomatic means, build a spectacular temple, and set up a monarchy based on Egyptian and Phoenician models. From then on, Israel as a nation called by God to be an example to the world began to adopt the world's ways to maintain itself. This form of secularism is illustrated in practical terms by Israel's constant struggle with idol worship. Probably the crisis came in the reign of Ahab, who provoked the Lord by erecting an altar to Baal. For us, secularism is much more complicated than erecting an idol. The scientific movement of the past three hundred years is secular, and it has brought us enormous benefits, especially in medicine. It has also brought power, including nuclear power, to our command. The issues with this form of secularism are related to the use we make of scientific knowledge and the degree to which we put our trust in the products of science. However, the basic issues of the meaning of life, the proper use of military force, and the moral obligations to share food and shelter have not changed because of our scientific achievements.

Sectarianism

Another reason why religious experience is constantly needed is that religion, when institutionalized, tends to develop a life of its own and be less sensitive to the leading of God. The problem is not so much a matter of sinful people as it is of the way human institutions tend to perpetuate themselves. Christianity started out with a charismatic person—Jesus—and after his death it was carried on by disciples and converts, of whom the apostle Paul was the best known because of his writings. For Christianity to endure in time, it had to become institutionalized.

Institutionalization does not necessarily mean a certain organizational pattern or a written set of rules and regulations; it simply means that a group of people develop understandings about how they are going to maintain a community based on what they believe to be important. But the process of institutionalization requires that some people have status as leaders and assume the role of reconciling diverse elements in the community so that the group can achieve the agreed-on purposes. The original revelation experienced by the person or group becomes secularized in the sense that it becomes adjusted to the world. Max Weber described this process as the " 'routinization' of charisma."[1]

Thomas O'Dea has analyzed the problems that emerge when religion becomes institutionalized. He uses the word "dilemma" to describe five areas where the requirements of being an institution within society compromise, weaken, or modify the teaching or vision of the original religious leader. "Dilemma" is well chosen, for in none of the five areas is it possible for religious organizations to give unequivocal leadership. In each area the requirement for an institution to endure in time goes counter to religious teachings. Compromises emerge that often result in a strong institution with an ever-weakening faith in God. The five areas discussed by O'Dea follow.[2]

The Dilemma of Mixed Motivation. A religion usually begins with a charismatic leader who personifies a very intense belief system. That leader is preoccupied with the importance of beliefs and the application of the beliefs to ordinary life situations, and disciples are attracted to both the beliefs and the explanations that the leader offers. During the early period the leader and disciples are so dedicated to their mission that they pay very little attention to society or to the future. As time goes by, they realize that the truth they have must be shared with others and preserved for succeeding generations, so some form of organization emerges. This means that authority to state, interpret, and apply this truth must be lodged in some individuals or groups. Such authority assigns status to certain leaders who—over time—"adjust" the original faith and teachings to fit the society in which the movement is trying to be a stable organization. The recognized leaders have a strong motive to keep the organization going, because this is the source of their recognition as important people. If the succeeding leaders become "professional"—that is, paid for their services by the religious organization—their role and authority are enhanced. The motive of lay people tends to undergo a subtle shift from a *search* for truth, which characterized the first disciples, to a more passive role of *receiving* the truth.

Matthew's Gospel presents a good illustration of this dilemma. Writing as the original disciples were dying off and a second generation of leaders was coming to the fore, Matthew presents many of the sayings of Jesus in the Sermon on the Mount. We are told that individuals are to endure personal insult graciously by turning the other cheek and, if sued for one's coat, to give up the coat plus a cloak (Matt. 5:39–40). But in the latter part of Matthew's Gospel, where the writer reflects the problems of the followers of Jesus as they attempt to organize the church, we are given different instructions. In chapter 16, Peter identifies Jesus as the Christ, and Jesus announces that Peter and his confession are the rock on which the church will be built. Having introduced the idea of the church as an institution, the writer then takes up problems such as the role of church leaders. In chapter 18 the topic is rivalry between disciples for the leadership positions after Jesus is gone. Moreover, the matter of how individuals should act when insulted has changed. A procedure for processing complaints is suggested, including the role of a church committee to process the complaint and appropriate punishment (Matt. 18:15–20). Later, the issue of dividing responsibility for church leadership emerged, criteria were established for officers, and many other practical problems were solved. The Pastoral Letters—especially First Timothy, written at least three generations after the crucifixion—show in spirit and content the churches' efforts to become institutionalized and still maintain faith in Jesus Christ.

The Dilemma of Religious Experience. The experience of people who originate a religion is so powerful that it redirects their lives. Because the original experience is sacred—the model of what can and ought to be—it is preserved in stories, rituals, and symbols. Such preservation honors the founder and first followers while at the same time assuming that succeeding generations will have something like the original experience if they repeat the stories, follow the rituals, and respect the symbols. Firsthand experience becomes secondhand when it becomes ritualized, for ritual is a rational planning of ideas and actions about a religious experience which originally was nonrational, supernatural, and deeply rooted in the life situations of people who had the original experience with God. As time goes on, rituals become formalized and thus more remote both from the original experience of the founders and from the everyday experience of later generations.

The Lord's Supper, for example, is central to the meaning of Christ's death and resurrection. We do not have an exact account of what happened on the Thursday evening before the crucifixion. It was probably a normal supper, filled by Jesus with extraordinary meaning. The first account is by Paul in his letter to the church in Corinth, written about twenty years after the event (1 Cor. 11:17–32). Paul's account documents the dilemma just referred to. The Corinthians, separated by time and culture from the Jewish tradition out of which Jesus came, had made the Lord's Supper into a banquet to satisfy their fondness for food and wine. Paul told the Corinthians that the Lord's Supper is a symbolic meal filled with theological truth, not a place to satisfy one's hunger (1 Cor. 11:33–34). He had to restore its symbolic value in order that the beliefs about Jesus' giving himself in sacrifice for sin could be maintained. Yet in the very act of insisting on the exact words of the institution, Paul set the ritual for later times.

The history of the Lord's Supper after the close of the New Testament describes how it became "the mass" to be administered only by priests—in an approved form, under carefully regulated conditions, and in a certain language. At the time of the Reformation, the church's ability to control access to the mass allowed the church power to punish those who disagreed with its teachings or decisions. By this time the Lord's Supper was an instrument of power rather than a reenactment of Jesus' last day with his disciples and a proclamation of his sacrifice for sin. The Reformers repudiated the mass because it got in the way of believers' having an experience with Christ through the Lord's Supper, and the Quakers eliminated all sacraments in order that no ritual stand in the way of experiencing the Spirit of God moving in their midst. However, the Reformers did not escape this dilemma; they too began to form rituals about their beliefs, and the process started all over again.

The Dilemma of Organization. As indicated in the first dilemma, those who follow the founder of a religious movement want to institutionalize it. To do so they move to some form of organization, which does, indeed, stabilize the institution. Organizations break up work into categories, each of which is to be presided over by people with an interest in that particular activity. Thus the natural drift of an organization is to perpetuate itself by justifying its roles of keeping the religion alive and keeping the believers working together in reasonable harmony. This situation is something of a paradox: the better the organization, the less it will represent the spiritual aspects of religion, since organization is primarily rational and religious experience is primarily nonrational. Moreover, the better the organization fits one time (era) and place (culture), the less it can adapt to another time and place. If the organization is not able to adapt, it tends to simply defend itself and lose sight of its purpose.

The New Testament does not cover enough time to give us many illustrations of how this dilemma functioned in the early church. I have pointed out how the church went from a Spirit-filled, spontaneous group of people described in the first few chapters of Acts to a group concerned for the selection and training of officers as described in First Timothy. But there is not much in the New Testament about the form of organization. After the close of the New Testament era, churches were gradually united under bishops. As early as A.D. 115, Ignatius, Bishop of Antioch, wrote letters to various churches, pointing out the importance of organization in the church. He likened deacons to Jesus Christ, bishops to God, and presbyters to the band of apostles. This linkage bestowed power on the organization and gave Christians a set of leaders to whom they could go for authoritative instruction in the faith and counsel as to how they should live.[3] By the fourth century a complex church organization was in place, based on the rational-legal bureaucratic Roman model. The inflexibility of this organization was seen long before the Reformation challenged every aspect of it.

The Dilemma of Communication. The original religious experience must be communicated in terms that succeeding generations can understand. Moreover, the meaning must be protected from misunderstanding and from criticism. Both processes require definitions in the common language and experience of believers. The more successful a religious group is in this communication process, the more likely it is to make its doctrine tenuous or prosaic. Yet if a religion cannot be expressed in fairly practical principles and procedures, it will not long endure. The ethical aspect of religion is most clearly at risk in this dilemma. If a religion interprets its ethical requirements in too precise a way—for example, in laws of conduct—it can easily slide into a legalistic stance alien to the mood and motive of the founder. On the other hand, if a religion cannot lay out what is expected in the concrete circumstances of life, then the followers drift away.

Paul faced this dilemma in his missionary work. The Greeks had no background in Jewish thought and worship, so Paul interpreted the gospel to fit their needs. This is illustrated by the Greeks' having a "bad" conscience about eating meat offered to idols. To these people, who thought that idols were important, Paul explained how idols possess no power; how love builds up a community rather than allegiance to a physical object; and how one should act in a situation when people one respects do not have the freedom of a Christian conscience. Paul's careful response to this problem shows how important he considered the dilemma of communication. Because he wanted the Corinthian Christians to understand the issue, he deliberately refused to lay down a law (1 Cor. 8). In his letter to the Roman Christians he deals with this dilemma again. He compares the law of Moses to the conscience of Gentiles, and in each case points out that true ethical conduct comes from obeying the spirit of moral principles rather than literal statements (Rom. 2:12–28). Unfortunately, Paul's instruction against legalism was not heeded; the church increasingly made many aspects of personal life a matter of law, with infractions punished by carefully calibrated duties.

O'Dea contends that this dilemma also extends to the doctrinal side of religion. The Roman Catholic Church and the Protestant denominations found it necessary to formulate doctrine in order to communicate their meaning of the gospel to people in a certain time and place. Such belief statements tend to become hardened into dogma, to which people pledge allegiance. Mircea Eliade, in his study of world religions, noted that symbols of the sacred over a period of time undergo a process "of rationalization, degeneration and infantilization . . . as it [the religion] comes to be interpreted on lower and lower planes."[4] Eliade describes two common ways in which this happens. One is for the symbol of a belief to be interpreted by the lower social strata in such concrete terms that the symbolic words become magic. His illustration is the Rumanian peasants' using the names of four rivers in the Bible (which symbolize the purity of the Garden of Eden) to relieve constipation: the peasants write the names of the rivers on a plate, run water over the plate, then drink the water. The other way is for a symbol to become sacred rather than point to the sacred. In this case people relate to the symbol and are satisfied. The Lord's Supper, for example, could be taken by people to mean that the bread and wine— rather than Jesus Christ himself—provide forgiveness. Eliade contends that this process of infantilization is inevitable and operates in "the most developed societies" as well as in primitive ones.

The motives of leaders who reduce religion to a simple creed may be good, but the results may lead people to a childish or superstitious reliance on words. The broad spectrum of American Protestantism contains some groups who attribute magical powers to the words of some verses of scripture, to certain answers in a catechism, or, more likely, to the affirmation of a Sunday school song such as "Jesus Loves Me." The issue is not that the meaning in these passages is wrong but that the passages may become objects of faith rather than pointing to God, the real object of faith.

The Dilemma of Power. To have any significance for a person, religion must be an experience that gives life both meaning and perspective. The experience can vary all the way from a vague feeling of what *ought* to be to a conversion experience in which a person has a clear vision of what *must* be. In every case religion has the role of putting all aspects of life together around beliefs, usually in association with a group. As religious organizations become institutionalized, they accommodate themselves to society, and their beliefs are often interpreted to fit the needs of that society and to support the secular authorities. Over a period of time, the beliefs become commonplace. When this happens, religion represents the core values of that society, resulting in two conditions. One is that religious beliefs become more open to question because they have drifted from the original experience to their accommodation with culture. The other is that the society may be more self-confident because its basic values have the approval of the religious authorities and, by inference, the power of God.

Under these circumstances religious organizations, which originally received their power from experience with God, tend to form an alliance with secular groups—even governments—to achieve status. From this alliance religious leaders gain concessions such as the right to educate children in partnership with the state, the right to conduct weddings, or the right to be seen and heard on ceremonial occasions. During the Catholic establishment in Europe and the establishment of Protestantism in Geneva, religious authorities were given the right to locate, try, and punish people who disagreed with prevailing religious beliefs. Following the Reformation, Western nations became involved in religious wars because the idea that a nation had to subscribe to one official religion was so deeply embedded. That period is now behind us, but the dilemma remains. Religion cannot help but be related to other aspects of society—at least through its followers. Since followers, by definition, believe that their religion is true, they seek support from all the agencies of society in which they are involved. The intermingling of religion and secular power seems to be inevitable.

Social Redirection

The above items—sin, secularism, and sectarianism—are related, for they all reflect the human inclination that allows religious experience over a period of time to be separated from God, formalized in some way, and used to support human needs and interests. This is an ancient problem and the solution is well known. Believers need to *renew* their allegiance to God and to seek God's will for the situation in which they find themselves. Most of the problems of the Christian life, both personal and ecclesiastical, are rooted in this human tendency to drift away from God's presence.

However, there are two matters of a different kind in which redirection rather than renewal is the result of experience with God. They are (1) matters in which God desires to lead believers in a different direction, thus creating a new tradition, and (2) matters in which humankind seeks guidance for problems for which there is no tradition.

In the first category one might cite the call of Moses to lead the people of Israel out of Egypt. This was literally a move in a new direction, to establish a new nation on the basis of a covenant God was preparing. When we read the Exodus account of the preparation and call of Moses, we see that it does not contain a reference to sin; the experience is simply about a new direction or a new mission for God's people and the call to Moses to be the leader (Ex. 1—4). The same can be claimed for the Protestant missionary movement that started with William Carey in the latter part of the eighteenth century. The religious experience of Carey and his contemporaries was a call to lead the church into a new awareness of God's will for all humankind.

In the second category one would cite the kind of ethical problems that have emerged as a result of scientific discoveries. The commandment "You shall not kill" presents us with unusual problems (Ex. 20:13). These problems are so well known I need only note the ability of medical doctors to keep people alive after all hope of conscious life is gone; the issue of who should make decisions about death under such circumstances is still uncertain. And the ability of doctors to start human life outside of a human body has caused many problems, as well as great joy for married couples who previously were unable to have children. These and related issues are not about human weakness but about new conditions in which we need guidance.

Self-Initiative

According to the biblical narrative, these matters are addressed by God's taking the initiative. A standard formula, used hundreds of times in the Bible, is that "the word of the Lord" came to a person to say certain things about the situation at hand. This occurred because there was a constant need for *renewal* of faith and often a need to *redirect* the community of believers.

There is, however, another side of experience with God that is not clearly defined in the passages where God takes the initiative: the aspect of religious experience in which a *person* initiates the effort to understand and do God's will. These may be two sides of the same coin, but each side is distinctive. This side shows a person who is acutely aware of the presence of God—often in ordinary life situations, including nature. Response to such awareness manifests itself in prayer and praise, in solitary brooding about the nature of God, in contemplation about events taking place, in extraordinary caring for other people, or in longing to be closer to the Divine.

The Bible contains a great deal of literature about this aspect of religious experience, especially in the psalms. Although there are several types of psalms, as collections of poems they are distinctive in that they represent humankind searching for God in the midst of ordinary experiences. The psalms are often lay people's response to an awareness of God. Many of them are about perennial human conditions, which makes it easier for people in succeeding generations to connect with the faith of the people of Israel. Psalm 23, about the goodness and guidance of God even in death, is a classic example of awareness of God's presence.

Christianity, like Judaism out of which it emerged, does not suggest that believers are to attain certain mystical states. However, the Christian religion has a mystical strand that is woven throughout the Bible and church history. In the first written record of Christian beliefs, the apostle Paul emphasized the importance of life in the Spirit: "Now the Lord is the Spirit, and where the Spirit of the Lord is, there is freedom. And we all, with unveiled face, beholding the glory of the Lord, are being changed into his likeness from one degree of glory to another; for this comes from the Lord who is the Spirit" (2 Cor. 3:17–18). The Gospel of John contains the most comprehensive statement of Christian mysticism; Jesus is identified as being one with God from the beginning. Moreover, the close association of the Son to the Father through the Holy Spirit is promised to be duplicated between believers and God (John 14; 15). This promise has attracted many mystics throughout the history of the Christian church.

If this book were written from a speculative or theoretical perspective, then the awareness of God's presence might be the first matter to consider; after all, it is thought by many to be the basis for religion in human life. Since religion of some sort has been a part of the culture of every known society, it is assumed that there is something in human life that seeks to resonate with whatever power there is behind and beyond the world. This innate desire—to link one's life with something that supplies meaning and hope, beyond what can be seen and understood—has coalesced into various forms of religious belief and practice. Although this hypothesis may be the correct explanation of why religion is a part of all human cultures, here we are concerned only to understand the Christian religion as it is embedded in the Bible and in the history of the church.

If there is a common human inclination to search for meaning beyond this life—and I think there is—then such inclination expressed in the Christian religion is open to critical analysis, as are all other claims of religious experience. The apostle Paul is our instructor on this point. The Greeks in Corinth grew up with "mystery" religions. During their celebrations some followers of these religions would become ecstatic and speak in an unknown language. The Greeks continued this practice, but Paul insisted on a critical analysis. In short, Paul required that speaking in tongues make sense or be interpreted to make sense, that what was said be for the purpose of building up the spiritual life of the congregation, and above all that the speakers take turns so the congregation could concentrate on what was being said while they searched for edification (1 Corinthians 14). Experience with God which came from a member's natural curiosity about God, or from an unusually acute sense of God's presence, did not have independent authority. Such experience had to make sense within the categories of what was already known about God and was so judged by the community of believers.

There is, however, a significant difference between religious experience that comes through this category of "awareness" and that which arises from the other categories. The difference has to do with the way a person feels inwardly. In the areas of sin, secularism, sectarianism, and social redirection, people are aware of the matter coming from outside themselves to which they are responding. Individual Christians are not always conscious of their involvement with these matters, but when they "see" their involvement they recognize three factors: the human situation outside themselves, their own feelings and mental judgments about the situation, and a sense of what ought to be said and done according to their conception of God. The category of sin is well illustrated by King David's taking Bathsheba and then having her husband killed so he could marry her. David must have been at least dimly aware of his sin, even though he was blinded by his powerful political position. However, when the prophet Nathan led him to see his sin, David realized that God, too, was an actor in the drama (2 Sam. 12:1–15). Secularism is more difficult to "see," since we have been so molded by secularism that we tend to interpret religion in terms of what it can do for our benefit, rather than to use religion in criticizing secularism. In our more reverent moments, however, we can perceive God's judgment on our enchantment with the things of the world. It is much easier to recognize the need for God's guidance in the categories of sectarianism and social redirection, for these are areas in which we are aware of our weaknesses and our need for help.

In contrast, individual Christians who are deeply concerned about the presence of God in their life are aware of two factors: their inward longing and their conception of God. These persons do not eliminate the human condition outside themselves, but they subdue or put such conditions on hold until they are confident they have "the mind of Christ" for their lives. Such single-mindedness in the pursuit of God distinguishes this kind of religious experience from the type in which God takes the initiative. The results, however, are the same. That is, *renewal* of faith in God often leads to a *redirection* of the life of the community of believers.

Communication of Experience

We can never communicate exactly the meaning of religious experience; it is so personal and so inward, we have difficulty explaining it to ourselves, much less to anyone else. We use words like "mystery" or "mystical" to describe what is indescribable. We might do better to label experience with God as nonrational, or transrational; then our efforts to understand it would be no more difficult than attempts to understand any other nonrational experience. In fact, what is revealed is not so much ideas or theological statements but aspects of God's will that relate to the human situation. For example, God reveals anger about sin or disbelief, sympathy for human weakness, commendation for righteousness, or purpose for national leaders. People who experience God's presence report something like a conversation with someone. At the deepest level the experience is vague—like the feeling we have about a person. At the conscious level the experience is expressed in words, but the words always seem inadequate because they are secondary and restrictive. Yet if we want the experience to influence other people, we have to use words to describe the experience and to communicate its meaning. Perhaps this is why so many biblical narratives about experience with God are reported as conversations or even as arguments.

On one occasion Teresa of Avila complained to God about her sufferings and trials. Through her prayers she heard the Lord say, "Teresa, so do I treat My friends!"—meaning that her suffering would bring purification and strength. Teresa already knew this would be the answer to her prayer, and she responded, "That's why you have so few [friends]." This kind of reporting—in conversation and with a certain kind of resistance and respect—is typical of those who are aware of God's presence.[5]

The priority of experience in the Christian life does not depreciate the role of theology. Theology, as Anselm said, is "faith seeking under-

standing." Experience and thinking about experience are in a dialecti-
cal relation to each other. Without experience, there is little religion
to think about; but experience, being extremely personal, needs critical reflection in order that it be instructive for other believers.[6]

Theology does not reveal truth but relates the mind to the truth
revealed. George Tyrrell, struggling with this problem within the
Roman Catholic Church at the turn of the century, concluded his
analogy as follows:

> Devotion and religion existed before theology, in the way that art existed
> before art-criticism; reasoning, before logic; speech, before grammar.
> Art-criticism, as far as it formulates and justifies the best work of the best
> artists, may dictate to and correct inferior workmen; and theology, as far
> as it formulates and justifies the devotion of the best Catholics, and as far
> as it is true to the life of faith and charity as actually lived, so far is it a
> law and corrective for all. But when it begins to contradict the facts of that
> spiritual life, it loses its reality and its authority; and needs itself to be
> corrected by the *lex orandi*.[7]

Theophanies

Experience and theology stand in a situation of mutual instruction
and correction. In between is the report of religious experience, which
is as near experience as we can get without actually being involved.
The Bible, as noted in chapter 3, is the believing community's written
record of what, over a period of time, that group found to be true
about God. One of the ways the community remembered important
experiences of God's presence is contained in a literary form called
"theophany," which literally means the appearance of God. In general
terms, a theophany is a "temporal manifestation of the deity to man,
involving visible and audible elements that signal God's real presence."[8] Theophanies transform people, and they are important to us
because they are intense, deliberate examples of religious experience.

Although theophanies are recorded from God's side—as is most of
the Bible—their purpose is to describe authentic religious experience
from a human perspective. This does not mean that theophanies are
peak human experiences such as Abraham Maslow thinks we should
aspire to. Although Maslow uses Christian saints as models, he states
that he wants to secularize and generalize their religious experience so
that it will become normative for anyone, regardless of that person's
faith in God. Maslow's goal is to maximize and enhance human experience.[9] But Saint Theresa, one of his examples, cannot be understood
apart from her conception of, and faith in, God. So theophanies are
not to be confused with exciting—or even creative—human experience.

Theophanies provide an example or a sample of authentic religious experience that transforms life. An example in this regard does not mean that theophanies as described in the Bible will be repeated today, for they are unique events. Rather, theophanies are illustrations of what God's presence meant in former times; they affirm the character of God's revelation and alert us to the possibility of contemporary experiences with God.

After a careful study of these self-disclosures of God, J. Kenneth Kuntz, author of the brief definition of theophany just cited, pointed out that they are also written "according to a definite literary form." Part of the literary form includes a "convulsion of nature" such as lightning and thunder, clouds, or unnatural occurrences such as a burning bush that is not consumed.[10] These convulsions of nature are important literary devices for saying that the experience is extraordinary and worthy of our most rapt attention. A theophany, then, is a condensed, intensive way of describing authentic religious experience.

The narrative style, or story, of how a person experiences the Divine is extremely important for the spiritual health of a community of believers. What is required is for the community to re-present the religious experience to itself so that it may be able to receive further revelations from God and be open to change. In short, the community needs to discover how a personal experience with God can be translated into directives for the community. Theophanies are such accounts. They certify the guidance of God within the events of history, thus prolonging the presence of God and providing expectations of further visitations. Theophanies are the classical biblical way of affirming the necessity of religious experience to the corroding influences of institutionalization from secularizing the community of believers.

Although each theophany is different, the literary form shows that there are three major elements in the experience. First, there is the situation. The event takes place in a certain place, at a certain time, and in relation to certain describable conditions. Second, there is a person or group who responds in fear, awe, and reverence. To that person or group the experience is real—real in the sense that they must do something about it. Third, there is a mission or work program in which they must engage, for what was revealed was God's *will* for them—not abstract ideas about God. The next three chapters will deal with these three major elements of theophany—situation, person, and work—so we may understand the full scope of religious experience.

5

The Situation

The idea of using theophanies as examples of authentic religious experience has been justified in previous chapters by showing that the community in which they happened believed them to be true. These occurrences of God's presence were remembered and recorded in stories that made telling and retelling them easy. The message from God was usually so specifically related to the historic situation in which it was received that it could not be used in a literal way again. However, the theophany story, which the community repeated over and over and over again, affirmed that God cared for and communicated with believers and that believers were to be alert to new revelations from God in their own circumstances.

Human Situations

When I first became aware of the value of theophanies as examples of authentic religious experience, I generalized the pattern in the following way: the experience came (a) to a person, (b) in a situation, (c) about events, (d) directing action toward God's purpose.[1] There is an attractive simplicity about this outline. Since religious experience begins with a person who is involved in a life situation, we can identify with that person and relate the biblical account to our own lives. Moreover, the biblical stories—with some exceptions, such as the giving of the covenant at Mount Sinai and the activities of the Holy Spirit in the formation of the church—are so identified with individuals that it is easy to focus attention on the person involved. Even in those two exceptions, Moses and Peter are the major actors in the dramatic events.

After further reflection, I decided to change the order and condense the analysis. Authentic religious experience comes (a) in a situation (which is the result of previous circumstances), (b) to a person or group, (c) directing thought and attention toward God's purpose for the person or group.

I now place the situation first, for the biblical account, although centered on a person, does not actually start with a person. The account always starts with a set of circumstances or a description of the prevailing human condition. The characteristics of the person involved are pictured as being formed by the cultural environment, but the experience with God results in the transformation of the person and often of the cultural environment. In fact, what believers learn from religious experience is directly related to the life situation through which the experience came to them. Let us look at theophanies related to Moses, Elijah, and Jesus for illustrations of the situational aspect of religious experience.

Moses

Perhaps the most important Old Testament theophany is the call of Moses, because that story describes how a group of slaves won their freedom and established a nation. The human situation is so well known it can be summarized briefly.

The Hebrew people had been living in Egypt in peace and dignity when a new king, or pharaoh, came into power. Apparently he was planning a conquest of neighboring countries or was fearful that other rulers would invade Egypt, for he came to believe that the Hebrew population might be a threat to his country's internal security. First, Pharaoh decided to oppress the Hebrews by forcing them to build fortifications. When the Hebrews continued to multiply, he asked the Hebrew midwives to kill all male babies; when they refused, Pharaoh ordered all Hebrew baby boys to be drowned in the Nile River.

When the baby to be named Moses was born and could no longer be hidden, he was placed in a basket in the river. The baby was discovered by Pharaoh's daughter, so Moses' sister, who was on guard, suggested that a Hebrew nurse be found for the child. Taking pity on the baby, Pharaoh's daughter agreed, and the sister selected Moses' mother to be the nurse. When Moses became old enough, he was given to Pharaoh's daughter to be raised in the palace. Thus Moses received the best education available, an intimate knowledge of Pharaoh, and an apprenticeship in statecraft.

Nevertheless, Moses identified himself with the plight of the Hebrews rather than with the Egyptians, as illustrated by his impulsive killing of an Egyptian who was abusing a Hebrew slave. This event forced Moses to leave Egypt. He settled in Midian, where he married and started a family. Perhaps that would have been the end of the story (and a story likely to be forgotten) except that Pharaoh died and his successor was even more cruel. The Hebrews could no longer entertain hope of any change in their condition of slavery, so they cried for help. The account at this point is both simple and profound: "God heard their groaning, and God remembered his covenant with Abraham, with Isaac, and with Jacob" (see Exodus 1—2). And there was Moses, trained and ready for leadership.

The story continues with God's revelation to Moses through a series of events both ordinary and extraordinary. Moses was keeping the flock of his father-in-law, as humdrum a task as a person at that time could have, when something extraordinary occurred: a bush began to burn, yet it was not consumed. We do not know the exact nature of the experience, but it was so momentous that Moses was transfixed. He became aware that the God of his ancestors and his people was speaking to him and that the Hebrews were suffering as slaves in Egypt.

If we pause at this point, we can appreciate the way circumstances have suddenly come together. The circumstances that described the slave condition of the Hebrews also accounted for the rescue of the baby Moses from death and his training in the palace as a potential leader. The worsening circumstances of the Hebrew slaves became related in Moses' mind to the promise of God to Abraham about a land where the Hebrews could live in freedom and dignity.

Elijah

The case of Elijah is important because of the general situation: a contest between faith in God and faith in idols. Such a conflict had been a constant problem with the Hebrews since the forming of the nation at Mount Sinai, but in Elijah's day the matter became so acute that the issue had to be decided. If Hebrews could worship local gods as well as the God of Abraham, Israel as a channel of communication between God and the people of the world would have no validity. Or, stated in another way, the temptation to worship idols or the local deity in order to placate the demands of a secular society cuts the nerve of the proper relationship to God—namely, awe, reverence, and obedience. It is not by chance that the first commandment states, "You shall have no other gods before me."

The human situation is complex, and much is lost in this condensed version. This particular episode in the life of Elijah starts with Ahab's becoming king of Israel. Apparently Ahab had some respect for God, for his two sons were given Hebrew-like names; but his wife, Jezebel, was the daughter of a king and priest of the god Baal-Melkart. After the marriage Ahab set up an altar to Baal. This public acknowledgment of other gods caused the writer to say, "Ahab did more to provoke the LORD, the God of Israel, to anger than all the kings of Israel who were before him" (1 Kings 16:33; see also 16:30). The Baals were local

village shrines of the sky god, Baal, who governed fertility by controlling rain.

Given these conditions, the contest was to be the control of the
weather. Elijah told the king there would be no more rain until the God
of Israel allowed it, and the resulting drought was in its third year
before Elijah confronted the king and challenged him to a public
contest between the Baals and God on Mount Carmel. The confrontation was dramatic: Elijah against 450 ministers of Baal; one altar
against another; one God against other gods. The drama was high-
lighted by Elijah's taunting of the Baal priests and by the deliberate
wetting of Elijah's altar before the fire came from heaven and the final
destruction of the Baal priests. Then the rains came, showing that the
Lord, not Baal, controlled the skies.

When Jezebel heard of Baal's humiliating defeat and the elimination
of the Baal priests, she was furious. She would not accept the defeat
of her god. Although she was probably not in a position to order Elijah
killed, she got her revenge by scaring him out of the country with the
threat to kill him. It seems strange that Elijah could challenge the king,
confront the Baal priests in public, eliminate them in the mass execu-
tion, and yet be afraid of the queen. But he was fearful, and he fled as
quickly as possible to Mount Sinai, where he hid in a cave. There the
theophany occurred—with some details that parallel the appearance of
God to Moses (see Exodus 33—34).[2]

This theophany is more important than the mere putting down of
fertility gods. The big issue is the nature and destiny of Israel. Is Israel
going to continue? The people might be saved at the moment from
worshiping Baal, but this was not the first time they had forgotten their
covenant with God. They seemed always to go back to idols. Elijah
realized that the dramatic events on Mount Carmel might have inclined the people to worship the Lord out of fear rather than from a
deep sense of obligation rooted in thankfulness. His despair and depression hit bottom: "and I, even I only, am left; and they seek my life."
Then came the convulsions of nature—strong winds, earthquake, and
fire—but the Lord was not in these things. The Lord was in "a still
small voice." (This narrative begins at 1 Kings 16:29 and continues
through chapter 19, where the theophany is recorded.)

The words translated "still small voice" are often interpreted to
mean conscience. This is a misunderstanding, for the experience is not
a psychological one. Kuntz, who translates it "a voice of a gentle
stillness," points out that this is an oxymoron, a contradiction in terms.
Silence and sound are put opposite each other. It is as if the mighty
convulsions of nature with all of their awesome power, noise, and fire
were necessary to produce the eerie silence through which Elijah could
hear the Lord.[3]

Peter, James, and John

A New Testament example of an intense religious experience will round out these illustrations of why the situation in which the theophany is experienced is the first element to which we must attend. Let us consider the transfiguration, since it confirms Jesus as the Christ and deliberately connects him with the great leaders of the Old Testament.

The narrative is simple and brief. Jesus took Peter, James, and John to a mountaintop for a prayer retreat. There Jesus was "transfigured"—changed into a figure with a bright, shining face and clothing as white as light. Moses and Elijah appeared and were talking to Jesus when a bright cloud came over them and a voice said, "This is my beloved Son, with whom I am well pleased; listen to him" (see Matt. 17:1–13; Mark 9:2–8; Luke 9:28–36).

In spite of its brevity, the narrative is rich in detail and full of allusions to the Old Testament, which do not make much sense unless we look at the situation in which the account is placed. In Matthew the story comes immediately after the experience of the disciples with Jesus at Caesarea Philippi, where—for the first time—it was made known in the words of Peter that "You are the Christ, the Son of the living God" (Matt. 16:15). Jesus then told the disciples that the church would be built on such confession, that he must now move on through the experience of death and resurrection, and that true discipleship consisted of loyalty to him and what he taught them. Since Mark and Luke placed the transfiguration in the same setting, we know that the story is related to the situation of the disciples. They had left everything to follow Jesus, they had learned from him, they had preached and taught what they had learned; but the idea that this Jesus they knew—as wonderful as he was—could actually be the hoped-for Messiah was not something they could easily accept. So this theophany, coming immediately after Peter's declaration, was a certification that Jesus was the Christ. Given this situation, the details and the brief story take on great significance. Moses represented the law, Elijah was symbolic of prophecy, and Jesus was shown to be the fulfillment of both the law and the prophets, thus affirming Jesus in continuity with God's previous revelations.

Situational Uniqueness

These three theophanies illustrate the uniqueness of each situation. The political, economic, and cultural conditions are different for each one. Even the religious tradition changes as it moves through time: it accumulates a literature and lore about a wider range of events. The story of Elijah had the Exodus events behind it, and the transfiguration had the whole Old Testament and the public ministry of Jesus in the background.

What we learn from the situational aspect of religious experience is the importance of the moment in which we live and the significance of the particular configuration of facts and events in which we find ourselves. Whatever religious experiences we have will come through and be related to our particular life situation. The specific circumstances for which we receive comfort or guidance will often change or pass away, but the experience of God's goodness toward us, or God's guidance for decisions we must make, will strengthen our faith.

Our time and circumstances are as potentially full of God's guidance as were former times. What is required is a faith that God is present and an alertness for the voice of God. This stance of openness to God is not easy, because circumstances of a job, family responsibilities, or the constant demands of social obligations take our time and force our attention on the matter at hand. But if we will distance ourselves from these pressing matters by scripture reading, prayer, congregational worship, and especially a quiet, deep, intense meditation during communion, we can gain God's perspective on the pressures of our life and begin to act accordingly.

There is nothing new about this process of seeking the presence of God. When Jesus was preaching to people caught up in the business of life and anxious about many things, he concluded his sermon with "He who has ears, let him hear" (Matt. 13:43). Jesus was reminding these people that God was present in their situation, but they had to take responsibility to stop and listen for God's voice. This listening can take place while one is washing dishes or mowing the lawn as surely as it happened to Moses while he was tending his father-in-law's sheep.

Experience

As far as the word "experience" is concerned, there seems to be no special problem. The word's Greek root means "empirical"; an experience, then, is something we know is true because we can see and understand it, and because other people can confirm what we see or hear. As rooted in the German language, the word means the knowledge one obtains by traveling or by exploring and finding out firsthand what things are, the kind of confidence seen in one who has actually been to the place described. And the Latin root means gathering data by trial and error or putting something to the test. Our word "expert" comes from this Latin source: a person who knows by experience, as an airplane pilot knows something by flying that cannot be learned by reading books about flying. All these meanings are carried over into English and form the basis of our extensive use of the word "experience." As soon as we move beyond root meanings and think about experience itself, however, we begin to pick up some of the underlying difficulties.

There is no commonly accepted theory about experience. We receive impressions about the world through our senses. As we identify an object through vision, for example, we differentiate it at once from other objects; we make a mental note that one thing is not another and thus start sorting out and relating objects. Since we do the same with feelings, sounds, and situations, experience is both a "differentiation and integration of perception and memories."[4] Many things go on as our mind takes a wide variety of experiences, collects them into categories, and forms concepts or judgments about them. At the same time the concepts and judgments condition what we see and hear.

Formative Power of Experience

The process of a person's responding to environment begins at birth. The baby responds to conditions created by parents, doctors, siblings, and neighbors, and to the interpretation that each of these groups provides. A baby born to an unmarried teenager who is a third-generation welfare recipient will have a different environment from that of a baby born to a mature married woman in a secure family setting. When we fill in the details for these two cases—such as the quality of affection the baby receives, the amount of encouragement to explore, the help with language, nutrition, health care, and all the other environmental factors that shape a growing child's life—we get a sense of how much the environment influences the development of a person.

Because experiences with environment begin at birth, they make a deep and lasting impression. The baby has little self-consciousness and no ability to speak. Small children can protest what they do not like, but they have so little knowledge of alternatives that their protests are often ineffective. Children also have many positive experiences with their environment, which give them good feelings toward parents or adults and a delight in certain activities. The results of a person's environment are established in early childhood and are expressed in that person's habits, self-confidence, moral standards, responses to new situations, attitudes toward other races and people, religion, and other human enterprises. The dynamic underlying the above elements is often unconscious because children incorporate them into their lives without conscious effort.

It is very difficult for people to change traits they have acquired through experience with their environment. One reason is that their interpretation of their environment continues to reinforce the traits they already have; another is that people are not able to analyze the conditions of their life situation until early adolescence. At that time they have the ability to reason in a logical manner and also the necessary background to make judgments based on how decisions affect themselves and others. But by the teen years persons are rather set in their outlook. It is difficult for the adolescent's newly acquired rational powers to bring about much modification of behavior that has such deep-seated roots.

Social Predispositions

Our social situation is also the situation in which we experience the presence of God. If we understand the way the social environment shapes our lives, we will be in a better position to gain a perspective on it and to consider ways the social environment should be changed to reflect more clearly the will of God in our common life. Chapter 2 outlines the historical and social reasons why secular individualism characterizes America today. If that analysis is correct, we are now in a position to define a more Christlike set of values to guide our congregational life.

Before we make comparisons, however, we must remember that society creates predispositions. This is a natural process, and these socially generated dispositions often show up in both congregations and other institutions. Whether they are good or bad depends on the criteria we use in judging. Let us pause for a moment to review this process and note how social predispositions provide an agenda for Christians.

Culture

One of the truly important developments of the twentieth century was the identification of the social nature of the mind. As with many developments in thought about human nature, this idea was not completely new, but in the teachings of George H. Mead it achieved a clarity and cogency previously unrecognized. Mead, interpreting life according to the pragmatism of his day, did not require God to provide humankind with a rational self. He showed how a small child's mind develops out of interaction with other people. Play, according to Mead, was the principal place where children learned their selfhood, self-control, and ability to organize life in a sensible way.[5]

Mead's work, in the first quarter of this century, explained how the mind is a product of the society in which it develops. Cultural anthropologists later showed how the mind by this process is conditioned at its deepest level by the beliefs and behavior of the people who nurture the child. Thus they could describe a tribe that was warlike and note the way small children were nurtured to develop this predisposition. Tribes not far away might be pacifists and have child-rearing practices that produced a peaceful predisposition in the adults. We have difficulty accepting this societal source of selfhood because our nurturing society—America—has taught us a special form of individualism. We affirm individual and political freedom as if we have thought of it all by ourselves rather than having come to an understanding of it as part of our heritage. This cultural process of forming general characteristics of the self creates distinctive personality patterns or inclinations, as mentioned in chapter 3 regarding differences in Japanese and American children.

Incidentally, these culturally induced predispositions are so deeply ingrained that they continue through all stages of development. For example, Japanese children may develop a capacity to do logical thinking at about the same age as American children, but their cultural predisposition for group approval, being social in origin, will not be affected by their increasing ability to do logical reasoning. Adult Japanese are just as group-oriented as children, for the adults developed this disposition when they were very young. Likewise, adult Americans are individualistic because they learned this outlook as children—in a way unrelated to their progression through stages of increasing capacity for logical thinking.

Although the data from social scientists illustrating ways that society inculcates general disposition in growing children continue to accumulate, the idea is not new. Recall again the story of Moses. Moses was unable to remove the mentality of slavery from the generation he brought out of Egypt; it was necessary for the Hebrews to wander for forty years until that generation died off and a new generation was raised with a disposition toward conquering the promised land (see Num. 32:13).

In our day, strong social movements have understood the problem and opportunity of mental predispositions. Three illustrations come to mind. The first was the civil rights movement of the 1960s, which originated among black Americans in the south. This movement had to deal with the predisposition of white Southerners to depreciate black people in general and to thwart their right to full participation in political and economic life. At the same time, Martin Luther King, Jr., and other leaders had to appeal to the conscience of the American public to create a new image of the worth of black people. This King did in several ways; his "Letter from the Birmingham Jail" and his "I Have a Dream" speech before the Lincoln Memorial in Washington are especially powerful examples. Many black people may think that progress has been too slow, yet from a perspective of social analysis the movement has succeeded, because the generation of children which has come of age since the 1970s is predisposed toward racial integration. If this change holds for one more generation, America will become a more integrated society.[6]

The movement for equal rights for women is not exactly the same as the civil rights movement. However, the problem and the opportunity of socially conditioned predispositions are the same. The problem is a male-oriented society in which women have had an inferior position. Pointing out discrimination in employment has improved the situation, with the result that now almost all positions are open to women—even heavy construction jobs. Developing in the rising generation a new mentality that will predispose both men and women to regard each other as equal has been more difficult. If we take as evidence the responses to the proposed equal rights amendment to the Constitution, the United States is not yet ready to support officially an equal gender society. Many women, however, are now aware of the social source of the predisposition problem. In their roles as mothers, teachers, and caregivers, these women are quietly establishing an inclination in both boys and girls to regard each other as equals. If this continues, in the next generation the equal rights amendment will either pass or become unnecessary.

Another illustration of the critical importance of culturally induced predispositions is the movement of peasants in Latin America for political and economic freedom. This movement is often in direct conflict with government, landowners, and some segments of the Roman Catholic Church. Paulo Freire, a professor of education, became interested in the plight of the peasants in Brazil. He soon discovered that teaching them to read was of little value, because they had accepted the judgment of their oppressors that they were inferior people and therefore society was right in giving them few rights and no opportunity to control their own destiny. This psychology in which the oppressed accept the judgment of their oppressors seems strange to middle-class Americans, because we have been trained to be assertive. But the phenomenon was first observed in a systematic way by Jewish social scientists in Nazi Germany. Under those terrible conditions some Jews who were given a little authority in the concentration camps began to act like Nazi officers, even against their own people.[7]

Freire realized that he must first help the peasants understand themselves as persons worthy of respect before he could make progress with any other kind of education. Like Moses, Freire had to exorcise the socially induced mentality of inferiority and help the peasants construct a different self-image before they could begin to take charge of their lives. This he did by raising their consciousness of who they were and what they could become. When they got a new perspective on themselves, they could gradually change their outlook. Then they would want to learn to read; reading became a means of self-esteem and a way to get the help they needed to achieve their rights.[8]

The movement for equal rights for women used the same method of consciousness-raising. Groups of women, through discussion of their situation, first had to understand the self-image imposed on them by society before they could begin the process of constructing a different self-image and insisting that society change its legal, economic, and social customs to match the women's new image of themselves.

Personal Circumstances

Chapter 3 outlined the way culture and religion are intertwined and how they communicate to individuals through many channels, including the church. We saw that the exact way people respond to the social-religious environment in which they are raised is different for each person. The discussion about predisposition explains why such deeply rooted nonrational inclination is important for the way individuals interpret the experiences they are having.

The particular circumstances of an individual are also a part of the social situation. This point is so obvious that we often fail to understand its significance. If we go back to the call of Moses again, however, we can see how those particular circumstances were crucial to the whole experience. The general condition of oppression of the Hebrews by Pharaoh resulted in the condition of slavery; Pharaoh's fear of a civil uprising, in turn, led to the policy of killing all male children in order to slow down the population growth of the Hebrew slaves. Moses' mother engineered his escape by hiding him in a basket in the river, an act which led to his adoption by Pharaoh's daughter. Finally, because Moses' mother became his nurse, Moses grew up with the Hebraic predisposition toward the welfare of his people, as shown by his defense of one who was being mistreated by an Egyptian (Ex. 2:11–12), and also a predisposition toward the rule of God in all of life (Ex. 3:7–10). Both predispositions were indispensable for Moses' experience of God's presence and the call to leadership.

In the same manner, the particular circumstances in which people find themselves are a critical part of religious experience. Such experience is not timeless, disassociated from the body, or unrelated to the hard facts of life. Rather, it is so tied up with the particular circumstances of people that those circumstances shape the nature of the experience, and the experience influences what one must do about the circumstances.

Religious Predispositions

I have been describing in this chapter how the human situation inculcates deeply rooted predispositions that govern every aspect of people's lives. Exactly how an individual responds to what comes from the outside is something of a mystery, especially if the experience is that of God's presence. This personal aspect will be covered in more detail in the next chapter. At this point, though, I want to continue the general discussion started in chapter 3 about the way religion and society are interrelated. There I pointed out that the two are almost inseparable and that congregations, according to their understanding of the Christian faith, harmonize the two for their members. At one extreme are congregations so like society that they hardly do more than bless the status quo and justify it against all other interpretations of life. At the other extreme are congregations which are cultlike in their intensity of belief and homogeneity. If their beliefs go counter to society, they will struggle for their right to be different. If not successful in such a fight, they will move the whole community of believers to another country where they can control the immediate environment. Here I want to identify four responses people give to religion as it comes to them from outside themselves.

The reason for dealing first with what is outside the self is that culture imposes itself on us in the early years before we are capable of imagining any other form of existence. Religion and society, in whatever mix our parents and mentors hold true, were presented to us as truth, and the practices associated with that mix were modeled before us in homes and congregations. Under normal circumstances it is not until adolescent years that we assay our inculcated religion and make some kind of judgment about our relationship to it. Often this process of evaluation and commitment does not take place until young people leave home for college or work. Under the circumstances of having to take charge of their life, make decisions about use of time and money, and become aware of different life-styles, they affirm or modify the faith that was presented to them as children.

Toward Secularism

As indicated in chapter 2, secularism is the dominant presupposition of American culture. This is not necessarily bad, nor does it automatically rule out a religious interpretation of life. Secularism ranges from a form that accepts scientific discoveries as gifts from God to a materialistic form in which religious faith has no place. Since American life contains all forms of secularism, the issue is the form that is supported in the community where a person is nurtured. If that form is one in which faith in God is absent or ridiculed, children will develop that predisposition and make it their own unless challenged by ideas or events of a different sort.

Toward Tradition

The typical kind of social conditioning that takes place in congregations and homes is respect for and participation in a religious tradition.

This array of experiences starts before a child develops self-consciousness, and it continues for church people throughout their life. It is not just the rite of baptism, which may be administered soon after birth, that counts here; it is the child's participation in whatever religious atmosphere the home provides, supplemented by church activities and the influence of friends and relatives with a similar religious orientation. Children can grow up in America having only nominal contact with a congregation and yet still obtain some understanding of the major theological beliefs of Christianity. They do so through the mass media, especially at Christmas and Easter, through literature courses and programs of public schools, and through association with peers who attend church.

Whether people absorb Christianity from society or are actually members of a congregation, their experience may be limited to their particular religious tradition. These people have learned, or experienced, religion in the same way they learn socially accepted manners; and it means the same thing. Religion is the sacred side of life. It has a role to play. It provides reassurance to cope with uncertainty, beauty to enhance drabness, forgiveness for guilt, fellowship for loneliness, and ceremonies for naming babies, for marriage, and for death.

We must be careful not to dismiss this kind of conditioning as merely a cultural form. People who use religion this way are accepting what is ready-made for the ordinary circumstances of life. Although they may feel estranged from God and neighbor because of their human inclination to sin, they also accept the religious tradition of family and friends as the way to restore themselves in God's favor. They do so because the religious tradition has prepackaged attitudes, responses, and ceremonies fitting all contingencies. Not motivated to probe behind the ritual, they accept what is already certified to be true.

It is incorrect to identify people who are traditional in their religion with persons who have a civic religion. The latter have one form of a ready-made religion, a form that absolutizes American values as the practical meaning of faith. But people can be conditioned by the religious tradition of a pacifist church or by a sect group that refuses to salute the American flag and still be affirming only what they observe and experience from people with whom they live. The crucial factor is this: people who have been conditioned by a tradition and who have closed their minds to anything else do not want new experiences, nor do they seek to know God in any way that would disturb their present situation.

Contemporary illustrations are not difficult to locate. Roman Catholics who do not understand Latin but insist on using it for the mass may be saying that they place the language higher than the meaning of worship. Protestants who glory in the King James Version of the Bible, even though the words in some passages now have a changed meaning, are giving more authority to the tradition than to the meaning of that tradition.

On many occasions Jesus contended with Jews who were conditioned by the tradition in which they lived and who seemed not to understand Jesus' meaning. Matthew, for example, points out that the opposition to Jesus began to solidify when the Jerusalem Pharisees accused him of not following the traditions of the past. Specifically, these critics said that Jesus' disciples did not wash their hands before they ate. Jesus replied by showing how these Pharisees had worked out a legalistic way to avoid their responsibility to their parents. He then berated them so severely that even the disciples were surprised (Matt. 15:1-20).

People who are conditioned by a religious tradition that leads to dogma can easily be faulted, but I have restrained from judging such people, for they have accepted and absorbed what the religious establishment has approved. They have a respected answer to the questions of life, death, and decision making. This form of religious conditioning produces an inability to adapt. Such people are confident of their experience and want their children and friends to have the same assurances from religious tradition that they have achieved. To these people, experience of the religious tradition is satisfactory; they feel their faith fulfills its proper niche in life's activities.

Toward Understanding Tradition

A third kind of conditioning is that which preserves the accumulated story of God's dealings with humankind in the past, with the expectation that the God thus described in the tradition can be found, understood, and enjoyed in the present.

The Bible provides our best illustration of these types of experience, for the biblical story is told from what the people saw as God's standpoint. Starting with Genesis, one can see that God had a plan for people to live in harmony and to enjoy the bounty of the earth. That plan was ruined by sin, yet God tried to lead the people into the way of peace and justice. The people wanted to use the earth and its products for their selfish desires. God started over again with Noah, but the results were no better. In the twelfth chapter of Genesis God starts a different strategy—the calling of Abraham to lead a people who will become God's model of what human life should be like. From that point onward, the account describes a constant struggle between people, usually prophets (who have experienced God through tradition) and others, usually rulers or priests (who have experienced only the religious tradition in its institutionalized form). The Baal worship lead-

ing to the theophany of Elijah provides a classic illustration of a
prophet who acted completely within the tradition. Elijah added no
new ideas about God, nor did he lead Israel in new directions. He
simply insisted that the first and second commandments meant, in his
day, an absolute resistance to worshiping a fertility god.

The life of Jesus furnishes us with even more dramatic illustrations
of how God can be experienced within or through tradition. Scholars
have often pointed out that very few of Jesus' teachings were original;
he either repeated or adapted ideas and stories from his scriptures, our
Old Testament. Matthew's account of Jesus' Sermon on the Mount
provides this formula: "You have heard that it was said . . . but I say
to you. . . ." Jesus then explained what the original commandment or
teaching meant when applied to circumstances of his day. Over a
period of time the tradition had made so many accommodations to
selfish purposes that the teachings had lost their significance. Jesus
showed what the teachings meant because he represented the God
behind the tradition. His auditors sensed this at once. Matthew recorded their astonishment: "For he taught them as one who had authority, and not as their scribes" (Matt. 7:28–29).

When Jesus wanted to explain the meaning of his death and resurrection, he used a story from Isaiah. The original story was so old that
it had already become a song in Isaiah's day. It described how God had
prepared a wonderful vineyard for his people, but the men of Judah
took it for their own pleasure rather than living the life of goodness
and justice God expected (Isa. 5:1–7). Although Jesus changed some
of the details of that story to fit the circumstances of his coming
rejection and to affirm his coming role in the salvation of humanity,
the force of the story is the same. The people had put their faith in
tradition rather than in the God behind tradition who was bringing
new things to pass (see Matt. 21:23–43).

The situation for us today is not widely different from that of biblical
times. We have a religious tradition; the question is whether we will
use it as a means of experiencing what it teaches. We must look at
religious tradition as the residue of how previous generations responded to God. The residue is not God, but it may guide us to our
own experiences with God.

To view tradition this way is not easy. It means that we honor
tradition and yet are ready to modify it when our experience of God
leads us to a different interpretation. A fine illustration of this attitude
is displayed by Gamaliel. When Peter and the apostles were brought
before the Jewish Senate to be tried for proclaiming that Jesus was the
Messiah, there was considerable demand that they be killed. In that
mob scene when passion was running high, Gamaliel, an honored
teacher, brought the Senate to soberness by his statement that they

should leave Peter and the others alone. He counseled that if "this undertaking is of men it will fail; but if it is of God, you will not be able to overthrow them" (Acts 5:33–39). Such an attitude of openness is the crucial factor that allows for an experience with God.

There are two ways a person may experience God in and through religious tradition. One is through conviction; the other is through conversion. Both ways are well known, so our discussion will be brief.

First, let us consider conviction. Experiences of conviction are those which correspond to what the tradition affirms to be true. In other words, we do not understand theology until we have the experience which theology explains. William H. Willimon, on the occasion of the two hundredth anniversary of the Sunday school, recalled an experience he had in his third-grade church school class:

> I remember the Sunday when, as Miss Lewis told us the story about Joseph and his brothers, I finally gave Stanley Starnes what he deserved and pushed him into the radiator at the back of the Sunday school room. As a result, Stanley had to be taken to the emergency room, and Miss Lewis had occasion to teach some theology of her own. When the dust had cleared and Stanley had been carried away screaming and bleeding, and I had started to feel deep remorse, Miss Lewis opened her Bible and looked at me and said, "Now William, you know what Joseph's brothers felt like. They had a little brother like Stanley, and they did to him what you would like to do to Stanley. But God loved them. And God loves *you*—even if you did push Stanley into the radiator."
>
> In the midst of my big and little adult sins, and my more subtle grown-up ways of pushing little brothers and sisters into the radiator, in moments of despair over my plight, sometimes I hear a voice in the darkness. It is Miss Lewis, speaking above the drone of my passionless academic theology, rising as it once rose above the din of 13 nine-year-old Christians, saying, "Now William, remember, God loves you."[9]

William now understands forgiveness because Miss Lewis related the doctrine to his need to be forgiven. Anyone who has experienced forgiveness by a loved one understands the common definition of experience as "I've been there; I know what it is like." People who are predisposed to experience God through the Christian tradition are also predisposed to seek God in prayer, to study the life of Jesus and order their lives by the ethical concerns he displayed, and to congregate with other Christians, discussing contemporary issues within a context of mutual concern and thus gaining spiritual strength.

The presence of God is also experienced in the sacraments. Those who prefer infant baptism believe that God is present to the child through the parents, while those who prefer adult baptism believe that God is present to the believer as he or she takes vows of discipleship. When we celebrate the Lord's Supper, we believe that Christ is present to us in the bread and wine. Communion is a reenactment of the Gospel, a time when believers are reminded of their salvation through the sacrifice of Jesus.

Christians often have experiences that they interpret as being from the Lord. These experiences, which provide guidance for decision making or give the individual a profound sense of God's protection, James E. Loder calls "transforming moments" because they bring "conviction beyond reason." Loder had such an experience as a result of an automobile accident, and although it did not change the outward circumstances of his life, in a sense it changed everything. He now lives with the realization that he has been spared for a while, a thought that permeates his whole being.[10]

Second, let us consider conversion. Although we tend to think that conversion is unique to Christianity, it is something that happens in many religions. Jesus knew about and took a negative view of conversion when it simply produced more legalistic Pharisees (Matt. 23:15). We should not think of conversion as being different from convictional experience except that it happens within a short period of time. It is one way of coming to a self-conscious decision about faith in Jesus Christ, but it is no more valid than a person's coming to that decision as a result of a set of convictional experiences over a period of time. In either case, one has a conviction of sin, an experience of forgiveness, a sense of fellowship with God, and a desire to love one's neighbor. Both processes produce a life commitment to Jesus Christ and a determination to resist the forces of the world that hinder the rule of God in our life.

The experiences of God described in this third kind of mental conditioning have one thing in common: they result in thought and activity in harmony with the tradition. Most of our congregational life is designed to help members experience the presence of God and to guide them into the life-style displayed for us in scripture. This does not mean that all Christians are alike. It means they have all experienced salvation in Christ, although that happened in a special way to each believer. Christians will have different ideas about the will of God concerning ethical issues, but they have a higher loyalty to maintain the integrity of the church, the body of Christ, while they search for a more harmonious judgment. Continuity in the tradition and continuation of the church as a body of believers are typical characteristics of this experience.

Toward Changes in the Tradition

The Christian faith, from its biblical base and its two thousand years of history, affirms that there are special times when experiences with God result either in changes in the tradition or in the commonly accepted interpretation of morality. The leadership of Moses, the vision of Isaiah (chapters 52 and 53), and the appearance of Jesus all come out of the tradition, and yet they all break with it. This fourth classification of experience does not come from conditioning different from the third kind; rather, the resulting experience is discontinuous with the past. When the discontinuity is theological—as with the appearance of Jesus—we have a different religion. When the discontinuity is a matter of interpretation—as it was in the Reformation—we have a new emphasis. And when the discontinuity is moral—as it was when slavery was finally identified as unchristian—we have a fresh understanding of the will of God.

In order to understand these experiences with God, we should look at the human situation from God's standpoint, as the Bible does. Biblical sources show that God cares for humankind yet allows persons freedom to choose their own destiny. This makes for an almost impossible position for God: if God is too aggressive, human freedom is overruled; if God is too passive, human beings will exploit the earth and each other for their own selfish gain. All this has been explained in the first eleven chapters of Genesis. Sometimes God solves this dilemma by breaking into the human scene to show God's will and how it may be achieved; sometimes, as we are seeing here, people have experiences with God that require the receiver to reform the tradition.

Present Situation

The three biblical stories I have used are major events in the history of the Jewish and Christian faiths. When we read the dramatic circumstances of these stories and see the decisive effect the presence of God had on the lives of the people involved, we are thankful for God's guidance in the past; yet we do not expect such events to happen today. If they do happen today, we assume they will happen to someone else—not to us.

Other stories, such as the conversion of Saul, could have been used, but more stories are not necessary to show the major features of experience with God. The biblical accounts affirm the situational aspects of God's presence. This means that our particular situation has the potential for being the place where we will become aware of God. When we experience God in our situation, we receive comfort, guidance, or assurance in relation to whatever the situation requires. This situational aspect of experience with God is what gives it power to change lives. Personal power is generated because questions must be answered, decisions must be made, or words must be spoken. If we receive help from the Lord in these matters, our faith is confirmed and our confidence in what we are to be or do is strengthened.

Exactly what happens in the moment of encounter with God is

difficult to describe. In Moses' case the encounter centered on a burning bush; with Elijah it was a voice; with Peter, James, and John it was a vision. These moments do not mean that God plays hide-and-seek, and is available only at certain times, but that we become conscious of God's presence in certain circumstances—usually conditions in which we are deeply involved—about which we must make some decision.

The moment of encounter is usually described in vague terms or in dreamlike language. It is so tied to the person's interior life and personal history that the description of the moment does not have much meaning for anyone else; nevertheless, we should let the description stand as the person wishes to state it, regardless of how unusual it may be. What is important is the situation in which the experience took place and what the person did with his or her life afterward.

Jürgen Moltmann's Case

Jürgen Moltmann is one of the top-ranking theologians of our day. Born in Hamburg in 1926, Moltmann belonged to the German generation that was caught up in the most intensive fighting of World War II. Although he intended to follow a scientific career in the university by studying mathematics and physics, he had to postpone that career when he was conscripted as a soldier. He took with him the "iron rations" of Goethe's poems and the writings of Nietzsche. In February 1945 he was taken prisoner by the British and for three years was moved from camp to camp in Scotland and England. During that period German prisoners saw the destruction of Germany. They learned of the efforts to exterminate the Jews. As their world fell apart, many men gave up hope; some even died from a lack of it, and Moltmann writes, "The same thing almost happened to me. What kept me from it was a rebirth to new life thanks to a hope for which there was no evidence at all."[11]

Moltmann did not have a sudden conversion. The old person died and something different began to build up: "At home, Christianity was only a matter of form. One came across it once a year at Christmastime." During his prison years a chaplain gave Moltmann a New Testament with Psalms; at that time, Moltmann explains, he "would rather have had something to eat. But then I became fascinated by the Psalms . . . and especially Psalm 39: 'I was dumb with silence, I held my peace, even from good; and my sorrow was stirred. . . . Hold thou not thy peace at my tears: for I am a stranger with thee, and a sojourner, as all my fathers were.' " Those words opened Moltmann's eyes to God because they described his own suffering. Realizing that God was with him "even behind the barbed wire" led him to experiences he expresses in these words: "I cannot even say I found God there. But I do know in my heart that it is there that he found me, and that I would otherwise have been lost."[12]

Moltmann looks back on his experience of the presence of God as the turning point in his life, yet he is unable to describe exactly what happened. He writes that "since it is impossible to convey mystical experience itself through doctrinal statements, the theology of mystical experience always only talks about the way, the journey, the voyage out to that unutterable experience of God which no one can tell or communicate." He adds, "Its doctrinal content . . . has never seemed particularly impressive, even down to the present day." Moltmann's story is fascinating because his life illustrates the thesis of this book and the comments made earlier about religious experience *of* the tradition and *in* the tradition.[13]

Other Cases

Hugh T. Kerr and John M. Mulder have edited a book entitled *Conversions.* Beginning with the apostle Paul and concluding with Charles W. Colson, they present fifty persons who experienced the presence of God, about twenty of whom lived in the latter part of this century and are well known to this generation. The book is of special value for the discussion in this chapter because Kerr and Mulder give a brief account of the social situation in which each person lived. With that set of circumstances in mind, we then have an account of the experience the person had with God and the way it changed his or her life.

For the people in the book who lived in the twentieth century—such as C. S. Lewis, Lin Yutang, Dorothy Day, Ethel Waters, Dag Hammarskjöld, Thomas Merton, Clare Boothe Luce, Eldridge Cleaver, and Charles Colson—the story is not so much conversion to Christianity as it is an experience that caused them to believe the Christianity they already knew. Lin Yutang, for example, was the son of Chinese Christians and had been educated in Christian schools, but he renounced Christianity and became a Confucianist. After he had finished his higher education, had held many high educational positions, had invented a Chinese typewriter, and had written a best-seller, *The Importance of Living,* he became a Christian. Why? Because while living in New York his wife asked him to attend church with her. When he heard Dr. David Read preach, he was moved to study the life and teachings of Jesus. That study so affected him, he said, "The scales began to fall from my eyes."[14]

6

The Person

Discussing the experience of God's presence by beginning with the situation in which it occurs is not an effort to affirm the superiority of society over the self; it is simply a recognition that, as far as written records provide us with information about human life, a person is always born into a particular cultural situation. We know life at the historical and geographical point where we entered and began to respond to it, so there is a sense in which knowledge, though personal, is always about and related to the world at large.

Experience of God

Theophanies help us understand how a person is involved in an authentic religious experience. These condensed versions of intense personal experiences with God are so dramatic we sometimes forget that the biblical person had the same kind of fears, anxieties, and desires that we have. Theophanies portray ordinary persons who are sinful, willful, and sometimes—as in the case of Peter—a bit slow to catch on to what is happening. Our biblical examples describe a four-phase process, which takes place usually in the following order: first, the individual has a prior knowledge of God; second, an event as a part of a larger situation arrests a person's attention; third, there is a call to the person that requires a response; and fourth, an engagement with God's desire changes both the person and the situation in which the event occurred.

Although the process follows approximately in the order described, these phases usually overlap. Furthermore, the phases may be longer or more detailed in one theophany than in another, according to the character of the person involved and the nature of the situation. Let us look at these four phases in the theophanies we have been using as examples.

Moses

In the story of the call of Moses, the prior knowledge of God is well established. Exactly how Moses obtained his knowledge is open to speculation, but we do know that his mother was with him during his early, formative years. The name "Moses," although of Egyptian origin, is explained in the story to mean "drawn out of the water," so Moses was constantly aware that he was a Hebrew saved from the cruelty of the Egyptian king. Moses received some instruction in the Hebrew religion, for his family was near and he could see his people every day. By the time he became a man, his self-identity was that of a Hebrew, for he attacked and killed an Egyptian who was abusing a Hebrew slave. Because of that occurrence he went into exile.

The event that formed the basis of the theophany took place during a humdrum, routine existence. Moses was doing the work of a hired hand as shepherd of his father-in-law's sheep. While walking in the fields one day, he saw a bush ignite and burn steadily without being consumed. The voice that called to him identified itself by saying, "I am the God of your father, the God of Abraham, the God of Isaac, and the God of Jacob." We do not know exactly what happened at the burning bush, and there is no point in trying to rationalize the event by saying it was a mirage or a bright reflection in the hot desert. The account is written to say that Moses was stopped in his tracks: he experienced himself in relation to God and began to realize that life was not just one thing after another but was something for which he was accountable.

The call of Moses is the most fascinating and profound phase of the story. Moses, although a believer in the God of his fathers and now one who had experienced the self of God, was by no means delighted by this turn of events. People who yearn for a religious experience in biblical terms should read this call of Moses carefully. Moses understood that he was in the hands of a willful God and did everything he could to escape; he knew what was being asked of him, for he had lived in the palace and had seen the brutality of Egyptian kings, who ruled by sheer physical power. Although our call from God may not be as dramatic as that of Moses, it nevertheless may be dangerous. This story affirms that an authentic experience with God will cause us to see that things are wrong and must be put right and we are being singled out to do so.

Today, at least three thousand years after this event, there are still oppressed people and there is much injustice encased in laws and customs. Thus an experience with the Lord may still be traumatic, for one may be called to set oneself in opposition to powers in society.

Because many Christians believe that a religious experience is a soothing, relaxing reassurance of their worth in the eyes of God, we may be surprised at Moses' effort to get away from God's call. His struggle shows that an experience with the Lord may be feared as well as prized.

1. Moses' first response was "Why me?" This reply is an adroit ploy we all use for a distasteful assignment. It assumes that the cause may be good but suggests that we don't want to be directly involved. Or the comment may imply that, although the cause is good, we do not have the background or preparation for this specific project (Ex. 3:11).

2. Moses' second excuse was more serious. "How can I be sure I have had an experience with the true God?" he protested. After all, he may have thought, this may be just something buzzing in my mind that will not make any sense when I go out to lead the people. The people need assurance that I have a true call. They are not going to leave their settled homes and guaranteed schedule of meals just because a self-appointed person stands up and says, "Let's go somewhere else." Tell me, God, what is your nature—what can I tell the people we can count on? God's reply is one of the most profound in the Bible. Its words, though difficult to translate, may be paraphrased as "I cause to be" or "I am the source of all that is" or "I am what is important in human affairs." This idiomatic description of God lies in the Hebrew word for God, which was considered so holy it was never pronounced aloud. But the account does not make a mystery of it, for the instructions to come confirm that God continues to be what God had been to the leaders of the Hebrews in former generations and that God is concerned for the future of the chosen people (Ex. 3:13–16).

3. With his main excuses demolished, Moses turned his mind to the people he was expected to lead out of slavery and conjured up a third objection: "The people will not believe I have a call from God." Here he was probably correct. Why should the people believe Moses—who had lived in the king's palace as a prince, who had never been a slave, and who had now come back from exile with a message that God had selected him to lead a revolt? The Lord countered that excuse with an array of miracles for Moses to perform as signs of God's presence (Ex. 4:1–9).

4. Not much was left in Moses' repertoire of excuses, but he came up with a fourth: "I'm not a good public speaker." This excuse was also cogent, for a leader must be able to communicate clearly and confidently. The Lord, growing impatient, replied that Moses would be told what to say, but Moses, having completely run out of excuses, continued his evasion: "O, my Lord, send, I pray, some other person" (Ex. 4:10–14). At this point Moses finally realized he was not going to escape the hands of a willful God, so he acquiesced. However, he did not accept this revelation from God wholeheartedly; later, when things went badly, Moses blamed God for giving him such a difficult assignment (Ex. 17:1–7).

The fourth phase of Moses' call, his engagement with God's purpose, was rather matter-of-fact. He went back to his father-in-law, asked for permission to return to his people, assembled his wife and sons, and went to Egypt. The experience changed Moses, and his leadership of the Hebrews changed the course of history (Ex. 4:18–20).

Elijah

The personal aspect of Elijah's experience can be told briefly. Because Elijah was a prophet, his knowledge of God from tradition was as complete as one could acquire. When the crucial moment came in the contest with the priests of Baal on Mount Carmel, Elijah called on the Lord: "God of Abraham, Isaac, and Israel" (1 Kings 18:36).

For most of us, the big event in the story of Elijah would be the dramatic scene of the prophet of the Lord against 450 prophets of Baal, each side praying for rain. Yet Elijah seemed to go through all this as though he were following the script of a play. Not until the furious Jezebel threatened his life did he fall into a state of depression—about himself, about the propensity of his people to worship idols, and about the secular spirit of his age. The event through which Elijah experienced God was undistinguished: he was at the end of his emotional strength, living in a cave, and brooding on his loneliness as the only person on earth who was faithful to God. In his desolation the voice of God came out of eerie silence to say that Elijah was not alone and that the nation would be saved.

In Elijah's theophany the sense of being called and being engaged in God's work was already present, so the issue was not so much whether Elijah would devote himself to God's cause as it was the way in which he would do so. Feeling sorry for himself for working hard without any sign of appreciation from God's people, Elijah was brought out of his depression into the real world—where there were still seven thousand people who had not bowed the knee to Baal.

Peter, James, and John

The personal aspects of the transfiguration are highly condensed. Peter, James, and John not only had prior knowledge of the tradition, they also had been with Jesus since the beginning of his public ministry. This experience of being alone with Jesus when he was transfigured into a glowing figure beyond ordinary understanding of time and space made an indelible impression on them. Peter was so struck with the realistic appearance of Moses and Elijah that he proposed building temporary shelters for them on the mountain. The exact nature of this intense mystical experience we do not know, but when it was shared with the other disciples and believers in the early church, it must have been a powerful way of affirming that Jesus was the long-expected Messiah.

Our Experience of God

Each theophany is a different story, but in all of them the personal aspect is pronounced. From these three illustrations we have found that the biblical model of authentic religious experience suggests four phases in one's apprehension of the Divine. We must be careful not to imply that these phases happen one after the other or in some other standardized sequence. Most likely they happen almost all at once, so any identification of phases or separation of one phase from another only helps us understand the way a person is involved in a religious experience. Such understanding may enlighten our own spiritual pilgrimage and aid our effort to communicate the Christian faith to others.

Prior Knowledge

First, one must have some prior knowledge of God. All our biblical examples show that a person who has a personal experience with God has been brought up in the tradition or has heard of God from some source. The only exception seems to be the story of Abraham, whose call is abrupt: "The LORD said to Abram, 'Go from your country and your kindred . . . to the land that I will show you' " (Gen. 12:1). This is a sharp change from the earlier chapters of Genesis, which tell the story of God's broader dealings. Beginning in chapter 12, God changes strategy (out of sheer frustration with a sinful and obstinate humankind), decides to form a nation that will be a model for the world to see and emulate, and selects Abraham to start that nation. Since he is to originate a new, God-loving nation, Abraham is presented in the story as a new figure, open to the guidance of God. Abraham's faith in God is proved by his willingness to sacrifice his son Isaac at God's command. But even this new strategy, new leader, and new tradition are not without a history. The eleventh chapter of Genesis opens with the story of the Tower of Babel—the scattering of the people and the origin of different languages—but it concludes with a genealogy that leads up to Abraham's family. Thus, by listing the generations who had continued to conserve a knowledge of God, the account makes a bridge from God's early attempts to deal with all people to the new strategy of building a model nation. In this sense even Abraham, the prototype of the new person of faith, had a prior knowledge of God.

Of course, at some point in history, there had to be an original revelation of God to humankind, but that is a speculative question we can bypass. As a practical matter, people who have an experience with God have in their background some prior knowledge of God. The writer of Hebrews put it this way: "For whoever would draw near to God must believe that he exists and that he rewards those who seek him" (Heb. 11:6).

This formula for drawing near to God requires familiarity with the concept of a God who cares about humankind, a knowledge that must come either from adults or from others who transmit this idea to children and to their peers. It is deeply imbedded in social custom, so it does not necessarily have to come to a person from parents. The idea of God is then used by a person to interpret events. Events by themselves, as previously noted, have little meaning; meaning is supplied by the mind as the events happen. Thus the concept of God, when used by people to explain events in which they are involved, is what starts their personal inventory of experiences with God.

Significant Event

A second element in the personal aspect of religious experience is an event that becomes significant enough to cause life to be seen in a new or different way. The event itself may occur while a person is going about daily duties, as in Moses' care of sheep; in a dream, as in the case of Peter (Acts 10:9–16); at a national celebration of God's guidance in times past, as in the case of the giving of the Ten Commandments (Exodus 19); or at the death of a ruler, as in the case of Isaiah (Isa. 6:1).

Because so much is made of the lives of saints and great religious leaders, we tend to set these persons apart as special and assume that religious experiences seldom happen to ordinary people. To remedy this failure to recognize how religious experience influences many people today, Sir Alister Hardy, Oxford Professor of Biology and Gifford Lecturer, invited people "who felt their lives had in any way been influenced by some power beyond themselves" to write about the experience and send the account to him. Now, after several decades of Hardy's collecting and studying such experiences at the Religious Experience Unit at Manchester College, it can be said that people in every vocation and at almost every age level have experienced a power beyond ordinary experience that influenced their lives. To many Christians, some of the experiences reported to the Religious Experience Unit might seem vague, but each experience was decisive for the person involved.[1]

The event that becomes significant is one that attracts attention. It may be that the event is sudden, such as a car accident that threatens one's life. It can also be an experience to which we respond negatively, such as a sickness that interrupts our schedule, or a marriage that dissolves. At the time of such an event or a series of closely related events, one might see nothing of value; but later, looking back, one may perceive in that experience a great deal of significance.

Singled Out

The third element is a sense of being singled out by God—for a specific task, a change of life-style, or a confirmation that what one is trying to be is what God desires. This singling out is like being called by someone. When called, we focus our attention on the caller and wait for the message.

Paul Minear uses the example of a drama to illustrate the meaning of a call. I paraphrase his idea this way: You are at the theater with a group of friends, sitting in a box; you are absorbed as a spectator of the drama taking place on the stage in front of you. Suddenly the author and director of the play steps out from the wings and, while the drama continues, shouts your name. "Joe Smith!" he calls. "Come here to the stage and get into the act; I have a part for you." The peculiar thing is, no one else hears him shout your name, and no one else moves or looks at you, for everyone is intently following the action on stage. Now you are aroused. You are embarrassed to leave your friends without a sensible explanation, but there is no logical reason for entering the drama except the compulsion from within. You begin to feel a panic, perhaps a cold sweat. What will you do? Will you suppress this urge to get into the play? Will you argue with the director? Will you leave the theater? Will you get up and throw yourself into the drama and try to influence the course of action according to the impulse that urges itself upon you?[2]

This sense of being singled out, or of being called, is highly personal. There is no explanation as to why one is selected. If the action required is dangerous or disruptive of our normal routine, our automatic response is exactly like that of Moses: "Why me?" Yet the event so changes the situation in which we live that we feel either a compulsion to act or a need to explain to ourselves why we will not respond to the call. We find ourselves being pulled by an invisible power, and we are obliged to be attentive to what the power is coaching us to do.

When a person feels singled out and called by God, time becomes altered. As we realize that the God who always was and always will be has visited *us*—creatures who have but a moment of existence—then *chronos,* or clock time, which goes on at a regular rate, becomes less important than *kairos,* or God's time. The experience we have with God's self may be exceedingly brief, but it is the moment which provides meaning for the clock time we have ahead of us. The apostle Paul, after his experience of God's presence while traveling on the road to Damascus, said that such an experience caused him to be reconciled with his past as he lived forward to a future with Jesus Christ (Phil. 3:13–14).

Thus God's time for a person is related to God's purpose. When one is touched by God's Spirit, one's whole life is quickened and time becomes precious—not to preserve life, but to be the means for serving God. Although chronological time clicks off minutes with sixty-second regularity, God's time is more a sense of the sacredness of God's purpose and of the holiness of life. In this sense, God's time has a tempo all its own and gives value to a person's life according to the manifestation of God in the events that make up his or her personal history. A person will therefore date his or her spiritual life by events which may seem trivial or uninspiring to others but which, for that person, become the means of understanding that "God loves me and sent Jesus the Son for me."

Becoming Engaged

The fourth element in the personal aspect of faith is a sense of becoming engaged with God and in God's concern for the world. No one has ever seen God, nor has anyone ever comprehended God's full nature. Theophanies, as the biblical narratives of people's experiences with God, disclose some of God's self; they show that God is like a person, and that we know God as we know persons. What we know of other persons are their interests (what things are more important to them than others), concerns (what they spend their time doing), and responses to life situations. Christians believe that the finest and final revelation of God was in a person—Jesus Christ. This human incarnation of God is what gives Christianity its power, for we can relate to a human being who has struggled with evil and who has demonstrated through his life and teachings what absolute faith in God is like.

The relationship to Christ is an engagement; that is, at the deepest level of our being we give ourselves to a personlike image who represents what we hold to be true and good. This is a subjective, introspective finding of our real self, but it is also a finding of ourselves in relation to God. John put it this way: "You did not choose me, but I chose you" (John 15:16). The image of God, formed by the person of Jesus and by the biblical tradition he incarnated, becomes something that knows us. We feel that our personal life has become holy. Then, as illustrated in the Gospel according to John, we realize an order of truth that is different from our human efforts to explain the physical world or to use reason in governing the affairs of people. We experience truth in the sense of being selected by God and set free to be what God would have us be (John 8:32).

Although this experience is personal, it is also objective. The biblical accounts are alike in describing the voice as coming from *God*—not from a generalized need, not from a desire of the community, not from a person's conscience, not from an idealized concept of what ought to be. It is a voice from a personlike image, beyond time, and thus it makes a person's time meaningful and precious. God is known not as a general principle, or as an influence for good, but as a holy Will which has interests and concerns about human life and human responsibility. "Why me?" No one knows. There is no logical reason. People who have this experience never know why they are chosen and are not able to justify God's attention to them. One's self-image is simply changed and, either suddenly or slowly, one begins to understand oneself in a different way. There are still fears, but they are less intense; sins are still committed, but their lure becomes less interesting as a person listens to the voice from beyond life. Paul captured the experience in one sentence: "Therefore, if any one is in Christ, he is a new creation; the old has passed away, behold, the new has come" (2 Cor. 5:17).

Problems

Communication of Christian faith (especially by educational methods) means forming the mind according to tradition in such a way that persons can experience the God of that tradition and also be open to experiences which may transform the tradition itself. In short, it is a process of *formation* looking for the possibility of *transformation*. The personal aspect of this approach raises two questions: (1) If religious experience is a personal experiencing of God's self, is not the result so vague that it will have little meaning for others? and (2) If the full meaning of experience with God is limited to young people and adults, what can we do with small children?

Vagueness

What we call religious experience is, as pointed out in chapter 5, the mind interpreting what the senses deliver. The mind responds to stimuli with images, feelings, patterned responses, ideas, idioms, or concepts supplied by the people who are raising the child. Culture has a ready-made response to all the normal problems of life and death. However, the mind also works out new and different responses: how, we do not know. We use words such as "inspiration" or "insight" to explain a process we do not understand. In every field—music, art, science, literature—people produce things that were not in existence before. Likewise, in the Christian religion we use the word "revelation" to describe the way God breaks through the normal predispositions of the mind to give an interpretation of human events different from those supplied by culture. From a psychological point of view, the vagueness of a person's experience with God is no different from the vagueness of the scientist's "hunch" about physical matter that he or she cannot prove, or the "feeling" that artists have before they produce their work.

Although an experience of God may be vague, the expression of what the experience *means* can be clearly stated and lived—just as the artist and the scientist can state in song, picture, or mathematical formula what their minds experience. Here our theophany model is helpful, for the biblical stories of people who experienced God's self were able to express that event in language and actions that could be understood and appraised by ordinary people. This does not mean that ordinary people, on hearing of the experience of Moses, Isaiah, Elijah, or Peter, accepted the message as true. In fact ordinary people, *because* they understood the message, often resisted or rejected it.

Clarity about the *meaning* of religious experience is important. It suggests that, although God is separate from humankind, God communicates concerns in ways which can be understood. The communication process within the self is like one person talking to another. There can be questions and answers, such as on the road to Emmaus (Luke 24:13–35); arguments, as illustrated by the call to Moses (Ex 3:10—4:14); explanations of symbols, as in the case of Peter (Acts 10:9–16); laughter, as at the ridiculous promise of a son to Sarah at age ninety (Gen. 17:15–17); or judgment on misguided behavior, as in Saul's persecution of Christians (Acts 9:1–19). Moreover, these matters can be communicated to others and discussed in a rational manner. When we do so, the vagueness of the origin gives way to the objectivity of language; then the substance of experience becomes common knowledge and can be dealt with, like any other matter requiring our thought and action.

Children

In chapter 5 I described four types of religious predisposition that may be inculcated by a person's environment. Children can experience the first three, and older children can recognize the fourth even if they do not understand it.

1. Children of all ages can experience the predisposition toward *secularism* if that is the environment in which they are nurtured. If they accept the major ideas of secularism when they begin to think and act on their own, a religious interpretation of life will seldom be open to them.

2. Babies and small children can absorb the *religious tradition* by learning the language of religion and the habits and customs of church people. They experience what is presented to them. They also experi-

ence a consciousness of death and the attending anxiety that will go with them throughout life.

3. Then, in middle childhood, they may experience the *understanding of tradition*. For example, they may feel loneliness and the love of God, sin and the forgiveness of God, beauty and the creation of God, awe and the worship of God. They may enjoy the friendship of children and adults in the church. Childhood—up to early adolescence—is an extremely important time for persons to experience what theology describes, even though the theology itself may be incomprehensible to them. The difference between learning the tradition, especially the stories, worship, and desired life-style (number 2), and having experiences of the tradition is not great and is difficult to judge. As a practical matter we should not belabor the point with children but should constantly assume that within the limits of their mental capacity they can experience "the fruits" of the Spirit of God.

4. The last predisposition, toward *changes in the tradition,* does not normally come about until people have had experiences of their own, usually in the early adult years. By middle adolescence, however, it is possible for individuals to have developed to the point where systematic, logical thinking is possible and they are capable of understanding themselves in relation to society. When this happens, individuals are confident enough to be self-directing and are capable of making some changes in themselves, in religious tradition, and in society.

The general developmental pattern from birth to adolescence is fairly clear. What is not so well known is the way an image of God is formed in the small child and how that image is re-formed or modified as the individual matures.

The Infant's Images of God. The mental conditioning already referred to (supplied by parents, friends, and peers) equips a person's mind to interpret the stimuli that come to it through the senses. But before this conditioning takes place, the baby, soon after birth, begins to respond to parents or other caretaking persons. Such relationships leave in the infant's mind a residue of images that will be there throughout life.

These images are psychic impressions; they do not have ideational content, for they are simply the sense of what one is in relation to life in general. As babies grow older they develop an inward vision of God, based on the relationships they have had and are having with parents and caretakers. These inward images are not God; they are an eidetic "starter set" of emotions of what God is like—according to the quality of the baby's relation to surrounding adults. Needless to say, these images are not arranged in any order, they are not easily sorted out or coordinated, and their strength varies considerably from person to person. However, one image or set of feelings will usually tend to regulate a person's outlook on life.

Since these images are a consequence of a baby's long period of dependency, they are present in everyone. They provide the emotional foundation for whatever form God takes in a person's life or for the rejection of a Godlike influence. These eidetic data are open to change as a person relates them to the image of God from the Bible and to the life of Christ.

One place to see these images at work is in a person's basic orientation. Some people, for example, have a highly developed sense that everything is worked out for them. The theological term for this is "special providence." Such folk revel in long and detailed stories about how things happen, words are said, and schedules are changed in an integrated way so that only a great computer in the sky (God) could have arranged for the matter to have been settled in so favorable a way. That these stories always have a happy ending should alert us to the self-centeredness involved. It is then useful to compare this image of God with that described by the apostle Paul, who, after praying three times for his illness to be healed, heard the Lord say, "My grace is sufficient for you, for my power is made perfect in weakness" (2 Cor. 12:9).

Another place to note the influence of these eidetic data is in our hymns, for music and poetry—especially the gospel songs—resonate with these images. There we sometimes find a celebration of the way God looks after a person: feeding, drying tears, holding hands, healing wounds, knowing and keeping a record of wrongdoings, or smiling on a person "face to face."

The idea of early images forming the basis for one's later image of God is not the same as that found in Freud's writings. The present view expects images from the mother as well as the father, it does not confuse infantile images with God, nor does it assume, as Freud did, that a person's image of God is frozen in early childhood.[3]

The Caregiver's Role. The caregivers' formative influence on the infantile images that influence a growing child's image of God has considerable importance for the church. It means that our efforts to communicate the Christian faith to children start with parents. The first contribution parents can make to their children's faith is the kind of loving care shared by all who value human life.

This view also means that parents, pastors, church school teachers, and adult friends of children are all responsible for shaping the child's image of God by the way they represent God in concrete life situations. Children do not have theophanies. They have experiences in which adults can represent what God is like and what God expects under those conditions. Somehow, in daily living or in the incessant coaching that parents do with children, some of the most important elements in the religious life are transmitted. A sense of justice, the rights of minorities, a concern for the sick and disabled, loyalty to the church as a human effort to be the body of Christ, or the habit of taking other persons seriously by listening carefully to them—these are all traits or sentiments that are absorbed by children from the adults with whom they live. In this sense, children learn Christianity as a way of life and assume its values long before they are capable of thinking about their religion.[4]

The problem of religious experience for children, then, is not with the children themselves but with the parents and other adults who take care of them. Children appropriate the affective aspects of religion before understanding the reasons for their faith. This is no different from the other areas of their life, where children accept diet and medicines because they trust the adults who are trying to help them, even though they do not understand the importance of nutrition or the way medicines affect the human body.

The goal for communicating the Christian faith to children is to help them experience God in such a way that they will be able to move into adolescence and adulthood confident in their relationship to God and open to God's guidance. The finest way to help this happen is for parents and other adults to provide a good model. This is a role adults tend to shun, but it is necessary if the child's faith in God is to develop properly.

7

The Mission

The Christian faith is based on the assumption that believers—through prayer, communion, Bible study, and the fellowship of the church—can experience the presence and guidance of God. Moreover, some Christians have a special experience of God that requires them to modify or change the tradition through which they learned about God. The question during and after either type of experience is, How do we know whether we—or any other persons who claim to have experienced God's presence—have had an authentic experience?

Chapter 3 noted that in the Bible the community decided if a claim was true. Over time a written record emerged, which contained all that was known about God's self-revelation. I have been using theophanies as models because they are accounts of intense experiences that were decisive for the history of Israel and the Christian church. Having discussed the situational and personal aspects of religious experience, we now need to examine mission, the third aspect of such narratives.

Assignments

The three theophanies described earlier all end the same way. In each account, the people involved were expected to do or say certain things in conformity with the will of God. They were caught up in an enterprise larger than themselves and in a program that also involved many other people.

Engagement

In the case of Moses, the assignment is clear: Moses was to lead the people of Israel out of Egypt into a land of their own, an assignment that took all his leadership ability and the rest of his life. The appearance of God at Mount Sinai, in the great pageant that we call the giving of the Covenant, resulted in God's demand for the nation to live devoted to the Lord and at a high moral level by observing the Ten Commandments (Exodus 19—20).

In the theophany of Elijah, the prophet was assigned to return to the wilderness of Damascus, to anoint kings, and to establish Elisha as his successor (see 1 Kings 19 and 2 Kings 2:1–11).

The transfiguration story is somewhat different in that its purpose is to identify Jesus as the Christ, the fulfillment of the law and the prophets of the Old Testament. Through the voice from the cloud that purpose was accomplished. However, the subsequent verses show that as soon as the group returned, Jesus healed a boy and used that event to demonstrate to his disciples that they needed more faith if they were to continue Jesus' ministry (Matt. 17:14–21).

Even Jesus is presented at the beginning of his ministry as one who has a set of goals to be accomplished (Luke 4:18–20). Later, when John—who baptized Jesus—was in prison and uncertain about whether Jesus was the Christ, he sent some of his own disciples to Jesus with the direct question, "Are you he who is to come, or shall we look for another?" Jesus' reply was in terms of the work he was doing, work consistent with the Isaiah passage he had used in his first sermon. Thus Jesus' way of claiming authority as the Messiah was to show that he was doing the expected work; anyone could observe the results (Matt. 11:2–6). Perhaps John pinpointed this phase of Jesus' experience of God when he quoted Jesus as saying, "We must work the works of him who sent me; . . . night comes, when no one can work" (John 9:4; see also John 5:36, 6:28, 14:11, and other places where Jesus refers to his message and mission in terms of work).

Enlightenment with Engagement

This biblical method of concluding an experience of God with a work assignment has several important implications for us. But before we explore those implications, let us look briefly at Peter's experience with God. His situation—like ours—shows how work must be constantly guided by the Holy Spirit.

Peter, like the other disciples, had a continuous relationship with Jesus throughout Jesus' public ministry. In that sense, he was constantly experiencing the selfhood of God—but without a clear understanding that Jesus was the Messiah. That experience came at Caesarea Philippi, when Peter, according to Matthew, had a revelation from God that Jesus was "the Christ, the Son of the living God." Moreover, Jesus promised, on that confession of faith the church would be built (Matt. 16:16–19). Peter was the first disciple to understand the divine mission of Jesus, and to whatever extent we can say a person is saved when making such a confession, Peter is that person. When we turn to Acts to pick up the story of the founding of the church after the crucifixion, we discover that Peter is the leader. He is the person who preached with great power, healed a lame man, and stood before the Sanhedrin to explain and defend faith in Christ.

The result of Peter's experience with the Holy Spirit was a work assignment he gladly undertook, yet the story is not complete because Peter had not yet been *thoroughly* converted. According to the first chapters in Acts, Peter was doing all his work with Jewish people, and he continued to observe their ceremonies and customs. We are not aware of how much of Peter's self is unconverted until we get to the tenth chapter of Acts, when a Gentile named Cornelius had a vision that he was to confer with Peter.

In the meantime, Peter had an experience with God in a dream, which told him that the old ceremonial laws were no longer pertinent. A few days later Peter went to Cornelius's house. There he displayed the tensions inside himself; he told Cornelius that both of them knew it was "unlawful" for him, a Jew, even to visit a Gentile—yet he was doing so because God had revealed to him in the dream that he was to lay aside his prejudice and "not call any man common or unclean." Peter then began his formal statement with these words: "Truly I perceive that God shows no partiality, but in every nation any one who fears him and does what is right is acceptable to him." After recounting the story of Christ, Peter had the honor of baptizing the first Gentile convert to Christianity. From that moment on Peter proclaimed the good news of salvation to all people, and Christianity, with the work of Paul, developed a theology toward becoming a religion for the whole world (see Acts 10).

It is difficult to overemphasize the importance of this event in Peter's life. He was already a Christian converted under the tutelage of Jesus. He was the human founder and recognized leader of the church; yet not all areas of his inner self were converted. In childhood Peter had been formed as a Jew, and his early training remained, even after he was converted. It took a special experience with God to break the formation of Peter's youth and transform his mind so that he could see life differently. Conversion, therefore, is not simply a goal of our efforts to communicate the Christian faith; it is the start of a process of spiritual awareness that must continually shape our minds as we do the work of Christ in the world.

Work

The word "work" needs attention. In some circles a person who works hard is called a "workaholic," one who compulsively puts work above family, friends, or even health. We should not allow this image of a compulsive person to tarnish the role of work; the workaholic could just as easily direct that compulsion toward recreation and become a "playaholic." The word "work" also connotes the idea of something difficult, exhausting, boring, or repetitious, something to be endured so one can use the wages for interesting activities. Certainly, some work is like this, although machines are increasingly taking over the more monotonous tasks. Yet all work, even work that a person enjoys, contains a certain amount of routine. Even an artist must prepare the canvas before starting the creative activity of painting a picture.

Work in the sense of the third phase of religious experience means the response one gives to a perceived call. A call is like a compulsion: the one called is dedicated to using time and energy toward a goal and feels discomfort with any obstacles in the path. A big difference, however, is that a person with a sense of God's call does not feel that he or she has the total responsibility for reaching the goal—that is God's domain. One only has to be faithful to what one is expected to do. Paul was labeled a zealous person before his conversion (Acts 9:1–3), and after his conversion he worked diligently, without pay, with a discipline carried over from his earlier days (1 Cor. 9:24–27). But he also realized that the prize for which he worked was approval by Christ rather than self-congratulation upon reaching a goal. We should notice that this is one of the few times Paul uses the word "mature." Within the context of Paul's letter, this means that Christians are always under work orders, and work is what helps us become mature in our faith (Phil. 3:12–16).

The argument about the role of work in the Christian faith has been misplaced. The debate is not faith versus works, with some insisting that it is faith alone which saves and others taking the position that without works faith is dead. That issue has been settled by the theophany stories, for all these stories end with a work assignment. One cannot experience the presence of God without a corresponding sense of changes that God desires in one's life and in the world.

The issue about work has to do with authenticity. The longing to know when one has obtained an authentic "word from the Lord" appears throughout the Bible. Today many people claim to have had a religious experience, but how do we judge the value of a person's claim? Part of the basis of judgment lies within the tradition of the Christian faith. For example, if a person had an experience with God which led to the belief that he or she should help people who needed health care, education, or an improved standard of living, and if the person who made the claim was competent in those fields, we would accept the experience as authentic because the resulting work is in harmony with the Christian tradition.

The problem emerges in a more acute manner with people who claim an experience of the fourth type: an experience requiring a change in the tradition. When anyone attempts to change accepted procedures or to reinterpret the contemporary understanding of the Christian tradition, that person will meet resistance—frequently of a fierce nature. This was true in biblical times with persons in the theophany stories. It was true of English leaders who tried to stop the slave trade, and of Christian leaders in the abolitionist movement in America before the Civil War. And it is true today, for if a group attempts to change tradition or to reinterpret it so that it is significantly different from the way most people have experienced it, that group will be resisted or rejected. This is so even though Christians know enough church history to realize that drastic changes have been made from time to time, including the great social upheaval caused by the Reformation in the early sixteenth century.

Need to Judge

Let us pause for a moment to justify judging. There is an attitude in the church that it is unchristian to judge or that we must make our judgments about claims of truth and religious experience so tentative as to be innocuous. This attitude is based on the affirmation that only God can judge, for only God can know people's motives or the struggles they are going through. These words of Jesus come to mind: "Judge not, that you be not judged. For with the judgment you pronounce you will be judged, and the measure you give will be the measure you get" (Matt. 7:1–2). Yet Jesus trained his disciples to make judgments (Luke 7:40–43), and he assumed that the crowds of people who listened to him teach were making judgments as well (Luke 12:54–59). Moreover, in Matthew's Gospel, Jesus' criticism of the scribes and Pharisees is a powerful demonstration to his disciples about how to judge those who would not accept his message (Matt. 23). When the church became an organized institution and met regularly in congregations, the task of judging what was a true experience of God became more acute. At that point Christians were told, "Beloved, do not believe every spirit, but test the spirits to see whether they are of God; for many false prophets have gone out into the world" (1 John 4:1).

These two positions—"do not judge" and "we must judge"—leave us in a quandary that cannot be resolved if we see them as judging the same thing. But if we note that the "do not judge" statement of Jesus relates to other persons' motives (which we cannot detect with accuracy) or to the salvation status of another person (which we cannot know) or to matters beyond our powers (such as the time for the world's end), then we see that the "do not judge" injunction is a caution not to make judgments where we do not and cannot have adequate data. The "we must judge" position is related to areas where we do have data and in which decisions have to be made.

One of these areas is our own personal life. We want to understand the presence of God in our life, even though we are not always able to express clearly what that presence means; however, we are able to translate the feelings we have into attitudes toward others and into actions for which we are responsible and accountable. These overt manifestations of covert sentiments are works that we and others can see and therefore judge. The other area where we must judge is in the response we make to persons who claim to have had a religious experience. That experience has probably led them into a work program—things to say and do—that may conflict with our own understanding of the meaning of faith. Granted that there is and will always be a certain amount of disagreement in the church, what can be done to judge the authenticity of those who claim that their position is correct? Since we must always be open to God's guidance and since it often comes to us through others, on what basis can we judge? We can judge on the basis of work, because (1) work is objective to the world and (2) work is objective to the self.

Work Is Objective to the World

This is a way of saying that work is life spent for a recognizable purpose. It is how we use our time, energy, and intentions—three elements that together produce something that can be seen and judged. It is the observable part of a life-style. One has only to look at Christian people who take their relationship with God seriously to see a pattern in the way they spend their time, money, and energy. What can be seen is objective to the world in that even non-Christians will note the pattern and what it produces.

We might take Martin Luther King, Jr., as an illustration since his life and work are so well known. In 1955 Mrs. Rosa Parks got on a public bus in Montgomery, Alabama, and sat down in the Negro section at the rear of the bus. When white people filled their section the bus driver ordered Mrs. Parks to get up and give her seat to a white man. This she refused to do. The driver called a policeman, who arrested Mrs. Parks.[1] In consequence, Martin Luther King, Jr., from his position as pastor of a Baptist church, organized a boycott against segregation laws, and a year later segregation in Montgomery buses was eliminated. King developed a national organization with the purpose of using nonviolent means to protest the segregated status of blacks. Event followed event until 1964 when Congress passed the Civil Rights Act and then, in 1965, the Voting Rights Act. King's unique work in bringing about social change in a peaceful manner is a lesson in how those who claim God's guidance must work openly so that their work can be seen and appraised.

The criterion of work being objective to the world also helps us decide what is not an authentic religious experience. As stated earlier, work is objective in that anyone can see the results and make judgments accordingly. On the other hand, thinking about or talking about religious experience is not the same thing as work. We might continue with Martin Luther King, Jr., to indicate how work is different from talk and thought. For over a quarter of a century Lawrence Kohlberg of Harvard University has studied moral development according to a six-stage theory. The first stage for the very young child, according to Kohlberg, is "punishment and obedience orientation." The sixth and highest stage is "universal ethical principle orientation," with justice as the goal of moral development. Kohlberg has developed a set of short stories that his subjects read and then respond to on the basis of what they *think* is the proper moral action. Kohlberg is fond of using Martin Luther King, Jr., as an illustration of stage six. But the irony of his classification system is that it is built on moral judgments, not on moral work. King could have achieved stage six on Kohlberg's scale by just sitting in his study and responding to the moral stories put to him by a research psychologist. But King did not come into prominence in American life, nor was he awarded a Nobel prize for the peaceful solution to a social problem, for sitting in his study and expressing proper attitudes. It was his *work*—to obtain justice by nonviolent means—that left a legacy for the world to see.[2]

We should not assume that every work in the name of Christ is good. As we look back in history, we find wars between Christian groups and also the persecution of Christians by other Christians, neither of which can be attributed to the guidance of God. The point is that work—that is, what people determine and want in the name of God—results in events and ways of living that stand independent of the person who created the work and must be judged on the basis of how the work affected human life over a period of time. We have no other way of judging the authenticity of an experience with God.

Work Is Objective to the Self

By affirming that work is the result of authentic religious experience, we can better understand the nature of such experience within the self. Religious experience lies close to the realm of feeling, intuition, hunch, sudden insight, or vague apprehension of what ought or ought not to be. Moreover, it is intensely related to one's self-regard. That is, persons who have an experience that might be religious in nature could—because they assume they are unworthy or incapable of understanding a message from God—suppress it. In such instances, nothing is shared with others; thus the meaning and value of the experience die for want of the nourishment that comes when urges from God are expressed, shared, and factored into ongoing life situations.

We need not solve the problem of the origin of religious experience within the self. Chapter 5 pointed out that experience, in the sense of stimuli reaching the brain, has little meaning. The meaning is supplied by the mind, which is conditioned in many ways—by the Spirit of God as well as by false spirits. Our problem is to "test the spirits to see whether they are of God" (1 John 4:1). This we can do in terms of what work is required by the Spirit's activity within a person.

The requirement of making experience objective to the self is part of the method the self uses to authenticate any experience it has. If we were to stop for a few moments and rehearse an experience, it would probably go something like the following: Somewhere from the depths of our being there bubbles up something that engages our conscious mind. We are aware of the insistence of the feeling, although we may, during business hours, suppress or "park" the feeling temporarily. We may wonder what it is that makes us feel glad, sad, threatened, troubled, or concerned about something we have seen, heard, remembered, or anticipated. Slowly or suddenly the "it" causing the insistent feeling becomes available to our conscious mind, and an internal dialogue ensues. Part of the dialogue, as indicated earlier, is whether the self assumes it is worthy or capable of having an experience with God; another part concerns what the experience means. The element of work is crucial for this dialogue. It is difficult, if not impossible, to forge meaning out of experience without the mind's testing what would happen if such and such were done. This question of "what would happen if" moves ideas, hunches, and feelings out of the self into discourse with the world. Although this discourse occurs first within the imagination, from this point on it can be examined and discussed as work.

We must note that this internal discourse is not restricted to strategy—how to accomplish a certain goal—though that is an important feature. As the imagination processes the feeling into work, the mind comes up against reality, including God's interests. The resulting dialogue, either within the mind or with other people, helps one understand the selfhood of God as well as the work assignment.

Religious experience that is turned toward the enhancement of a person is not authentic. People who claim to have had a religious experience but whose experience seems to do nothing more than elevate them above others or promote their self-interests have not had an authentic encounter with God. A genuine experience with God exhibits itself in a struggle with personal problems, with unjust social conditions, or with religious people who are unwilling to open their minds to new truth. People who have an authentic religious experience are confident about the presence of God; they report that the relationship was initiated by God and is independent of any special worth on their part. The resulting achievement has made for the increase of the rule of God in life rather than a glorification of the ability of the person by whom the work of God was done.

Ongoing Construction Work

The idea of work includes more than activity or a way of earning money to provide the necessities and pleasures of life. In the biblical idiom, work is the construction of a proper human community. The outline is worth recalling. After the creation of the world and humankind, sin became a part of each person, causing the person to protect and enhance the self rather than to live for the common good. God tried various ways to shape human life, but with little success. Then God called Abraham to form a people who would be devoted to God and thus produce a model nation for other nations of the world to emulate. That plan, too, met with little success. There were moments when Israel lived up to the calling; but the record shows that Israel's people wanted a king and a kingdom built on power and political alliances, which eventually led to political defeat and exile (recall the stories of King David and King Solomon).

Has God's purpose for humanity changed, now that Christ has come? No. In the Old Testament, individuals who had the great theophanic experiences were led to work that was related to the spiritual health of Israel. In the New Testament, individuals' experiences with Christ or the Holy Spirit drew them toward works and actions that strengthened the church. But in both Testaments, the work assignments were related to a community and its task, and both matters are of crucial importance. In theology they are discussed as the kingdom of God. One can make a convincing case for the kingdom of God being the overall theme of the Bible.[3] Although I want to support that case, I am reluctant to use the phrase "kingdom of God" in spite of its widespread biblical usage. My reasons are linguistic rather than theological: the word "kingdom" has come to mean a geographic place, a country with boundaries; yet the kingdom about which Jesus prayed is a spiritual outlook that is open to all and unrestricted in territory. Richard R. Niebuhr has correctly pointed out that the word translated "kingdom" really means "the rule of God"—a state of affairs, rather than a ruler with an army for protecting a land.[4]

Now that Christ has come, God's goal for the believing community has become both easier and more difficult. It is easier in that Jesus, growing up in ordinary circumstances and facing actual human problems and opportunities, has shown us exactly what a God-directed life is like. It is more difficult in that Jesus' life reveals how much opposition there is to the rule of God. Religious leaders often use their position for self-advancement rather than as a way of serving God, and political leaders tend to think in terms of doing what is necessary to stay in power rather than using power for civic justice. Ordinary people, although interested in the rule of God in human life and capable of understanding how the common life can be improved, most often succumb to the words or weapons of the rulers rather than give up the personal security these rulers provide. Now that Christ has come, we know what is expected of us as Christians: we are to continue the ministry of Christ in the world.

Has God's strategy in reaching this goal changed since the appearance of Christ? No. The strategy has always been the creation and maintenance of a community of believers who work to establish the rule of God in its own corporate life and in the world. Christ's coming has established the church as the community expected to live by the rule of God and to be the means of extending it to the world.

There are two meanings of the word "church." One is a mental image of what ought to be, because the church is the body of Christ; this theological conception is the ideal toward which we work. The other meaning of the word is the local congregation of believers, an actual congregation of a certain size, location, and leadership, living by a certain interpretation of the Christian faith. Both meanings of the word are important, for each influences the other. It is always easier to think of the church in ideal terms because they provide such a lovely description of potential human relationships, rather than to face the actual conditions found in most congregations. We must resist that temptation and follow Paul's example. His letters make up more than half of the New Testament, and each letter either explains or reflects the ideal nature of the church; yet the letters were addressed to particular congregations about practical problems. Paul's theology—which came out of his experience—was put to work in congregations, where spiritual activity takes place. This work is thus of two kinds.

Maintenance

The first kind of ongoing construction work is that which creates and maintains the fellowship of believers. There are all sorts and conditions of people in the church, but all are required to love and respect one another—or else nothing Christian can flow into or out of the congregation. In addressing the congregation at Corinth, Paul used the illustration of the body. The foot has a function and so does the eye. The functions are different. Neither of the parts is a body; but each, in doing its job, contributes to the body's work. So the congregation as the body of Christ is both greater than and different from the individuals of which it is composed, but all individuals, regardless of gifts and functions, must work to make love the aim of the church (1 Cor. 12; 13; 14:1). Later, Paul used the same basic idea but tailored the words to fit the congregation at Ephesus. There he insisted that all believers, regardless of their ability, work to build up the body of Christ so that they might become mature. The image of the people's growing up and becoming mature is dependent on their working together as a community of people dedicated to Christ (Eph. 4:1–16). The work of a Christian, then, is to help build a congregation into a community where Christ is honored and his ministry reenacted. Nowhere in the New Testament writings do we have a description of a church building, of retirement plans for clergy, or of detailed church government. The work of the church is primarily to build human relationships of a quality and kind which, in the words of the hymn "The Tie That Binds," create a "fellowship of kindred minds . . . like to that above."

Mission

The second kind of work flows spontaneously from the "fellowship of kindred minds." As previously indicated, it is a continuation of the ministry of Christ in the world. If a congregation avoids this type of work, then it will become little more than a society for its own enjoyment. Although the book of Revelation is difficult to understand, the seven churches evaluated in that book clearly are all judged by their works. The church at Laodicea seems to be the most severely criticized because it is "neither cold nor hot" (Rev. 3:14–16). We have little difficulty today in judging a congregation by its works: if the life of a congregation is centered on itself, its building, its production of fine music and other programs for the use and enjoyment of the members, and if it spends all its budget for its own upkeep, we can—by those observable facts—say that it lacks a sense of being called to ministry in the world. Although this is a sad situation, it presents no special problems of judgment.

Teresa of Avila

It seems fitting to conclude this discussion of religious experience with some comments from one in the front ranks of those who have sought to unite their souls with God. Teresa of Avila (1515–1582) not only achieved widespread recognition of her spiritual journey during her lifetime; she wrote such lucid accounts of her experience that she was proclaimed "Doctor of the Church" by Pope Paul IV in 1970. Although Teresa's roots are in medieval Catholic culture, twentieth-century Christians can learn from her writings, especially *The Interior Castle* (1577).

Teresa appropriated the grandest edifice of her time—a castle—and used it as a metaphor for the spiritual life. She described seven dwelling places within the castle. The first is the place where most people are. There people mill about. They know there is something better, but they are so busy with everyday things they do not search for the truth about life and death. The second dwelling place is where people have started a prayer life and are attentive to the grace of God as it is described in worship, sermons, books, and good friends. In the third dwelling place, people have become sensitive to God's presence and begin to include God in their daily thoughts. By careful use of time and money they begin to order their lives after a consensus model of religious living. They pay attention to the needs of other people by acts of charity and mercy. However, these people do not have strong commitments, for they are unwilling to give up their wealth and status. Some of these people seek wealth because, they say, if they become wealthy then they are more capable of giving to the poor![5]

These first three dwelling places are reached by human efforts to know God. The next four are reached by a gradual union of a person's soul with the Divine. In the fourth dwelling place, for example, Teresa begins to separate the activities of the mind from the affections and gives a definition of the spiritual quest. To enter this dwelling place,

> the important thing is not to think much but to love much; and so do that which best stirs you to love. Perhaps we don't know what love is. I wouldn't be very much surprised, because it doesn't consist in great delight but in desiring with strong determination to please God in everything, in striving, insofar as possible, not to offend Him, and in asking Him for the advancement of the honor and glory of His Son and the increase of the Catholic Church.[6]

In the fifth dwelling place the soul unites with God. Teresa uses the silkworm as an illustration: the silkworm grows in warm weather, encloses itself in a cocoon, and then dies, but a white butterfly later emerges. This situation, in Teresa's comparison, is like that of people who accept all the benefits of the church and the guidance of the Holy Spirit, build a good life, and then die—except for their souls, which are transformed and united with God.

The sixth dwelling place is where the person betrothed to Christ gets ready for union with Christ. Much courage is needed in this dwelling place, for here one encounters severe trials. Gossips may say, "She is just making out she's a saint." Although others will praise you, this can be an even greater trial than censure. There will be illness, fears, and, above all, apprehension over God's possible rejection.[7]

The seventh and final place is the dwelling for a soul that is spiritually married to Christ. This union is different, in that "when the soul is brought into the dwelling place, the most blessed Trinity, all three persons, through an intellectual vision is revealed to it through a certain representation of the truth." In this dwelling place a person is able to say with Paul, "For to me to live is Christ" (Phil. 1:21).

Many ideas in *The Interior Castle* have great value for our understanding of Christian experience. For our purpose, however, I will note only (1) the role of work in each dwelling place, and (2) the way faith in God has the possibility of becoming the dominant element in one's life.

Work

I was surprised at the role of work in all the dwelling places, for I had thought that Christian mystics tended to get further and further from practical problems and concern for ordinary life situations as they increasingly turned inward, had visions, and yearned for a union with God beyond time and space. Within her own visions, Teresa built her whole spiritual life on the plan of reaching the central room of the castle where she would marry Christ, but this plan did not distance her from our ordinary problems, illnesses, misunderstandings with spiritual advisers, jealousies, or the work of the church in the world. For example, in describing the fourth dwelling place she notes that some sisters spend so much time in prayer and keeping vigils they become weak and "fancy that they are being carried away in rapture. I call it being carried away in foolishness because it amounts to nothing more than wasting time and wearing down one's health. These people feel nothing through their senses nor do they feel anything concerning God."[8] Under these circumstances the prioress should help the sisters get enough sleep, see that they eat well, and give them work in the monastery. From Teresa's standpoint, when there is something from God there is "no languishing in the soul."[9]

When Teresa describes the seventh dwelling place where the soul is married to Christ, she says that work is the criterion by which one knows one has achieved this final goal. There is little value in being alone with the Lord "proposing and promising to do wonders in his service" if, when the opportunity comes, one does not do them. Her advice is to fix one's eyes on the crucified: "If His Majesty showed us His love by means of such works and frightful torments, how is it that you want to please Him only with words? Do you know what it means to be truly spiritual? It means becoming the slaves of God."[10] Being a slave of God, to Teresa, implies doing God's will. She uses the term as Paul did many times to show that the ultimate goal of Christian life is to be so conscious of Christ in our life that we become his slave (see 1 Cor. 7:21–23; Gal. 1:10; Eph. 6:6; and Paul's identification of himself as a slave of Jesus Christ in Rom. 1:1).

Faith

Teresa of Avila considered faith something that becomes stronger as one comes closer to God and more completely a slave of God's will.

As faith strengthens, it takes over more and more of one's life. Teresa was puzzled by the role of the intellect in the strengthening of faith. In her account of the fourth dwelling place she describes how it was only four years earlier (when she was about fifty-eight years old) that she learned that the mind (or imagination) is not the intellect. This helped her a great deal because she found the intellect to be restless, flying about many interesting matters while she was trying to get her mind (imagination) focused on God.[11] To her, faith was not something that developed in stages along with the development of the intellect.

Faith, to Teresa, was a relationship to God, a relationship that had both a history and a goal of union with Christ. It did not, however, proceed by stages so that persons could say at the seventh dwelling place that they were morally better, or wiser, or had a finer quality of faith. For example, in the section on the sixth dwelling place Teresa warns about nuns who have visions. Such persons should not be considered better than others; a vision is just something that happens and is neither to be approved or condemned.[12] The goal is holiness, and judgment about the quality of holiness is to be made only on the basis of who serves the Lord with greatest humility and purity of conscience.[13]

Humility was important to Teresa because it was related to truth. Teresa wanted the sisters to walk in the truth—that is, to live as accountable to God. But such upright living should not make others regard those sisters as especially good or holy. The Lord is fond of humility, according to Teresa, because God is the Supreme Truth. Therefore, as we walk in the Truth, we cannot but be humble; we must look only to see if we please the Truth. People who have progressed to the seventh dwelling place do not have a faith that is more altruistic or universal than when they were in other dwelling places. Rather, their faith has made them more aware of God's interests and more determined to be God's agents.

Teresa does not support the common idea that people who live saintly lives in the seventh dwelling place are in a dreamy world protected from ordinary life situations. Faith in God does not bring personal peace, physical comfort, or miraculous solutions to problems. Instead, those closest to Christ have the greatest trials. Teresa cited as example the situations of Mary, Peter, and Paul: "Did Saint Paul by chance hide himself in the enjoyment of these delights [his vision of Jesus on the Damascus road] and not engage in anything else? You already see that he didn't have a day of rest, from what we can understand, and neither did he have any rest at night since it was then that he earned his livelihood."[14]

8

The Residue
of Experience

Experience is not only the great teacher; it is also the great unifier of all the diverse things that make up our lives. By its very nature, experience starts and stops with a set of circumstances. Some experiences—say, an automobile accident—are brief, although the meaning of the accident may linger for years. Other experiences, such as a war or a marriage, may last for decades. But what we call experience can usually be described as having a beginning and an end, even though it flows along with many other events in the stream of time. Because experience is a unit of life that has arrested our attention, it is scrutinized by our mind for signs of special meaning. If no sign is identified, the experience slides into forgetfulness. When we reflect on experience, we net something that stays with us until other experiences change the set of our mind. After an automobile accident, for example, we may say to ourselves, "Drive cautiously." We may gain a feeling of confidence in our investment advisers if their suggestions continue to turn out to our advantage. Or we may build up a philosophy over a period of time about how people will behave under certain circumstances we have observed. If the experience is significant, we will receive something from it that has bearing on the way we live.

Experience that is religiously interpreted is similar to any other experience; the difference lies in the interpretation and in what we conclude from it. An automobile accident may be just an accident to a person who considers herself "lucky" that her injury was not serious. Another person hurt in the same accident may consider the experience a sign of God's presence; he may receive courage to continue his life along the path he was following but with a new confidence in God.[1] A third person involved might be a sincere Christian who does not believe in "special" providence. Although that person does not attempt to relate his survival to a special act of God, nevertheless he has been sobered by the event and is thankful to God that he has been spared.[2] So once again we are faced with circular reasoning. The three people in the accident have three different beliefs about the event, and each has seen in the experience confirmation of the belief he or she uses to interpret such occurrences. Each person's belief is a composite of previous experience, family influence, opinion of friends, beliefs from the church, independent thinking, and the brooding one does about one's self in relation to powers outside one's control. But once the circular reasoning starts, how can other ideas break in? I pointed out in chapter 3 that communities inevitably engage in circular reasoning. There I indicated from the sociology of belief how communities that are gathered around certain beliefs manipulate interpretation of what happens to fit their beliefs. Religious communities do likewise unless they pay attention to the biblical account of Israel or the church. The Bible records God's breaking into circular reasoning because God has a will for the people that is different from their own will. In somewhat the same manner, the circular reasoning of individuals about a religious interpretation of an event may be broken into if they pay attention to biblical stories of individual religious experience.

These biblical stories are all God-centered: after the person's religious experience is over, the residue is faith in God as a presence and power in life. Faith was present before the experience too, but the quality of faith afterward is what the stories emphasize. This is not a blind, undifferentiated faith that somehow everything will turn out all right. Such faith is self-centered. Faith resulting from experience with God is animated by a holy Will for the world, a Will that moves us forward with confidence that we are able to influence the future. We feel as if a gentle pressure, like a wind or current from an unseen source, is moving us along. As a result, faith—the residue of experience—is like a divine companion who will be with us as we attempt to help establish God's rule in the world. We cannot, therefore, describe what faith means apart from the situation in which it functions. The meaning of faith comes from the ongoing series of events in which we look for guidance from God. Faith in God, according to the biblical account, does two things: it (1) unifies a person's life and (2) orients activities. Both functions become apparent in the lives of people who interpret experience through their faith.

First, faith as the residue of experience with God unifies the divergent interests, instincts, and other forces we feel within ourselves pulling one way and another. It brings together the affective and cognitive domains of the self. The person of faith does not stop to differentiate between love of God or concern for God's rule in the world and thinking about God, for the two go on simultaneously. Faith joins self and society in that a faithful person knows God is concerned for all people of the world. One's self is not a separate thing; it is always related to service in and for the world. Past, present, and future are coordinated, for faith comes to us out of the community of believers living by tradition from the past; but our experience with God is in the present for the future. The phrase used to identify God ("the God of your Fathers, the God of Abraham, the God of Isaac, and the God of Jacob" or its equivalent) appears repeatedly throughout the Bible and is included in Jesus' genealogy (Matt. 1:1–2). That formula identifying God's action in the past is always the sign that something important is going to happen in the present, as indeed it did in the birth of Jesus.

Second, orientation comes from God, in whom one has learned to trust. Faithful persons, who base their thoughts and actions on God, plan their lives and live them in a way different from people who have no such reference. Observe the way faithful people use their time, money, and influence. In these matters we can manage our Christian life with a high degree of certainty, because they are areas in which we have considerable control. However, when it comes to acting in the world in the midst of social problems—such as war, unfair distribution of food, strikes, boycotts, and the like—the will of God is harder to determine. Our desire to help bring about God's will is clear, but the question of what decisions to make often eludes our most honest efforts. We shall deal with such conflicts in Part Three. At this point, we can note that an environment of faith is essential for our decision making if we are to act according to the prayer Jesus taught his disciples: "Thy kingdom come, Thy will be done" (Matt. 6:10).

Faith

Faith as the residue of experience with God is not a doctrine but a feeling or a sense of confidence that one is related to an unseen holy Will that is concerned for the conditions of human life everywhere. As such, faith is an underlying mood, outlook, or stance toward everything. Yet, as a *word*, it has liabilities. Perhaps a brief discussion of these difficulties will help us understand faith.

The word "faith" is often used as a synonym for religion. In ordinary speech we use "Christian," "Jewish," or "Catholic" to identify a specific form of faith. Thus "faith" has come to mean certain beliefs or a particular religious affiliation. This common way of associating the word "faith" with religious beliefs is not wrong so much as it is inadequate for the purpose of understanding the faith of Christians. We can readily recognize this use of "faith" as a synonym for a particular religious group or as the equivalent of certain doctrinal beliefs, so it should not give us trouble.

Faith is often contrasted with reason. One way of speaking is to say that we know God by faith and we know the world through experience, which, like science, can be verified by anyone regardless of religious belief. There is some truth here, for faith is a different way of knowing, although it is based on experience as all knowledge is. Perhaps it would be better to say that faith is experiential knowing in a realm different from science—the realm of human relations where we deal with our relation to each other, our responsibilities for each other, and our goal for human society, including the way we use the resources of the earth.

Faith, Paul Tillich noted, "is continually being confused with belief in something for which there is no evidence, or in something intrinsically unbelievable, or in absurdities and nonsense. It is extremely difficult to remove these distorting connotations from the genuine meaning of faith." Tillich's way of clearing up the confusion is to provide a "formal" and "material" definition of faith. His formal definition is for "all religions and cultures": Faith is "the state of being grasped by that toward which self-transcendence aspires, the ultimate in being and meaning." In this sense everyone has faith, because everyone lives by what he or she considers important, even if what that person considers of "ultimate concern" might be deemed unworthy by others. Tillich's material definition of Christian faith is "the state of being grasped by the New Being as it is manifest in Jesus." Christian faith, according to Tillich, is created by the Spiritual Presence and not by our human "intellect, will, or feeling." Therefore, it is not subject to verification by experiment or trained experience. This means that faith "as a kind of independent reality has biblical support."[3]

Faith in the biblical sense is sometimes confused with or equated to what Erik Erikson terms "basic trust"—the first sentiment to be developed after birth. He describes this sense as an "attitude toward oneself and the world derived from the experiences of the first year of life. By 'trust' I mean what is commonly implied in reasonable trustfulness as far as others are concerned and a simple sense of trustworthiness as far as oneself is concerned." He then goes on to point out that "basic" means a deep fundamental attitude that is not especially conscious. Erikson uses "a sense of" to mean what we have in mind when we say "a sense of health" or a "sense of not being well"; such "senses" pervade surface and depth, consciousness and unconsciousness. Although "sense of" seems imprecise, it has three dimensions: it can be an experience of which we are conscious, it can be a way of behaving that others can observe and identify, and it can be an inner state of which we are not aware.[4]

Such trust is not religious faith. Rather, according to Erikson,

> Trust, then, becomes the capacity for *faith*—a vital need for which man must find some institutional confirmation. Religion, it seems, is the oldest and has been the most lasting institution to serve the ritual restoration of a sense of trust in the form of faith while offering a tangible formula for a sense of evil against which it promises to arm and defend man.[5]

From the viewpoint of one who has compared many religions, Wilfred Cantwell Smith has likewise separated faith as a normal human experience from religious forms of faith. Smith writes, " 'Faith,' then, I propose, shall signify that human quality that has been expressed in, has been elicited, nurtured, and shaped by, the religious traditions of the world. This leaves faith unspecified, while designating its locus." By this separation of human faith from a particular religion, Smith is able to contrast various forms of religion that have emerged from and are nourished by a condition of faith that is common to all humankind.[6]

This identification of trust or belief as a quality of human life which may or may not become religious is not a modern idea. The biblical words translated as "trust" or "belief" do not ascribe any special value to the person who has faith. In Proverbs we are reminded that the simpleminded person (fool) will believe anything (Prov. 14:15). The Queen of Sheba did not believe the reports of Solomon's wealth and wisdom until she visited his palace (1 Kings 10:6–7). Jesus, likewise, observed that people could have trust in—and belief about—things that were not worthwhile. Probably the most common object of trust or belief was money, for Jesus warned his hearers not to hoard it. Rather, he said, "Lay up for yourselves treasures in heaven, where neither moth nor rust consumes and where thieves do not break in and steal. For where your treasure is, there will your heart be also" (Matt. 6:19–21). Paul's version of the same idea is that people who live for their own excitement and pleasure in an attitude of "This world is all we have" will "reap corruption," whereas the people who live by the Spirit "will from the Spirit reap eternal life" (Gal. 6:7–8). Biblical writers had no difficulty sorting out differences between trust or belief as a quality that all people have, and faith as a trait of those who had had experience with God.

Christian Faith

The foregoing description of faith suggests that faith always has a reference. Trust arises out of human relations; its meaning lies in a person's life experiences. The reference in such cases is life as it is lived here and now, and the beliefs that are formed will reflect this reference.

In the Christian religion the reference is God as revealed by Jesus Christ and as defined in the Bible. The belief statements of a person or group will reflect what it means to trust in God. Beliefs are like the tip of an iceberg: they can be seen, identified, and compared to other beliefs, but underneath is a vast unseen body of sentiment that supports them. And—like an iceberg—beliefs move in a slow and ponderous way, but with such power that they can hardly be stopped. This power is well expressed toward the end of the New Testament era. The writer of Second Timothy, an older, time-tested minister, was giving his final words to a younger minister. Recalling how he had suffered while preaching and working in a hostile environment, he wrote, "But I am not ashamed, for I know whom I have believed, and I am sure that he is able to guard until that Day what has been entrusted to me" (2 Tim. 1:12). Here one sees the fundamentals of Christian faith: confident knowledge (trust) in a person (Christ). The beliefs are what the person, Christ, means to the one who has the trust. Throughout many experiences and in many different situations, the trusting and believing have proved true. And there is absolute assurance that what is done in Christ's name and for his sake will be established because of that truth.

This definition of Christian faith is in sharp contrast to today's popular expressions of religious faith. Even in churches one often hears that faith is believing things that are not sensible, or that faith is what we have left when our mind has exhausted all possibilities of explanation. Amid tragedy or threatening circumstances it is sometimes said that we "still have our faith"; but this may be said in tones of desperation, indicating a conclusion that must be simply accepted rather than understood. The word "faith" is also used when a person undertakes a course of action with an unclear goal or an uncertain outcome. Although under such circumstances a person may have "blind" trust based on his or her deposit of trust left over from infancy, this is not Christian faith.[7]

Biblical Hebrew does not have a noun that can be translated "faith." The word usually translated "trust" or "faith" is a verb meaning "to be certain in one's mind."[8] It is noteworthy that the Hebrew word for faith in God is never used for faith in false gods.[9] In Christian worship this word is our familiar "amen." We use it to conclude our prayers, for our prayers represent our clearest affirmation of God's glory, our deepest yearnings, our finest hopes, our most earnest pleadings, and our most sincere pledge of allegiance. We address our petitions to God with confidence that some response will come into our consciousness. Because prayer is the supreme act of our conscious self, we conclude it with "amen." We want to declare that we are "certain" about God's rule and God's power to protect and guide our lives. "Amen" to a Christian's prayer is the exact opposite of a vague religious faith concerned with human goals in the here and now. It is likewise correct to say "amen" to belief statements about God, for in so doing we confirm what we know. The practice must have been well known in the Corinthian church, for Paul argued that a person who claimed the guidance of the Holy Spirit must speak so others could understand. Then, if there was agreement about what was said, the congregation could say "amen" (1 Cor. 14:13–19; see also Ps. 106:48).

Old Testament Illustrations

When we go to the Bible for illustrations, we must remember that its writers attempted to speak from God's standpoint. The important thing is God's purpose for humankind. Faith in a broad sense is a commitment to God's purpose and an identification with the community of people who share that commitment. In a more precise sense, faith is what happens to individuals as they relate to God. The stories of faith are therefore situational; that is, the faith experience is intense because it relates to a decision that must be made about specific life conditions or to an action that will cause a person to pledge his or her life one way or another. These episodes are also historical, for they happen at a particular time and under certain conditions, and they produce results that can be described and communicated to others.

Faith is powerful because it functions in specific human situations, a fact that makes faith difficult to define. The situation Abraham faced, for example, was different from that of Isaiah, and both were quite different from that of the apostle Paul. Thus it is almost impossible to compose a single definition of faith that is true to the biblical record. Rather, we must try to understand what faith in God meant under particular circumstances. To trust in God will have meaning in terms of God's desire for a person or group of believers at a particular moment. At another time and under other circumstances the meaning might be different. We can, however, observe some characteristics of faith at work in human life and draw some conclusions about the range of meanings that emerges.

Abraham

The first stories of the Bible—those of Adam and Eve, Cain and Abel, Noah and the flood, the Tower of Babel—are mainly about disobedience. We learn from these stories that God tried to deal with all humankind but that human willfullness and self-gratification at the expense of others (i.e., sin) thwarted God's design. The twelfth chapter of Genesis records that God changed strategy and called Abraham to start a nation of people who would obey God. Through this people, all peoples of the world would be blessed.

The story is well known. When the Lord called seventy-five-year-old Abram to leave his country and kinfolk, Abram took his wife, Sarai, a few friends, and all their possessions and went to the land of Canaan to start a new nation. Abram became rich and powerful, but he was deeply troubled because he had no children. Soon the Lord appeared in a vision and promised Abram a son: "And he brought him outside and said, 'Look toward heaven, and number the stars, if you are able to number them.' Then he said to him, 'So shall your descendants be.'

And he believed the LORD; and he reckoned it to him as righteousness"
(Gen. 15:5–6). The word translated "faith," "trust," or "believe" is
used here for the first time in the Bible, in verse 6. The idea is "to
affirm, recognize as valid" the promise God has made.[10]

We must remember the story of Abram against the background of
the previous stories in Genesis, which tell how God tried to work with
all humankind. Although human beings knew the difference between
good and evil, they were unable to order their lives by that knowledge.
The lesson we learn from the first eleven chapters of Genesis is that
whenever human beings try to live independently of God—in a state
of disobedience—disaster follows. Against that background, Abram
suddenly appears. The contrast is obvious: Abram is a model of obedience, a person who lets God control his life in order to achieve a future
God has in mind for all humankind. The "curse" (Gen. 3:14–19) that
resulted from disobedience can now be cured with a "blessing" because Abram obeys.

Abram seems to have had no special preparation for his role as the
founding father of a people. Neither his parents nor the people of his
home tribe are reported to have known the Lord. There seems to be
no special background or unique conditions pointing to Abram. His
faith is without motive, except that he believes the promise. "So Abram
went, as the LORD had told him" (Gen. 12:4).

Abram's obedience is radical. In those tribal days, people found
their emotional well-being, their physical safety, and their economic
welfare bound to the group. Outside that group, people were aliens,
with little hope for themselves or their children. Abram gave up his
tribal security for an unknown future, except that the Lord promised
that the future would be desirable. Thus faith means a willingness to
be disassociated from all that makes life comfortable and certain in
order to do what God desires. This is a drastic reorientation of one's
life. It is an adventure into a future where the Lord works things out.

We are well into the story of Abram when we are reminded that he
still has no offspring (Gen. 15:2–3). How could the promise of God be
achieved when Abram was old and his wife, Sarai, far past the age of
childbearing? Sarai understood this incredible situation. Taking matters into her own hands, she supplied her Egyptian maid, Hagar, as a
mate for Abram. A son, Ishmael, was born of this alliance, but he was
predicted to be "a wild ass of a man" (Gen. 16:12). Why? We can only
surmise that it was because Sarai tried to step in and solve a problem
that God was going to solve another way. This event within the larger
story is full of pathos. Sarai was trying to remedy what she perceived
as her weakness, and she did so within the rules of her society at that
time. Yet her action was seen as impertinent, part of the recurring
theme of human disobedience.

We must be careful not to discredit Sarai. The events should be seen as a mirror of ourselves, for she represents humankind's impatient way of trying to solve problems without waiting for a clear signal from God. We must also be careful not to credit Abram as a model moral leader just because he was selected to be the founder of Israel. Abram's use of Sarai as a sex partner for Pharaoh in order to save his own life was so crude that even Pharaoh was angry when he learned of the deceit (Gen. 12:10–20). In this event Abram reflects our image: regardless of how productive we may be in God's work, or how full of faith we may be, there are segments of our life that are selfish or immature.

God's promise is renewed in chapter 17. Abram's name is changed to Abraham, Sarai's to Sarah; they are promised a son, to be named Isaac, and a covenant will continue with his descendants. At this point, since the story is about to have a happy ending, we breathe a sigh of relief. Then in chapter 22 we realize that nothing has been settled—everything can be ruined. The account of Abraham's impulse to offer Isaac as a sacrifice is incomprehensible to the modern mind. But within Genesis' explanation of faith, the story is a cautionary tale of Israel's precarious position before God.

Isaac, the son and heir, has been born by the intervention of God against the laws of nature. He represents an Israel that exists because God wants Israel to keep the covenant and live a life of righteousness, thus blessing all nations of the world. If this does not work out, God can start over again. Israel, then, is perpetually in danger of being cut off by God if it is not faithful; yet God, as represented by Abraham, loves Israel and will spare it. The tension and ambiguity of this story convey a generalization about God and the people of promise.

The story of the sacrifice of Isaac shows that God is making the ultimate and final test of Abraham's faith. God told Abraham to take his beloved son and offer him "as a burnt offering" (Gen. 22:1–3). When Abraham obeyed and was in the act of making the sacrifice, the angel of the Lord stopped him because "now I know that you fear God, seeing you have not withheld your son, your only son, from me" (Gen. 22:12).

This passage closely associates faith with fear. In the Old Testament the words "fear" and "trust" are rather evenly balanced, each being used about 150 times.[11] Although fear may have been originally used to express terror in the presence of God, it came to mean a sense of awe and respect, as in the proverb, "The fear of the LORD is the beginning of knowledge" (Prov. 1:7 and 9:10; see also Job 28:28). Fear in this situation is not so much fear that God will harm Abraham if he disobeys as dread that Abraham may not do what God wants done. Fear, faith, and love describe three aspects of a relationship with God that are present simultaneously. All three are often assumed in a faithful relationship.[12]

Abraham's first test of faith—whether he would leave the security of his tribe—was difficult, but there was a promise of glory in the future to lure him on. The proposed sacrifice of Isaac was the ultimate test of faith, for if God had required Abraham to carry it out, there would have been no descendants and all his hopes and dreams would have been canceled. It is no wonder that Abraham is used throughout the Bible as a model of faith, for he was willing to give up everything, even a promise from God, for God's glory.[13]

Isaiah

About 733 B.C., the Northern Kingdom, Israel, allied itself with the Syrians and wanted the Southern Kingdom, Judah, to join the alliance. When Ahaz, the king of Judah, refused, the allies marched against him. In desperation Ahaz asked the Assyrians for help. They were willing, at the price of Judah's becoming a client state, paying tribute to the Assyrians. Ahaz went even further and set up an altar in Jerusalem to the Assyrian god.

This scenario in which a political alliance furthers the self-interest of nations is familiar. What is extraordinary is the way faith functions in such an environment. The prophet confronted the king while the king was inspecting the defense of the city's water supply. Isaiah, standing with his son, told the king to "take heed, be quiet, do not fear, and do not let your heart be faint." This political power move would fail, Isaiah said, for God would not allow it to happen. He concluded with these words: "If you will not believe, surely you shall not be established" (Isa. 7:4–9). This sentence plays on the word for "faith," and it is difficult to translate. A paraphrase would be, "If you are not steady of soul, completely confident of the trustworthiness of God, and certain that his word will be fulfilled, you are (i.e., your physical existence is) not firm and enduring."[14]

Ahaz ignored Isaiah's appraisal of the situation and refused to ask God for guidance in this crisis of his government. This was not new. For years Ahaz had paid less attention to God's concerns than to political alliances that might strengthen his kingdom. Nor was Isaiah's protest new; several years before, he had named his son "A Remnant Shall Return." Isaiah had seen not only that the nation, under an unfaithful king, would drift into bondage, but also that a few would be faithful to God and would someday return to their homeland.

The confrontation was Ahaz's last chance; there was still time to select the way of faith. Here the situation of Ahaz is similar to that of Abraham preparing to sacrifice Isaac: if he opts for faith, the descendants of Israel will be saved.

The king finally decided against faith and in favor of military assistance from Assyria. In poetic terms, Isaiah wrote that the people had refused the gentle waters of Shiloah and that the mighty waters of Assyria would sweep over Judah, even up to the neck of the people. This desperately gloomy situation is important for our understanding of faith. Isaiah's faith was stripped of everything except the fear of, and hope in, the Lord. Feeling helpless, he wrote his account of these events on a scroll so future generations would understand his anguish. Only catastrophe, misfortune, and misery lie ahead, he reflected; there is nothing one can do except "wait for the LORD, who is hiding his face from the house of Jacob" (Isa. 8:17).

Although God seemed unavailable, Isaiah had faith. This primordial faith was a certainty so passionate that it overpowered what he felt more deeply than anything else in life—his concern for the whole people of God. "The LORD," he affirmed, put "his strong hand upon me, and warned me not to walk in the way of this people" (Isa. 8:11). Isaiah's faith forced him to separate himself from his nation and turn his attention to his little band of disciples. There, in an arena where he could to some extent control events, the prophet lived by faith. This is one of the few times in early biblical history that a group is called to be apart from the larger body of believers because of the intensity and substance of its members' faith.[15]

The book of Isaiah gives us one more major demonstration of how faith in the Lord creates beliefs. The historical situation was as follows: Jerusalem was destroyed in 586 B.C., and the people of Judah were taken into Babylon as exiles. Generation after generation lived and died there. They had no country; they had no political autonomy; they had lost the temple and its power to symbolize their religion. In short, they had a miserable present and no hope for the future. Their defeat, interpreted by the mentality of that day, meant that the Lord was helpless. Conquered nations of that time lost their identity, and individuals were assimilated into the larger and more powerful culture.

This historical situation raised the basic theological question, Is the Lord the one true God or merely a tribal deity? Since there was no hope of returning home and nothing but dreary work ahead, should they not give up faith in the Lord? Out of this desperate situation a prophet emerged, about 550 B.C. Urging the people to remember and trust the promise to Abraham and Sarah, he spoke from God's standpoint: "Fear not, for I am with you, be not dismayed, for I am your God; I will strengthen you, I will help you, I will uphold you with my victorious right hand" (Isa. 41:10). The Lord, the prophet claimed, would liberate the people, because God made the world and is in charge of it:

> Whom did he consult for his enlightenment,
> and who taught him the path of justice,

and taught him knowledge,
and showed him the way of understanding?
Behold, the nations are like a drop from a bucket.

Isaiah 40:14–15

Here certain characteristics of God express faith. God created the earth; God does not give up when things go wrong; God will strengthen the weak, and all who wait for the Lord will fly like eagles (Isa. 40:28–31). Faith—with its reference to these qualities of God—helped the prophet see beyond the misery of Israel to the whole world's need for salvation. God was responsible for the entire world. In the past the Lord had depended upon Israel to be the major witness to God's will for the world, but now the Lord was reasserting divine initiative. God was promising that all who "wait for the Lord" would be strengthened. Salvation would come, but it would not depend on Israel, for the Lord was now going to open salvation to all the world without waiting for Israel to be the agent. Israel, still beloved, would continue to be an object lesson to the other nations—but an object lesson of how God loves and saves disobedient people.

At this point Israel's role in God's drama of salvation changed; now, wrote the prophet, other people seeking this relationship "may know and believe" (Isa. 43:10). The relationship described by the writer is "suffering love." God loves, gives, and forgives; humans seeing and experiencing this love may then have faith. Faith, then, is a response to this gracious suffering love shown by the Lord in the midst of sin and disobedience (see Isa. 43:8–13). This love comes to a climax in the well-known "suffering servant" passage (Isa. 52:13—53:12). Isaiah describes how a person lives a life of suffering love and gives himself for the sins of others.

Faith, functioning in the desperate circumstances of a people torn from their land and forced to live under foreign rulers, found a way for people to relate themselves to God, a way that became the dawn of a new strategy of salvation.[16]

New Testament Illustrations

In the New Testament the basic idea of faith, with its meaning as shown in Old Testament stories, is assumed. Here the word "faith" is used frequently and is also given special meanings having to do with salvation in Christ, belief in the resurrection, being a believer, and acceptance of church beliefs. Faith is closely associated with the will of an individual to believe in Christ and to become a part of a congregation, the "new" Israel.

According to Gerhard Ebeling, the Septuagint translation of the word "faith" carries the idea that "Real is what has a future." To elaborate that idea, he quotes Von Soden:

The peculiarity of the Hebrew concept of truth is . . . on the one hand its temporal determination, its specifically historic character. It is always a case of something that has happened or will happen, not of something that by nature is, is the way it is and must be so. To that extent truth and reality would here not be distinguishable at all, but truth is reality seen as history. Truth is not something that lies somehow at the bottom of things or behind them and would be discovered by penetrating their depths or their inner meaning; but truth is what will transpire in the future. The opposite of truth would so to speak not really be illusion, but essentially disillusion (in the commonly accepted sense of disappointment). What is lasting and durable and has a future is true, and that holds supremely of the eternal as being imperishable, everlasting, final, ultimate. The law of history would be truth for the Hebrew not in the sense of a regularity or natural law that is always confirmed in all that happens, but in the sense of the fulfilled determination of its unique course, of its divinely appointed rightness.[17]

This idea—that faith can be translated to mean the equivalent of the Hebrew understanding of truth as that which will come to pass in the future—leads naturally to Jesus Christ as the fulfillment of the Old Testament expectation so well represented by Isaiah.

Earliest Christianity and Paul

Paul's letter to the congregation he started in Thessalonica about A.D. 48 is the first written record we have of Christianity. The letter indicates that there was an oral tradition about Jesus already in creedal form. Paul quotes the oral creed concerning the dead—"For since we believe that Jesus died and rose again, even so, through Jesus, God will bring with him those who have fallen asleep" (1 Thess. 4:14)—and the rest of the paragraph describes the immediately expected return of the Lord. This statement is a short version of the tradition Paul handed on to the believers in Corinth. In the first Corinthian letter he is explicit about the tradition: "For I delivered to you as of first importance what I also received, that Christ died for our sins in accordance with the scriptures, that he was buried, that he was raised on the third day in accordance with the scriptures" (1 Cor. 15:3–4).

These terse creeds imply that the first Christians thought of faith as a response to what God had done in Jesus Christ. It was in continuity with, yet was a break from, God's previous way of relating to believers (see 1 Cor. 8:6; 1 Thess. 1:9). God's word remains the same, but one must now relate to Christ "who is the likeness of God" (2 Cor. 4:4). Faith is not only the way one comes to God; it is also the word used to describe the central message: "If Christ has not been raised, your faith is futile and you are still in your sins" (1 Cor. 15:17; see also Eph. 4:5).

But Paul did not limit his theology to beliefs about death and eternal life. To him, faith was the way to live. When people have faith in God, they understand life and are enabled to live in a manner acceptable to God. The problem is how people can live a good life. The religion of Pharisaic Judaism said that a person became good just by following the law of Moses. The law was a gift from God, and people could keep the law if they tried. Paul believed that he himself fulfilled the law in a "blameless" fashion (Phil. 3:6). But Paul, as a Christian, found the law was inadequate—that only faith in Jesus Christ would bring true righteousness. He offered two major reasons for this radical shift.

The first is an argument from experience. Paul respected the law as the highest moral code, for he knew that God expected the whole world to be blessed by the exemplary living of the Jews. Did it happen? No. The law the Jews had had for centuries had not produced the expected moral achievement. Sometimes the Gentiles, who did not have the law of Moses, actually lived closer to the spirit of the law than did the Jews (Romans 2).

The second argument is theological. Paul analyzes the human situation on the basis of our insecurity before God. In the depths of our being we are aware that someday we will cease to be; this fear of death, coming early in our life, "stains" (Paul Ricoeur's word) all our thoughts and actions. The terror of losing our self-consciousness in death causes us to affirm ourselves in every possible way. The human self is, therefore, a bundle of energy striving to maintain itself. Although this energetic anxiety is not sin, it is the condition that leads to sins. People protect their pride by lying; they enhance themselves by moving against other people to obtain money, property, or prestige because these things seem to have permanence against the day of death. The law, according to Paul, is unable to change this insecurity before God. Keeping the law will not justify a person. "All have sinned and fall short of the glory of God," Paul declares; righteousness can come only through faith in Jesus Christ (Romans 3).

This theological point rises out of psychological insight. Later in his letter to the Roman Christians, Paul says that the law introduces a person to sin because it tells what one should not do (Rom. 7:7). This description of what is wrong just excites one's natural passions. It should not do that, of course, because the law is holy, just, and good; but people want physical gratification and social status, and they will work around the law to get what they want. The struggle of the self between gratification of impulses and doing what is good is nowhere better expressed than in these words: "I can will what is right, but I cannot do it. For I do not do the good I want, but the evil I do not want is what I do." Paul said that sin living in us causes this condition (Romans 7) and that the remedy for this condition of sin is faith in Jesus Christ.

God has taken responsibility for this human dilemma and has offered righteousness in the person of Jesus to help humans achieve what they cannot do on their own. Humans have done nothing to deserve this gift: it comes only because God's nature is to be compassionate and to save the whole world that God created (Rom. 11:29–36). The only way humans can accept this gift is through faith (Rom. 3:21–31).

Paul's insistence that one is saved by faith and that faith is a gift of God was radical (see Eph. 2:8–9). It separated him from the Jewish interpretation of the law as the way of righteousness and changed the basis on which one could live at peace with God. The way of Judaism was a form of self-discipline in which one could have certainty because one could keep the law. The way of Christianity, by contrast, depended on faith in Christ and participation in the church that was the continuation of Christ's ministry in the world (see 1 Cor. 12).

Paul, as indicated, found this theology in the Christian church when he became a believer. His role was to enlarge and explain it. Perhaps we should pause to observe what the first Christians remembered and wrote down about this drastic change in their own religious beliefs.

The first community of believers in Jerusalem interpreted Jesus as the promised Messiah, and they continued to go to the temple daily (Acts 2:46). They may also have paid the temple tax (Matt. 17:24–27). Thus the very first Christians were a sect within the Jewish communities, and as long as they observed the Jewish law, they were not disturbed. Apparently they kept the law. The Christian group grew in numbers, attracting Jews who were raised in a Greek environment and spoke Greek. One of these Greek-speaking converts, Stephen, believing that faith in Christ was enough, deprecated the law and Jewish customs. In a speech before the high priest, Stephen traced the history of the Hebrews, showing that religious leaders seemed always to resist the prophets and now they had betrayed the "righteous one." This so enraged the Jewish audience that they took Stephen out of the city and stoned him to death (Acts 6 and 7).

So the first Christians faced a life-or-death situation in the way they interpreted the role of the law. Peter observed the law until he was led by the Holy Spirit through dreams and through a relationship with a Roman soldier, Cornelius, to realize "that God shows no partiality, but in every nation any one who fears him and does what is right is acceptable to him" (Acts 10:34–35). But the group of Christians that thought they could stay within Judaism did not give up easily. The conflict was resolved by a conference in Jerusalem about A.D. 52, and the Peter/Paul theology, requiring only faith in Christ for salvation, became the church's belief.

Given the central importance of Abraham for the Hebrews, Paul realized that he must relate his theology about Christ to the ancient beliefs of the Jews. Paul's forensic skills are well displayed on this matter in Romans, chapter 4, and Galatians, chapters 3 and 4. Although the passages are too long and too carefully designed for his Jewish readers to be summarized briefly, we can note how Paul's faith interpreted scripture.

Paul uses the passage "Abraham believed God, and it was reckoned to him as righteousness" many times in these chapters (Rom. 4:3). He points out that Abraham had faith before he was circumcised, so that circumcision was only a sign or a seal that Abraham was faithful. The promises of God are therefore based on a relationship of faith, not law. Abraham knew he had no chance of a son, yet he maintained his faith. His faith passed the test; thus "it was reckoned to him as righteousness."

The Galatians section is a more precise attack on the role of the law. The law, Paul states, does not rest on faith. We have the law because that was the only way God could control human life. It was like a caretaker until Christ came. Now that we have Christ, all people regardless of race, sex, or status are "Abraham's offspring, heirs according to promise" (Gal. 3:29). Thus we see how faith in God—the God addressed in the Old Testament—is carried forward through the centuries and used to secure meaning for the present. Paul is more explicit about this method in Romans. There he says that the faith that was "reckoned" to Abraham for righteousness was not just for his sake; it was for us, too. If we have faith in the God of Abraham, we will believe that the same God raised Jesus from the dead "who was put to death for our trespasses and raised for our justification" (Rom. 4:23–25).

Paul's insistence that the law was no longer binding created a crisis in the lives of believers and an ethical problem for Christian theology. Paul deals with both these matters.

Living by faith in God's goodness and mercy, without the restraint of the law, could logically lead one to say that sin did not make much difference, since God in Christ was ready to forgive (Rom. 6:1, 15; see also 3:8). Paul opposes this logical deduction with the psychology of affection. If we love God for what he has done for us, we will be thankful to God and will want to please Christ. Therefore, we will no longer be slaves to sin.

The matter of ethics in daily life is much more involved than the sin/forgiveness issue. Faith is not a one-time affair but the beginning of a new life. Obedience shifts from the law to Christ. This leads to "holding to your faith" (2 Cor. 13:5) or "standing firm in your faith" (1 Cor. 16:13; 2 Cor. 1:24), which is the same as "standing fast in the Lord" (1 Thess. 3:8) or "standing in the gospel" (1 Cor. 15:1). Being "in Christ" causes a person to be "a new creation" working for reconciliation of all people (2 Cor. 5:16–21). In fact, what is important to

Christ is "faith working through love" (Gal. 5:6; see also Eph. 1:15–23; 3:14–17; 6:23).

Matthew, Mark, and Luke

All of Paul's letters were written by about A.D. 70. Jesus had not returned, and the disciples who had been with him were getting along in years. There was a need and desire to record information about Jesus before those who knew him personally were gone. Considerable evidence suggests that an oral tradition existed, perhaps even some documents containing the sayings and parables of Jesus. The Gospels, as we have them, were written thirty to fifty years after the crucifixion, at a time when the believers may have become discouraged because Jesus had not reappeared. If so, we can understand the enormous emphasis on faith—a kind of faith, Jesus said, that is available to anyone and is powerful enough to do almost anything. The quality of faith in the Gospels reminds us more of the Old Testament than of Paul. We could argue that Paul had done the necessary theological work on faith with the first generation of Christians, so this second generation did not attempt to duplicate what Paul had already done. Regardless of the reason, faith seems to have a somewhat different character in the Synoptic Gospels than it does in the writings of Paul.

The principal meaning of faith in the Gospels is trust in God's power to do wonderful or miraculous things. Reading the stories gives one an image of God as a gracious power just beyond our consciousness, available if we only have faith in God. Having faith seems to be a matter of a person's will, something anyone can have if he or she wants it with deep desire. Moreover, the power of God is available in specific life situations here and now—in contrast to the concern for life after death that was featured in Paul's letter to the Thessalonians. Jesus did not give or imply a new definition of faith; he demonstrated how faith can utilize the power of God (Heb. 2:1–5; Rom. 2:12–16).

Perhaps the most spectacular and incredible illustration of how much power faith in God can produce is this declaration:

> And Jesus answered them, "Have faith in God. Truly, I say to you, whoever says to this mountain, 'Be taken up and cast into the sea,' and does not doubt in his heart, but believes that what he says will come to pass, it will be done for him. Therefore I tell you, whatever you ask in prayer, believe that you have received it, and it will be yours."
> Mark 11:22–25; see Luke 17:6 and Matt. 17:20 for other versions

It is assumed that this statement is part of an old tradition, for Paul alludes to it (1 Cor. 13:2). The conclusion to the equivalent remark in Matthew's Gospel states, "and nothing will be impossible to you." Hermisson and Lohse say that "never in the Judaism of that period was faith described with this turn of phrase."[18] Thus we can assume that the Christian community remembered this striking promise just as Jesus gave it.

If we assume also that Jesus' conception of faith was as a connection to the power of God, it is natural to relate faith to prayer just as Mark did in the passage about moving mountains. Prayer is a way to express faith, a meditation about what one wants by reason of having faith.

There are so many stories in the Gospels about healing and about miracles of nature occasioned by faith that we need not provide an inventory. The stories of healing are often followed by the words "your faith has made you well" (Mark 5:34; Luke 18:42). A different twist is given in some stories, such as in the healing of the epileptic boy. The father first asked for help from the disciples, but they could not heal the child, and Jesus rebuked them and others because they were "faithless." When the father asked Jesus for help, Jesus replied, "All things are possible to him who believes." The father professed his belief, and the boy was healed. Later the disciples asked Jesus why they could not cast out the demons. Jesus replied, "This kind cannot be driven out by anything but prayer" (Mark 9:14–29). Jesus' comment is puzzling. Is prayer more than a means of communicating with God? Or, in the context of the whole story, is this Jesus' way of saying that prayer helps develop faith for believers so they can have the power of faith? The latter seems to be the point of Jesus' explanation to his disciples.

A full inventory of Gospel stories about the power of faith to change things radically would include those of raising people from the dead (Luke 7:15) and of storms stilled (Luke 8:22–25). Moreover, the role of faith in these unique events is heightened by the report that, when faith was not present, Jesus was unable to perform miracles (Mark 6:6). Faced with evidence of intense faith, however, Jesus was able to heal the centurion's servant who was not present and who was not even aware that his master was seeking a cure (Matt. 8:5–13).

John

John's idea of faith has some of the features of Paul's, but it is different in that John's Gospel is written to create belief that "Jesus is the Christ, the Son of God, and that believing you may have life in his name" (John 20:31). John is concerned with knowing Christ, and therefore he relates faith to knowledge.

In contrast to the Synoptics, John's Gospel does not use the word "faith"—only the verb "to believe." Nevertheless, the idea of faith as it is used in the other Gospels is present. For example, in chapter 3, verse 16, we read, "God so loved the world that he gave his only Son, that whoever believes in him should not perish but have eternal life."

Here "believe in" has the same meaning as "have faith in," a formula John uses a number of times (John 4:39; 12:44; 17:20).

An important difference between John and the other Gospel writers lies in their portrayal of faith's role in life. In the Synoptics, a person is to have faith in God and then wonderful things will happen; in John, one is confronted with a sign and then responds with faith. The sign is a "mighty work," usually a miracle, that certifies Jesus as the Messiah and causes people to be aware of God's presence and power. When one's attention has thus been arrested, one is expected to have feelings of awe and respect, resulting in faith (John 6:26; 14:11). Some people resist the sign or fail to respond with faith, and they are lost (John 1:11; 11:45–48).

Although John usually pictures people as either accepting or rejecting Jesus, he also describes two other responses. One is that of the person who barely believes, the one who is almost forced to accept Jesus because the miracle overpowers him. In the story of the nobleman's son, Jesus said, "Unless you see signs and wonders you will not believe" (John 4:48). The same idea is applied to Thomas, who would not believe unless he could literally see the nail holes in Jesus' hands (John 20:24–25). The story of Thomas brings out the other response—that of the person who has not seen Jesus, yet believes. These people seemed to have a stronger or better faith because they did not need physical evidence (John 20:29).

Blackman points out that the way John uses belief *in* Jesus is unusual, resulting in a distinctive idea of faith.[19] This comes about because Jesus is so closely identified with God that to believe *in* Jesus is to believe *in* God. The image is that Jesus was with—and was a part of—God at the creation of the world. Because of God's love he came to live on earth for a while, and now he has returned to heaven to make a place eternally for all who believe *in* him. Blackman cites the story of the woman at the well as an illustration of this point. The woman was secular in spirit, but she had some knowledge of religion. Not wanting to commit herself, she tried to divert Jesus to generalizations about religion. But Jesus told her he was the Messiah and, in the context of the dialogue, that she should believe in him. Since this woman was not a Jew, the story shows Jesus as the savior of all the world. Indeed, "Many Samaritans from that city believed in him because of the woman's testimony" (John 4:7–42).

John's idea of faith continues one of Paul's major points; namely, that faith is a way of life. The difference is that John relates faith to knowledge rather than to love and hope. If a person believes in Jesus, that person will continue in Jesus' word and will know the truth, and the truth will set the person free (John 8:31–38). Here, believing and knowing are about the same thing because what is known is Jesus. But the idea is not that one believes and then one knows, with the implication that knowledge increases; sometimes John puts knowing Jesus before believing in Jesus, so the two go together (John 16:30; 17:8). Within the meditative mood of John's Gospel, the idea is that knowing Jesus leads to faith, and faith is intensified by that knowledge. The two are combined in one's devotion to Jesus, the son of God.

Hebrews

When one thinks of faith in the New Testament, one's mind goes automatically to the book of Hebrews, chapter 11. There we find a paean of praise to faith's role in Hebrew life, from the Cain and Abel story up to Jesus. In Hebrews, faith is portrayed as a heroic quality of human life. That quality is the special characteristic of the Hebrew people, a trait that keeps them going in spite of persecution, trials, tribulations, and other adversities. This heritage of heroic faith will help the people endure persecution—especially now they are "looking to Jesus, the pioneer and perfecter of our faith" (Heb. 12:2). By this analysis, the people of God are asked to rally around Jesus as they endure by faith whatever they must. Faith, in this letter, means "holding firm," "patient endurance," or "steadfastness." The required loyalty is to God, who has a future for all people. To the writer of Hebrews, as to Paul, faith is the beginning of the Christian life—not something one works toward.

Latest Christian Writings

By the year A.D. 100, all the people who had been with Jesus were dead. The churches were made up of second- and third-generation Christians. Beliefs and practices were based on oral traditions, and perhaps on written collections of Paul's letters or of the Gospels. Out of this situation came a number of short letters that are extremely important for our purpose, for they indicate how the churches were settling down into a routine after the days of charismatic leaders described in the first chapter of Acts.

First Peter reflects the mood of that era; its writer is thankful that God has guarded the faith so the readers know that Jesus' resurrection has prepared an inheritance for them. They may have to suffer some trials, but these will merely test their faith. They are to be commended because, without seeing Jesus, they love him and believe in him (1 Peter 1:3–9).

Believers still live in hope of Jesus' return, but they are equally conscious of themselves as the bearers of the "mystery of the faith" that must be handed on to the next generation through an organization (1 Tim. 3:9). If they struggle personally to "keep the faith," they will receive a "crown of righteousness" from the Lord (2 Tim. 4:6–8).

The prevailing mentality of the people during this historical situation was to hold on to what they had, to protect the faith, and to separate themselves from unbelievers. The word "faith" was used to mean a cluster of doctrines that were "given" to guide their lives and were to be passed on without change to their children and converts (1 Tim. 4:6–12). The fear was that one might "depart from the faith by giving heed to deceitful spirits and doctrines of demons." This departure from faith as correct doctrine would lead to immoral living, and the people would thus become "liars whose consciences are seared" (1 Tim. 4:1–5). Although the wrong doctrines were not precisely identified, the false teachers were called by name, and what they said was described as a "gangrene" that would poison the souls of true believers. The readers were urged to be good workmen, rightly "handling the word of truth" (2 Tim. 2:14–19).

There is nothing in these later epistles that contradicts the teachings of Paul, but their mood and emphasis are significantly different. In Paul's writings we get the feeling that faith describes a relationship with God. What comes of that relationship might be—probably would be—different from the past. Moreover, in human situations where ethical choices must be made, there would be a sense of a person's meeting the situation with fresh understanding, unencumbered with the accumulated theology of the past. In these later epistles we get the feeling that faith is a set of beliefs to be defended. Jude said it this way: "I found it necessary to write appealing to you to contend for the faith which was once for all delivered to the saints" (v. 3).

Understanding Faith

As far as biblical teaching is concerned, faith in God is something a person either has or does not have. There is no speculation as to its human source. What is important in the biblical view is the way faith *functions* in persons, causing them to seek and understand God's will for the world and their responsibility to bring it about. We cannot, therefore, find in the Bible a psychological theory of faith; nor can we find anything very precise about its relation to mental development or to other facets of a person's psychic life. What the Bible describes are situations in a historical setting and individuals who try to enact God's concern within that milieu.

There is a strong element of will in faith. Persons or groups living in faith are trying to bring about a future they believe God desires. Because situations differ, a general *meaning* of faith cannot be constructed. We have seen that each biblical illustration had a different meaning in accord with the situation in which faith was exercised. However, we can form some generalizations about the way faith functions in the Christian life

Faith Is a Gift

Faith is something one receives in the beginning of the religious life, not something toward which one aspires as a goal. The goal is to do God's will, or—in the language of Paul—to be "in Christ." Faith is the means to that goal. There are variations on this theme: some people have deficiencies in their faith (1 Thess. 3:10); a person can be weak in faith (Rom. 14:1), or can grow strong in faith (Rom. 4:16–25).

The proper mental image of faith is that of a journey or pilgrimage, an image suggesting that faith is a quality or characteristic a person has in facing life situations. Faith is the disposition of mind and spirit that finds a way to live with and through the vicissitudes of life. In this sense, people with religious faith have a history; they can describe how different things happened to them and what meaning they extracted from those situations. Religiously speaking, a person can be a failure (be "lost") up to the end of life and still become successful (be "saved")—as the story of the thief on the cross affirms. Thus faith is an awareness that becomes activated by life situations and helps a person understand God's will in them. Practicing the presence of God leads to more confidence, but not to more faith. Similarly, practicing faith as an awareness of God reduces fear, doubt, and uncertainty, but it does not increase the amount of faith one has.

What these conclusions deny is the theory that faith develops in certain predetermined stages that can be known in advance. This theory, based on structural developmental psychology, identifies six stages of faith. Although this is not the place to challenge that theory, I want to emphasize that its conception of faith is different from the one that has been described. Development deals with regularities of life (age gradations), the average person's thoughts and actions, and progression toward a predetermined goal. Faith in God, on the contrary, deals with irregularities of life (sin), a person's uniqueness in relation to God, and the creation of a human community with Christian characteristics.[20]

Faith Describes a Relationship

"The faith that you have," Paul said, "keep between yourself and God" (Rom. 14:22). Faith is not something to be displayed or measured, for it describes a relationship. Because of the nature of God, the relationship will take on different qualities according to the circumstances the person is facing. The characteristics listed below are not types of faith but more like facets that shine brightly when a person of faith is in certain situations. Often two or more facets of light meet the eye and fuse into a different hue when we look at a faithful person striving to find and do God's will.

Struggle. This characteristic of faith was displayed by Abraham, Isaiah, Paul, and others. They defined what might be called a "problematic situation" for which conventional theology offered no possible solution. Because they had trust in God, they struggled with God for a solution different from those of former times.

Acceptance. This quality of faith was evident in those who were healed by Jesus. Paul's insistence that we are saved by grace—and that grace, too, is supplied by God—is a form of resignation. We can note this same attitude described in Acts as people waited for the guidance of the Holy Spirit.

Obedience. Although best defined in the late New Testament epistles, this style of faith is a feature of Abraham's situation as well. Similarly, when Jesus said to his would-be disciples, "Follow me," he expected them indeed to leave everything and go with him.

Confidence. This facet of faith, explained in the book of Hebrews, is a certainty of mind that overcomes all obstacles. It expresses the profound hope that all things are working toward a future God has designed. There is a timeless, abstract quality to this type of faith; persons who exhibit it often do so without even being aware of it. Many of the people mentioned in the book of Hebrews, for example, neither used the word "faith" nor claimed that they had it.

Because the biblical word for faith means "to be confident in one's mind," confidence is often dominant in faithful persons. Such confidence comes from the object of faith, God. People who have faith have committed themselves—meaning that they conduct their lives in the most sober and careful ways they can command. They are not easily shaken by adversity, for their perseverance is based on what they know in their heart to be true. External problems or logical arguments against their beliefs only spur them to bring into being the future they know to be right.

Serenity. John best illustrates this aspect of faith in his Gospel, where we find a timeless Christ combined with a compassionate Lord who wants to come and dwell within a person. If a person believes, she or he will have a special peace that the world cannot give. Paul also referred to this characteristic of serenity, for he said that he had acquired a peace beyond understanding.

Faith Creates Beliefs

The faith relationship produces beliefs that express the meaning of a person's or group's relationship to God during a particular historical moment. However, we must not equate faith with beliefs in an absolute way. Faith is a reality greater than any documented beliefs, a fact with weighty significance. Let us identify two results of the faith relationship.

Beliefs, as we have noted, are what we can define and discuss from a faith relationship with God. Under ordinary conditions it is difficult to separate beliefs from the underlying trust, and in ordinary circumstances we need not try. In fact, to believe that a certain thing is true is the proper way to combine faith and the meaning of faith. From our analysis we have observed that faith functions in specific human situations. This is why faith is so powerful; the persons involved are confident that they are being led to speak and act in a certain way. Beliefs, then, are the manifestations of what is real and important in the way we order our lives.

Abraham and Isaiah faced different situations, and accordingly the beliefs of each man were different. Jesus' beliefs, saved for us in his teachings and parables, reflect the needs of that time; to the extent that our human condition is the same, they also apply to us today. A community of faithful folk over a period of time tests beliefs, modifies some, changes some, and at certain historic moments formulates fresh conceptions of what faith means.

Faith Re-creates Beliefs

As previously indicated, ordinarily we need not separate faith from beliefs. But as a theological matter, we must allow for the possibility of new beliefs or for a fresh or different way of interpreting old ones. Isaiah's searching for the meaning of life in exile and his feeling of being abandoned by God forced him to formulate beliefs about God's purpose that were fresh, if not new. The profound theology of the "suffering servant" and the idea of salvation for all the world resulted when the belief system of the past failed to account for the plight of Israel (Isaiah 53). In this case we see that faith is a deep desire to go on living even when previous meanings of life have broken down. It is an elemental urge to keep on trying even when we cannot make much sense out of the events that are happening.

The role of faith in re-creating beliefs is most often evident during adverse circumstances. In times of crisis, conventional answers may be unsatisfactory. When anxiety erupts in acts of destruction or when a person's passions get out of control, former beliefs may not apply. Under these conditions a person may be forced to review his or her relation with God and seek an understanding that was not there before.

We must remember that, although faith may live in the realm of the affections, it operates in our lives through our perceptive system. The person of faith sees things and evaluates the forces in human situations differently from a person with no trust in God. For example, Psalm 73 tells the story of someone who saw wicked people prosper and almost went over to their ways. When he went to worship, he saw himself— during a moment of meditation—in relation to God, and realized that the people who built their lives on power and prestige were living in a dream world. Their feet were on a slippery place. After a prayer of confession for his shortcoming, he concluded, "It is good to be near God" (v. 28).

PART THREE

Experiential Religion

The line of thought runs as follows: we inherit our religion mingled with culture. In America secular individualism is the dominant theme. Unless this mixture is analyzed critically, it will be communicated as true religion by society and congregations to church members and their children.

The biblical story of humankind confirms both the above situation and the constant drift of individuals and societies away from God's will by way of sin, secularism, and sectarianism. However, the Bible also recounts stories of individuals and groups of believers who, experiencing God's presence and guidance, maintained a community of faithful people who were resistant to secular culture and who were led to change the meaning of their tradition in order to meet new conditions.

The problem of practical theology, therefore, is how to help people experience the presence of God as described in our tradition. The solution is a congregation where the leaders create an awareness of God's will for present life situations through worship, education, and service. Amid such congregational life, an individual's faith will mature through shared experiences. The question of how this can be done is the subject of the final three chapters.

9

Life Together

The distinctive feature of practical theology is its involvement in contemporary life situations. Such concern creates a fuzzy field of study and activity because human life is so complex and uncertain. There is hardly any issue in our lives where we have absolute confidence about what to say or do, whether it be love, hope, forgiveness, decision making, the role of law or restraint, mental images of God, the occurrence of evil, a sense of God's will in a particular conflict, transcendence of ordinary duties in order to see what ought to be, identification and opposition of selfish motives, or communication of faith to children. All we have to go by is the biblical record—believers' experience with God over a long period of time in many different situations—and our own experience, yet we have to deal with many practical aspects of faith every day. Moreover, if we describe an actual life situation in which some decision must be made, disagreement will inevitably emerge between equally sincere and devout Christians. This happens because individuals with varying past experiences interpret current situations differently. How then should church leaders proceed to plan worship, education, and service?

Mainstream Denominations

This discussion of how faith matures is written for mainstream Protestant denominations in America. What is said may also fit some Catholic or Orthodox congregations; but if it does, adjustments will need to be made in the recommendations that follow, for congregations in those traditions differ significantly in governance and worship. Additionally, what is said may fit some congregations in other Western nations where a middle-class way of life is well established; if so, again, some changes in the recommendations may be necessary to fit the different cultural context.

Congregations of Christian sects, small residential communities, or congregations made up primarily of people of the same race or similar ethnic background will probably find little help in these last three chapters, because they may already be doing much of what is proposed. For these congregations or groups the issue is not so much the communication of their beliefs and practices (for they do that rather well), but their inability to critique those beliefs and practices because they are so deeply committed to the special interests that hold them together as a congregation.

Although mainstream American Protestant denominations differ in governance and theological tradition, they have become so much alike that they often use the same church school materials. When members of such denominations move to a new community, they may join whatever congregation is conveniently located or has the kind of services they desire. The interpretation of the Christian faith in the mass media at Christmas and Easter reflects the beliefs of this middle-class segment of society. Because these mainstream denominations have been decreasing in size for the past twenty years, a great deal of attention has been given to their plight.[1]

Many suggestions have been made as to how to stop the decline in membership. This book does not deal with this problem directly, for an assumption of this study is that the church is always in tension with culture. We are not exploring here how Christians can increase in number, but how Christians can experience the living God and relate that experience to events in the arenas where they have some control—family, friends, community, and work. The story of the founding and expansion of the church in Acts has little to do with the matter of how to recruit new members or how to influence society. That account is about what happened when a small group of disciples and friends were convinced they had experienced the risen Christ in their midst and were commissioned by him to preach the good news that "in Christ God was reconciling the world to himself" and to continue Christ's ministry in the world (2 Cor. 5:19). The conviction that they had experienced the presence of God changed their perspective on everything. From their convictional experience in an informal association of believers, they formalized a simple organizational plan to establish the church as a social institution; they began to develop a more systematic belief system, a more coherent pattern of worship, a distinctive lifestyle called "the Way" (Acts 9:2), and an educational program.

Wayne A. Meeks, in his study of the earliest Christian writings, has pointed out that all New Testament writings "had as their primary aim the shaping of the life of Christian communities." Although these writings contain many rules and exhortations to live by certain moral standards, we will "fail to understand the force of the arguments and rules if we take them out of the contexts in which they stand." New converts were to participate in congregations, for there they would learn a new identity as "those for whom Christ died." Additionally, new converts were to bring moral issues to the congregation, for that was the context in which morality was to be formed.[2]

These terse summary statements about the New Testament church illustrate the process by which the Christian faith lives. We learn about God through the tradition, but experiencing the presence of God provides both the perspective by which all things are to be judged and also the power to live by that perspective. In the church the tradition is transmitted from the past, and in the congregation we formulate the meaning of faith for the present. The issue is how religious experience can become more integrated into congregational life.

Congregational Uniqueness

Let us first recall the uniqueness of congregations. They are like no other social institution, for they are a voluntary association of people and therefore are not subject to government regulation except in matters of public morals and safety. They sponsor schools of various sorts, yet the church itself is more than a school. They evaluate the quality of social life and often lobby legislators for laws or social programs, but they are not primarily a political organization. And although they sponsor many services, such as child-care centers, homes for the aging, hospitals, soup kitchens, and shelters for runaway children, they are not founded for social service. For thousands of years the churches worked incessantly to formulate moral codes and instruct people about them, yet church leaders insist that Christianity is more than morality. Even the sermon (which is used to inspire, to instruct, to proclaim God's love, and to announce God's will for particular life situations) is not considered by preachers to be the most important part of worship. The sacraments—especially the Lord's Supper—are more important. Church members might affirm that ongoing goals—developing a perspective by which they can judge history and current events, learning how to suffer and how to react when evil occurs, and achieving a hope beyond death—are the distinctive features that set a congregation apart from all other human organizations.

The reason for this uniqueness is the nature of the church as a community of people sharing a belief in Jesus Christ as their Lord and Savior—with all that phrase means in the biblical record and the history of the church. However, since Protestants broke away from the Roman Catholic Church because of differences about fundamental beliefs, Protestants tend to place correctness of beliefs over community, as if the two were separate matters. But the two are never separate, for community is a component of beliefs. In crisis situations or in tense times when people feel that their beliefs are in danger, they will split from the dominant group and form their own association. So, ultimately, beliefs are stronger than community. It is extremely important to note, however, that when a split occurs, it is a *group* that effects it, and that group immediately forms a community to preserve the belief that caused the split. The Reformation is a good illustration, for those protesting against the Catholics disagreed even among themselves, and each segment consequently formed its own church. If we are acquainted with a local congregation where a split occurred, we will notice that the split-away group almost always forms a congregation to support each other in its beliefs.

Today mainstream congregations are recovering the special theological significance of the community. Community is more than an inevitable concomitant of beliefs: community, in Christian terms, must take on the character of the religion it embraces. This means we must take seriously the way Jesus went about being the Word of God to humankind. Because Jesus was a teacher, beliefs were central; however, he also spent considerable time forming the disciples into a community. He could have written books about his beliefs and left us a definitive statement of truth, but instead he used his time to show his disciples how to live the beliefs he taught. The community became the place where the disciples could gain further insight into Jesus' teachings, support each other in their ministry, formulate administrative policies by disputation among themselves, and share the experiences they were having so that their faith might become more mature. I have already referred to the example of Peter. Although according to Matthew he was the first to declare Jesus as the Christ, Peter denied knowing Jesus at the crucifixion; and he needed to learn after the resurrection that Gentiles were just as much the object of God's love as were the Jews. It was the community of believers who supported Peter, as he slowly learned from his experience.

We learned from the letters of Paul how, when the small group of disciples became the church, the community functioned to reflect Christian beliefs. Since most of Paul's letters are about this, there is little need to cite examples. In general terms Paul saw the community as a group of people gathered because of their beliefs, but he also recognized that members of the community held different versions of the common belief statements. In fact, some church members had basic misconceptions, and others failed to live up to their beliefs. Yet Paul called the church the "body of Christ" (1 Cor. 12:12–27; Rom. 12:4–5; Eph. 4:15–16; Col. 3:15). It was a place where people learned to live their beliefs just as the disciples did under the tutelage of Jesus, except that Jesus—now represented by the Holy Spirit—was the invisible head of the church. It was also a place where a person could share doubts and have hurts healed. Since this book is primarily about the congregation as a place where religious experiences may be shared in order to help people's faith mature, I will not deal directly with the uniqueness of the congregation as a place where people can associate with others while they are working through their doubts, finding guidance for their lives, or adjusting to events about which there is great sorrow. Going through such experiences creates profound learning, but the people involved often cannot bring themselves to discuss the matter with anyone. However, the congregation through its ordinary work and worship brings stability and a reconstruction of hope. Ministers who are close to the life situation of members know such growth is going on, but they often cannot say much about it because people's feelings are too sensitive for conversation.[3]

This hidden aspect of the pastoral function of a congregation came to my attention a few years ago when I was a guest professor at San Francisco Theological Seminary. One semester I held seminars on Christian education in three off-campus centers on the Pacific coast. The group was made up of ministers with responsibility for education and of lay people who had become so interested in a church that they were employed part-time as educational leaders. In order quickly to bring up the matter of experience in education, I asked the members to write a description of an experience they considered important for their own Christian growth. I thought such experiences would show us how faith was communicated more through life situations than through conventional schooling methods, but only a few members of the seminar described the kind of experiences I expected. Most of these highly dedicated people interpreted the assignment to mean, "What experiences have I had that caused me to be interested in the church?" This question is more profound than the one I had asked. They interpreted the question that way because they were living in an extremely secular region of the United States—Seattle, San Francisco, and Los Angeles—so their being associated with the church as leaders meant going contrary to the culture around them. They thought they should show why they had this special interest in the church. It turned out that although about half these people came from nonreligious families, their parents had sent them to Sunday school. There they had found a teacher or a pastor who accepted them in a way they had not experienced anywhere else, and they learned to appreciate these leaders as persons who were concerned about their life in a special way. A rather high percentage of these people had gone through a divorce or experienced the death of a loved one. They found that church attendance gave them unique perspective and hope. Of the other seminar members, most were people who had serious doubts about Christian beliefs. Some had dropped out of the church in college days and then returned to take a last look before giving up religion entirely—but discovered that the congregation was a place where they could rethink the meaning of their faith. Others had had a smattering of information about religion and then almost by accident—such as going to church a few times with a friend—had found the life-style of the congregation pleasantly different from what they had expected.

In these cases the members of the congregation, while going about their ordinary work and worship, provided a pastoral ministry of which they were largely unaware. The individuals who received help were only dimly aware of their need, and what happened took place in an unplanned, unpretentious way. We cannot know how often people with ill-defined needs are helped by just sharing in the life of a congregation. Since such occurrences cannot be scheduled, we tend to forget that congregations can be helpful just by being a "fellowship of kindred minds."

Congregational Realities

Congregational uniqueness has been described in general terms and from the standpoint of what congregations can be and often are. However, from the standpoint of practical theology, we must always keep the actual congregational situation in view. We cannot know in a precise way what the total congregational situation is or exactly what influence it has in the lives of its members. We can know some facts that describe the congregation—such as size, location, history, wealth, and the qualifications of the leaders. Each of these facts has implications for the life of the congregation, but taken together they can do no more than suggest what life in a particular congregation is like. If we know something of the beliefs of the members and their style of life together, we can begin to form an image of what a particular congregation communicates.[4]

Congregational Personality

When applied to a particular congregation, the set of objective facts plus the subjective aspect of beliefs and life together create a corporate personality. We have very few studies of actual congregations over a period of time to which we can refer.[5] Only by living in and working with a congregation can one get a sense of the way that community interprets and lives the Christian faith. Many ministers, after having served several congregations, know a lot about the corporate personality of a particular congregation. Such ministers seldom attempt to systematize their knowledge, but they are keenly aware of the dynamic interaction within the congregation that establishes and maintains a certain ethos.[6] Several recent studies of congregations may prove very helpful in an understanding of particular ones.

Researchers in Hartford, Connecticut, surveyed the 413 Protestant, Catholic, and Jewish congregations in the Hartford area. From that group they obtained data on 177 congregations, much of which related to each congregation's mission orientation. As defined in this study, (1) activist congregations were those most interested in the here and now as the arena of God's redemptive activity; (2) civic congregations were those who, though concerned about the community, were inclined to support the status quo; (3) sanctuary congregations tended to withdraw somewhat from the trials and conflicts of daily life; and (4) evangelistic congregations tended to emphasize a future world and to convert individuals to their beliefs.[7] The researchers then studied in more detail a group of churches within each of the four classifications. The study of each congregation is a brief story that covers history, location, size, program, and theological self-understanding. A thoughtful reading of these ten accounts will illustrate how congregations develop a corporate personality. Such an analysis may also help readers begin to sense how they could estimate the corporate personality of a particular congregation.[8]

Although the Hartford researchers were mainly interested in mission orientation, the corporate personality they describe shows within each of the congregations a variety of forces at work; thus we can get a rather clear image of what life together in that particular congregation would entail. Carl S. Dudley reports a similar diversity within the congregations he has studied in the Midwest. Dudley's work with congregations was over a period of time in which he and the leaders were thinking through many issues related to each particular church. From such associations he identified eight images that motivated members as well as the congregation as a whole. Personal relations characterized those churches which thought of themselves as (1) the Christian family or (2) a nurturing community. The tradition was determinative for congregations which considered their church (3) a representative of a historic denomination or (4) a sanctuary where members could experience the comfort and personal faith of the tradition. A smaller percentage of congregations thought of themselves as (5) a citizen church active in community affairs or (6) a servant church in which members received strength and guidance for their own service to people in need. The least frequent image related to changing the world, as expressed in (7) the prophetic church, seeking to relieve oppression and injustice, and (8) the evangelistic church, seeking to convert individuals and bring them into the congregation.[9]

Dudley's discussion of each of these eight types is important. The way the minister relates to people, the way decisions are made, and the way teachers are selected and trained are all influenced by the image that dominates congregational life. Dudley is careful to report, however, that several of these images may exist within a particular congregation. Indeed, several of the images may exist within one church member, so we must understand that we are dealing both with a dominant image which shapes the congregational personality and with subsidiary images that may ascend in importance to modify or replace the dominant one. Moreover, the images are in a dynamic relation to each other. When the congregation is planning for the future, for example, church leaders think and act in terms of "good" images. They may recall the servant image when planning to help the needy, but if conflict breaks out over such plans, then they may begin to point out that "those people" attracted by the servant church do not really belong to their congregation.

The Hartford researchers and Dudley's account of congregations reveal that each congregation is unique, because within each congregation there is a special configuration of leaders and members who hold varying images of the church. Thus the corporate personality of the congregation in each period of its history depends on the dynamic interaction of its leaders and the specific situation to which they are responding. Some situations are forced on the congregation—such as the closing of a local steel mill or a sudden influx of people because of a military base opening nearby. Other situations are what the leaders, from the perspective of their beliefs, deem important. Situations such as the housing needs of the urban poor, evangelistic opportunity with local high school students, and day-care centers for small children or older adults are "there" only if congregational leaders include them in their interpretation of Christianity.

James F. Hopewell has also made extensive studies of congregations. Although Hopewell is interested in how congregations can and should change, he is mainly concerned in understanding their inner life. He believes groups should do this by first listening to members and then forming a narrative or story of their self-understanding. Seeking a story for each congregation led him to literary categories and finally to Greek myths as a way of capturing the richness and depth of meaning found in congregational life. How helpful his analysis will be in practical theology is unknown, but Hopewell's insistence on considering congregations as corporate personalities made up of complex forces and motives comes closer to the truth than does rational analysis.[10] In the light of these modern studies of congregations, the term "corporate personality" is well chosen. Not only is each congregation different from others, but each congregation is composed of elements that exist in a dynamic relationship. The comparison with human personality is apt. We all know that each person is different from others, but we also know that inside each person is a set of elements that are constantly struggling. We experience ourselves internally as a struggle between uncertainty over what or what not to do, pride of achievement, shame for not keeping commitments to people we love and respect, and guilt over doing things for which we repent. These feelings, perhaps vague yet always present, are buffeted about in our conscious mind with ideas we pick up from various sources. Our interior life is like a debating society over which our conscious mind presides. As this condition of conflict both within and without is normal to a person, so it is to a corporate personality such as a particular congregation.

Congregational Conflict

The conflict just referred to can never be completely eliminated; it is endemic to the congregation as a social institution. There will always be differences of opinion between people who have different images of what the church ought to be. So the question is not so much how to diminish conflict—although a certain amount of that can and should be done—but how to understand and live with conflict in congregations.

Mainstream Attitudes

Mainstream denominations are made up of professional people, merchants, teachers, governmental employees, and the like. They include Americans who are knowledgeable about our history, and who have high educational achievement and a sense of responsibility for the nation's welfare. They vote. They are the volunteers who are associated with all kinds of community organizations, including the church. Given their position as caretakers of the American way of political and economic life, mainstream Christians personify certain attitudes toward conflict.

Some of those attitudes come from our political history. We know about the conflicts in the minds of the nation's founders that led to the compromise in having a House of Representatives and a Senate. Other compromises in our history, in our civic enterprises, and in our labor disputes have laid down the principle that in a democracy we have to give and take. Yet we must understand that compromise is not a resolution of conflict. It is a way to handle issues between contending parties: both parties agree that the unity of the community is more important than a prominent rupture.

Additionally, some of our attitudes can be traced to our family situation. "Family" here means the household in which people of various ages and relationships live as well as the close relationship of one family to other families. Some families in mainstream Protestant congregations have developed an atmosphere of non-conflict; that is, conflict between family members is denied or suppressed because it is considered out of keeping with the affection family members should display to one another.

Many mainstream attitudes come from business and the law courts, where competition or an adversarial relationship is assumed. In these relationships, custom or law provides the rules by which conflict is legalized and the assigned boundaries beyond which it may not go.

Some attitudes, finally, derive from the American idea of secular individualism as recounted in chapter 2. Even if Americans affirm a Christian faith, they are so surrounded with the socially approved striving to get ahead that they can easily justify conflicts with persons or institutions that hinder progress toward their self-centered goal.

Each of us possesses some—if not all—of the attitudes toward conflict mentioned above. Attitudes, we must remember, have a nonrational basis and are not arranged in logical order, so any or all of them may emerge in conflict situations. Probably the most common stance toward conflict in mainstream congregations is a desire to minimize its presence. This happens because the church emphasizes the importance of a loving and forgiving relationship between people and because we consider the congregation an extension of our family life. These are desirable qualities to which I will return in a moment.

Most courses at workshops on conflict for church leaders have as their purpose the restoration and maintenance of tranquillity. To many ministers, having a conflict-free congregation is a proper goal; only under such circumstances, they think, can the congregation devote its energy to its mission. The opposite—a contentious congregation—is usually feared by ministers, who dread having to devote too much time to managing disputes. Moreover, ministers know from their study of church history and from their own experience that controversy rooted in religious beliefs can lead to bitter battles and church splits. Given these attitudes, we can understand why ministers and congregational leaders tend to avoid matters that are disruptive or why they seek some compromise if contention arises. However, to avoid or suppress conflict in congregational life is to create a false sense of security and to forget that part of the mission of the congregation is to seek the will of God for current and ongoing events.

If we take that mission seriously, the congregation will inevitably have conflict with the community, for secular society neither shares all the values of the church nor pretends to listen to a voice beyond itself for guidance. Within the congregation there will be varying opinions because members have different backgrounds, religious experiences, images of the church, and hopes for the future. Conflicts will emerge as leaders maneuver to assert their will in order to gratify their personal need for recognition. The interests of different age groups within a congregation often vie with each other for space in the building or for amounts of money they can expect from the budget. Occasionally there will be episodes of immorality and lying in the congregation, and members will have different opinions about how to deal with the people involved.

It should be a considerable comfort to recall the writings about the first Christian congregations. The history of the founding of the church, as told in Acts, is a brilliant flash of God's presence on the day of Pentecost, filling Peter and the other disciples with the powerful message of God's saving grace in Jesus Christ. The enthusiasm for and devotion to Jesus were so great that the people shared all things in common. But a few chapters later on we read of Ananias and Sapphira attempting to cheat on their commitment (Acts 5:1–11), and later still we find a conflict developing about admitting Gentiles. This was such a serious matter that a consultation was held in Jerusalem between contending parties, and a formal letter was sent to churches recording the compromise that eased the tension (Acts 15). Moreover, because false prophets appeared, congregations were expected to test prophets to see whether or not they were true (2 Peter 2, and 1 John 4:1–6).[11]

Educational Potential of Conflict

Since conflict is always present in congregations, the issue is how we deal with it. I propose that we consider conflict as an opportunity for education, a chance to relate actual human situations to the faith we profess. I titled this section "educational potential" because learning under such circumstances is by no means certain, and the experience is of a kind not often labeled "learning."

Educators often identify learning as that which a person absorbs, accepts, relates to, or identifies with, out of his or her experiences. The experience is the key to what the person learns. Teaching, however, is a deliberate act in which a leader tries to transmit knowledge, skill, attitude, or insight to someone. The key to teaching is the knowledge and ability of the teacher. For example, two students in a chemistry class may respond differently to the work of a teacher. One may absorb by rote enough information to pass the course but may also learn that she does not like the subject and resolves never to study chemistry again. Another may also memorize a lot of equations but may be so thrilled with the idea of understanding and controlling part of nature that she resolves to major in chemistry. "Education" is the word we use to include the process of teaching and learning.

Education is going on whenever the congregation meets or whenever some part of the congregation, such as a class or youth group, engages in some activity. Sorting out exactly what is happening is almost impossible, although we are more confident about teaching than about learning because the leaders prepare the worship, the committee agenda, or curriculum in advance with rather clear goals in mind. Exactly what people learn from the planned experience is far from certain—not only because each person brings a different background and expectation to the gathering but also because when people gather there will be a lot of conversation which is unpredictable in character and uncertain in effect.

Let us consider congregational conflict in the light of our definition of education. How are conflicts managed? The tendency in mainstream congregations is to avoid controversy, to compromise, or to postpone decisions with the hope that contradictory views will diminish or go away. This political way of responding deals with the effects of conflict but does not attempt to address the cause of contention. Such political process is inappropriate because (1) it fails to respect the nature of the church and (2) it misunderstands the way people learn from what they experience in the congregation.

1. Politics in the secular world is largely the management of power. To treat a matter politically is for a person or group to deal with a situation so they will stay in power or get more power over others. Those in politics often have power because of their position. In the church, things should be different. The church is a community based on beliefs about God; these beliefs include the idea that God can and frequently does communicate God's will to the body of believers through individuals other than official leaders or those with power. That is why Jesus singled out children as having the attitude of trust and hope needed to enter the kingdom of God (Matt. 18:2–5); on another occasion, when wise secular people could not or would not respond to his message, Jesus gave thanks to God that some humble people ("babes") accepted what he said (Matt. 11:25). The congregation, seeking to learn and do the will of God in relation to present events, has an orientation to God and therefore should listen to any of its members. In conflict situations there must be openness to ideas from any source, regardless of the "power" the individual or group may have within the congregation.

2. To manage conflict by dealing only with its effects is to misunderstand the way people learn from experience in the church. Experience is not neutral. People who participate in congregational life are learning both by what is said and done and also by what is not said and done. If, for example, a congregation through the preaching, worship, and program of activities never mentions the plight of poor and hungry people in the community, church members will "learn" that such a concern belongs some other place—such as the United Way or the Salvation Army. This kind of learning is weak because it is learned through absence, but that very absence implies that these concerns are unimportant or are outside the mission of the church. Therefore, if controversial matters are always suppressed or compromised, church members will slowly get the impression that such issues are not "religious." It is precisely this reluctance to engage in serious debate about pressing social and personal issues that turns many young people away They are accustomed to dealing with such matters in college,

with business colleagues, or in civic organizations and cannot understand why the congregation will not deal realistically with the same issues.

It is true that many of the pressing issues of the time are addressed by the national organization of the church, but those positions are not real to church members until the congregation to which they belong has worked through the debate and arrived at a decision in which they have an intellectual and emotional investment. Mainstream Protestant denominations and the Roman Catholic Church make official pronouncements on current issues with some regularity. I think an adult class in a congregation should take those pronouncements and documents and work through them section by section to arrive at their own stand on the same issue. Such a curriculum would be interesting because it deals with the public aspects of faith in a timely fashion. It would also teach theology and biblical interpretation, for both are involved in establishing positions on current issues.

Learning from Conflict

For a long time sociologists viewed conflict as a negative factor in community life, a disruptive force that would tear a group apart. It is true that conflict about the basic assumptions of a community—such as a difference of opinion about whether all property is to be owned by individuals or held in common—is disruptive, for a community cannot hold both views. In church history we have accounts of groups that have split over basic beliefs, such as God's relation to the world, the person of Christ, sacraments, biblical interpretation, or style of church government. But if the basic issues are settled, as they are in congregations of mainstream denominations, the conflicts are likely to be either on the surface or about matters that can inspire divergent views without destroying congregational unity.[12]

Lewis A. Coser's study of social conflict has turned our attention away from conflict's disruptive potential to its more positive role of forming and unifying groups of people. By applying to congregations some of Coser's observations about the role of conflict in community life, we can uncover both educational opportunities and also the possibility of a more unified congregation.

Boundaries

A group of people defining itself by drawing boundaries between itself and the surrounding culture, or by distinguishing itself in dress, customs, and beliefs, must be as old as recorded history.[13] Certainly the biblical story of the Hebrews and Christians portrays these groups' struggle to maintain their unique beliefs and style of life. This in-group mentality sometimes produced (for the in-group) ethical standards that did not apply to the out-group, as illustrated in the lending of money: Hebrews were not to lend money at interest to other Hebrews, but they could accept interest on loans to "foreigners" (Deut. 23:19–20). Christians in New Testament times defined themselves not only in terms of what they believed but also in terms of how those beliefs distinguished them from Jews or worshipers of Greek and Roman deities (see Rom. 12:2–21 for an example of an atypical church).

Congregations by their nature and mission are different from other social groups, and the differences are seen at the boundaries. Educational opportunities lie in the way those differences are understood. If the boundaries are dimly marked and seldom referred to, such congregations are hardly more than societies of people interested in religion; however, church leaders can use the boundaries to educate and strengthen the ties between members.

The educational potential is great. Public worship, with its prayers, scripture, hymns, and sermon, can be focused on the differences between believers and nonbelievers. This should not be done either in a triumphant spirit or with an attitude of moral superiority. Rather, it must be done in terms of the church's mission to the world. This stance brings up many important issues, about which abundant biblical and historical data exist to help us address our contemporary boundary situation with the secular world. National denominational agencies must face these issues in the world mission enterprise; congregations can participate in those discussions. However, in keeping with the thesis of this book, let us consider how the congregation relates to the community. Is the relationship only in terms of service, or are there issues of economic injustice, such as affordable housing for the poor, social values, such as the availability of pornography, or other matters about which the congregation should take a stand? If adults discuss such issues and take a position either officially as a congregation or as an adult group within a congregation, they are defining themselves as having a different outlook from that of the secular community.

The boundaries between a congregation and other religious groups in the community offer wonderful opportunities for education. Adult and youth groups could work extensively on those boundaries. The conflict in belief between mainstream congregations and Christian sect groups is not well known and is often dismissed as being unimportant. Yet the differences are extremely important, and they should be identified. Furthermore, the boundaries between Protestant congregations and Jewish groups in the community deserve constant attention and analysis. Forming boundaries with Jewish groups will evoke fundamental theological issues that need careful research and extended debate. Also, the boundaries between mainstream beliefs and some particular practices—such as speaking in tongues, which has emerged in many Protestant and Catholic congregations—need clarification.

There are two kinds of educational potential in locating a congregation's boundaries, the first of which is in helping members understand the meaning of their faith in practical terms. When a congregation compares and contrasts itself with the larger community and with other groups as suggested, a great quantity of information about Christianity is reviewed and absorbed. Perhaps more important is the process of working through biblical and historical data in order to arrive at beliefs that relate to other people in our community. This is serious study designed to clarify the beliefs on which congregational decisions are made, and part of the process requires biblical interpretation. If adults in a congregation make interpretation itself a matter of study, they will become aware of how the Bible should be used in relation to current life situations. Teaching adults and young people to interpret the history of the church and the Bible in terms of everyday issues is probably the most practical way to learn such a method. They can then use that method to formulate a Christian point of view about other issues.

The second educational possibility in locating boundaries is in the attainment of greater congregational unity. This learning, although more elusive and less measurable than the first, is equally important. When adults and older teenagers in a congregation go through the process of locating their boundaries, they not only establish reasons for the distinction of their faith, they experience a comradeship that draws them together. The unity of a congregation lies in its belief about Christ. But such cohesion does not emerge if people interact about beliefs merely on an intellectual level. Only when individuals work through the meaning of faith in their own lives and share that meaning with others can they feel a sense of solidarity with one another. Because this learning is emotional, it is not like more concrete information or ideas; it is the intangible glue that holds the congregation together.

Challenge from Outside

A social group that has located boundaries between itself and surrounding society will often be challenged by groups from society.[14] In the case of a church, the challenge will be to the church's beliefs or activities. At first thought this attack from outside seems dangerous, for it would seem to weaken the church and discredit its ministers and lay leaders. But on second thought we know that such a challenge has almost always had beneficial results. The New Testament is a good example: Christians had to deal first with persecution by Pharisees— such as Saul—and later with Roman authorities. It was challenge from outside groups that forced Christians to sort out their beliefs and write down their theology for the guidance of all believers; most of the New Testament books, especially the letters of Paul, were composed for the first generation of Christians. Challenges from outside the church result in educational opportunities.

First, the church must review its theology and put its beliefs in priority order and then compose new statements for new situations. The creeds most widely used in Christendom illustrate this point. The Apostles' Creed in its present form probably dates from the eighth century, but its earlier form goes back to baptismal vows of about A.D. 200. Those vows, in turn, are probably based on Matthew 16:16 and 28:19. It is important for us to note that the Apostles' Creed contains a strong statement of Christ's humanity—one who was born, suffered, was crucified, died, and was buried. This was a strong declaration against Docetism, a theology that was declared a heresy at Chalcedon (A.D. 451). Docetism held that Jesus was not truly human, that he only appeared to have a body and therefore could not have suffered and died.

The Council of Nicaea (A.D. 325) declared Arianism also a heresy, because it considered Jesus as an exalted person worthy of worship but only the adopted Son of God—not One with God from the beginning. Wanting to preserve the deity of Jesus, the Council adopted a creed to test orthodoxy. The present version of the Nicene Creed developed over time, but it was obviously written to establish Jesus as One with God from the beginning of time.

It is probably true that all the creeds and confessions of faith that have developed since the Council of Nicaea were provoked by a challenge from outside the church and written to define a position and to exclude unacceptable ideas. From the Reformation to the present, Christians have produced many confessions of faith, usually to defend particular theological positions. The Barmen Declaration (1934), for example, adopted by representatives of the Lutheran, Reformed, and United Churches of Germany, was written in defiance of Hitler's National Socialism; the Confession of 1967, adopted by the United Presbyterian Church, was designed to show the church's concern for social situations, such as racial discrimination, poverty, war, and prejudice based on gender. John H. Leith recorded the rationale for such creeds when he wrote, "Generally speaking, creeds have not been written in the quiet periods of history but in those moments of historical intensity when the Church has been engaged by foes from without, or when its mission or life has been endangered from within."[15]

The educational possibilities of creeds are enormous. A study of the major Christian creeds, starting with the short ones that were already developed by the time Paul founded churches, would be an important church project (see 1 Cor. 15:3–8 for an example of an early creedal statement). Such a study would have to take into consideration the historical factors that caused each creed to be written.[16] It may, in fact, be necessary to study creeds in order for adults (1) to learn major Christian beliefs and (2) to gain a historical perspective. Most adults in mainline congregations are so shaped by our secular society that they need instruction in the distinctive Christian beliefs. A few carefully selected creeds studied slowly with opportunity for full discussion and constant examination of biblical references will help adults see the assumptions they have absorbed from secular society. Gaining a historical perspective is also important, for that may help persons see the present as the arena in which God is at work. The Barmen Declaration shows the Spirit of God at work among Christians in Nazi Germany. But Nazi Germany is gone, so what we learn—other than the way these Christians resisted Hitler in the 1930s—is that God is always present and is attempting to bring about a form of human life in which individuals can live with dignity.

To understand the present from a historical perspective is necessary if a congregation is going to be serious about doing God's will in its community. This activity of the mind and heart could be formalized by a congregation's undertaking to write its own creed—composing an informal statement of belief designed to interpret the life of the congregation to new members. A less difficult task, but one that would require the same kind of careful thinking, would be for a congregation or adult class to compose a commentary on the Apostles' Creed or some other historical statement of beliefs. Such a commentary should have as its purpose an explanation of the creed in conversational terms, with implications for modern life. If, for example, the Apostles' Creed is used, the class will note that there is nothing in it about the life or teachings of Jesus, because such was not germane to the challenge from outside the church when the creed was composed. Today the secular world is a challenge to the teachings of Jesus and to the moral principles of the Bible, so Christians today need to include such beliefs in their commentary.

A more aggressive way to compose practical theology about the present from the perspective of the Christian tradition would be to follow the pattern of the Barmen Declaration or of the Confession of 1967. That pattern was to identify a threat from without the church and then to compose a Christian response. What that threat would be is dependent to some extent on the community in which a congregation is located. To some congregations the threat could be community conditions, such as inadequate housing, inadequate public health services, or substandard schools. In some congregations there are a few adults who understand the image of secular individualism that informs much of our education, advertising, and social life. A group of this kind could sponsor a study that would enlarge the number who can rise above such secular values. When enough adults are able to see that

Christians are in, but not of, the world, they can systematically compose their beliefs in relation to the outside challenge they perceive.

Second, a challenge from outside the congregation will promote a review of leadership and program. A congregation will want to be reassured that its leaders are ready and able to articulate the issues and have a cogent plan for dealing with them. If not, other leaders will emerge. Given the way that churches drift away from the meaning of the experience that formed them and tend to become concerned primarily with maintaining themselves (as described in chapter 4), occasional challenges from outside may be necessary to jolt a congregation to review itself and its mission.

Third, a challenge from the outside almost always rallies people to defend their group.[17] Why this is so is not easy to understand, but it is a rather common occurrence. Apparently we all have a deep sense of obligation to the groups that nurture us. Although we may have considerable reservation about the value of the group with which we are associating, if that group is challenged we will usually rally to its aid. The church is a special illustration of this principle, for it serves a wide range of interests and promotes help for people in difficulty as well as high standards of conduct for humankind. If a congregation is challenged by outside forces, its members will become more unified; they will then give more time, money, and attention to their church. Moreover, if individuals are selected to represent the congregation to outside groups or agencies, those members will speak and act with more than normal boldness because they feel they embody the congregation's power and purpose as they distinguish their beliefs or interests from those on the outside.

Challenge from Inside

A congregation will always experience two kinds of conflict within itself. The first is primarily personal; some people do not like certain other people. The second is primarily about policy; some people will disagree with others on matters ranging from property management to biblical interpretation. These two types of conflicts within congregations often overlap. For example, a person who dislikes another person may resist that person's ideas about the use of church property. However, for both types of conflict there is an emotional basis that cannot be easily diagnosed or treated. In normal congregational life we will be unable to get to these emotional bases, but we can note the educational potential within each type.

The first type—conflict caused by a personality clash or a personal outburst based on inner tension—is to be expected. People cannot control all their emotions all the time. Coser calls this the "safety-valve" function of institutions; they serve as places where people can blow off steam rather than blow up.[18] Such conflicts happen regularly in classes of small children, and with some frequency in youth and adult groups. Skillful teachers have learned how to deal with such outbursts. With children the leaders often separate the ones in conflict and talk with them about sharing toys or taking turns. This can provide important social learning, for the children involved may not have had any home experience in sharing toys with others or any opportunity to learn how to play in a group. With youth and adults, personality clashes are expressed verbally and often in subtle ways. The group leader can often defuse such conflicts by paying attention to the substance of the argument, rather than the personalities involved, and thus may bring out into the open something in which all members of the group can participate.

The most important educational opportunity for personal eruption in a congregation is the response to such behavior. With small children the competition for a toy may be brief while rules are being worked out for sharing. The child learns a lot about the role of rules in human relations, and also that the church is the place where people are fair as well as loving. Young people and adults may also learn how to accept hostile behavior from members and how to understand and make allowances for whatever causes such disruption. This is profound learning that goes to the depths of one's self. It greatly intensifies one's feeling of solidarity with others and also with Jesus, who continually forgave other people. So the environment of acceptance in which individuals are listened to and respected—even though they may be acting more from personal bias than for the good of the community— is a powerful learning experience for all the people involved. There are few social institutions where this type of learning is possible, but the church with its commitment to mutual forbearance is the place where personal idiosyncracies will be tolerated because of the church's devotion to its mission (Eph. 4:1–7).

The second type—conflict caused by differences of opinion about policies—is more common and can be handled in a more direct way. All of our mainstream denominations either have a book of parliamentary order or they accept *Robert's Rules of Order* as the basis of handling differences of opinion about policies, practices, and theological statements. Such rules were invented to provide a process for decision making when people disagree. Moreover, such rules provide ways groups of people from a larger body can maintain contrary opinions on one issue while agreeing on other issues. Since rules of order are observed in all organizations to which church members belong, there is nothing unique about this aspect of congregational life.

In congregations when people express differences of opinion, two learning opportunities should be noted and celebrated. The first is the exchange of opinions and information when people are ready to make

decisions. Under these circumstances people speak their true convictions, for they are trying to persuade others. In other contexts, such
as conversations or discussion groups, we often test ideas in which we
are interested but not necessarily the ideas we use for decision making.
During decision-making exchanges—whether in the washroom or in
formal meetings—we relate theology to practical life situations. Sometimes we use our theology to form a decision. Sometimes we are so
emotionally involved that we use our reasoning ability to find a theological rationale to justify the position we have already adopted. Occasionally we are so confused or uncertain that we avoid meetings where
decisions have to be made. What causes us to use one of these responses is the requirement that we take a stand. We are very careful
about our commitments because they become a part of our identity
and therefore part of the way we are addressed and treated by others.
This situation—of being known as a certain kind of person—provides
the educational opportunity. People are far more alert to information,
new ideas, ways of perceiving a problem, or the influence of respected
leaders when they must take a public stand on an issue. Thus conversations, debate, or formal arguments used in a decision-making context
are exceedingly important curriculum materials for a congregation.
Such expressions display the real beliefs of people and have the power
to influence church members deeply.

The second learning opportunity when people express conflicting
opinions is in the way these conflicts are handled. Open meetings
regulated by rules of order must be seen as teaching opportunities in
human relations. By maintaining a friendly and fair demeanor, the
presiding officers can go a long way in seeing that everyone is respected, that everyone is given a chance to speak, and that the process
is not rushed to a premature conclusion. Although conflict of opinion
in a decision-making meeting can result in the members' becoming
displeased with one another, the opposite can also happen. If the
leaders prepare people for the debate by explaining both the procedure and the methods for deciding issues when everyone does not
agree, there will be an atmosphere of expectation rather than a contest
in which some people win and others lose. Church leaders should take
time with decision-making groups to discuss the theology of the
church. This is a wonderful opportunity to let biblical, historical, and
creedal material show that the church has a commitment to Jesus
Christ and his ministry. Our goal is to do God's will in the world. Since
we are all under God's judgment, our problem is how to discern the
leading of God in the decision-making process. This theological context is what makes conflict of opinion in congregations different. None
of us can be absolutely certain that he or she is right. All of us must
listen to one another, because the Spirit moves in its own way and all

decisions must be tested over time to be sure they represent the gospel we profess.

If congregations have a conflict of opinion, congregational life will be an experience in which members learn to respect each other even if they differ. They will get to know each other at a deeper level, and they will demonstrate in many ways the unique situation of a community that lives in the world but has its own source of inspiration and direction from outside the world.

Challenge with Outside

The sociology of conflict views a challenge with outside groups as an educational opportunity. People within a community who challenge another group get to know themselves more realistically because their concerns are at stake, they must learn more about the outside group in order to compete, and they are alert to forming alliances with other outside groups in order to succeed.[19] For example, in wartime a nation draws in on itself and tests its leaders and way of life more vigorously than in peacetime. It studies the enemy's social and economic situation to find weaknesses. During war a nation will also search for allies of any kind, as the United States did in World War II when it welcomed the Soviet Union in the struggle against Nazi Germany even though the United States did not trust the U.S.S.R. and disapproved of its economic and political system. Churches do not often challenge society except in extreme situations, such as that of Nazi Germany in the 1930s and of South Africa today.

The trouble with mainstream churches in the United States is that they do not recognize their relationship to society as an "enduring problem."[20] Fundamentalist churches acknowledge the difficulty and try to resolve it by resisting culture, or else they try to get laws passed to support their views. Evangelistic churches distinguish themselves from the surrounding culture by their efforts to convert people to their beliefs, and liberal congregations are active in the political arena as they try to shape society to ideal goals of peace, justice, and individual rights. Mainstream congregations, although they often include some members who hold to each of the above views about society, often consider themselves to be in tune with the values of the community. This comes about because the membership of mainstream congregations is made up of doctors, lawyers, accountants, teachers, public officials, and others who are the managers and administrators of the community. They see the church as the supporter of general community values rather than as the challenger of those values.

Since mainstream congregations have an easy alliance with culture, they are not open to the learning that comes when a congregation challenges the laws, customs, or practices of the community, except in the most obvious differences of life-style. Mainstreamers recognize the plight of the hungry, the homeless, and the victims of catastrophes such as fire, storms, and earthquakes. Because they have a deep-seated concern for helping the less fortunate, they respond with money or other forms of aid. However, they do not expect their religious faith to put them in serious contention with some part of society. So the learnings that would flow normally from a congregation's challenge to some segment of society do not often occur.

Given the conditions just described, how can church leaders help congregations understand that they are in and of the world of human affairs but that their faith puts them in contention with that world? This question cannot be answered unless some church leaders gain a Christian understanding different from what their culture has communicated. When ministers or lay leaders begin to orient their faith toward God as incarnated in Jesus, they will begin to see distinctions between the congregation and the secular community and will help the congregation draw boundaries based on those differences. Although this sometimes happens when one or more persons have a special religious experience, it most often happens over a period of time when a small group of people "grow in the grace and knowledge of our Lord and Savior Jesus Christ" (2 Peter 3:18). It is important for a congregation to become conscious of itself as challenging the culture at some point, so we will look at the possibilities in more detail.

Congregation as Counterculture

The term "counterculture" came into prominence during the struggle for civil rights in the 1950s and 1960s and the response of college students and young adults to the war in Vietnam. In each case people coalesced about a cause or vision and in close association developed a life-style or set of values different from the laws and official concerns of the nation.

The idea of Christians' being different from the world is discussed throughout the New Testament, especially in the writings of Paul and in the later writings, such as James and First and Second John. The idea has been expressed in different ways during the church's long history, but especially in the monastic orders that continue to influence the Roman Catholic Church. Protestantism, by its resistance to the Catholic Church and the state, set loose the notion that a church could and should be formed around special beliefs. As a result a proliferation of denominations formed to express their special beliefs and to be "counter" to culture and to all other denominations. However, as pointed out in chapter 2, denominations in the mainstream of American life have become so similar to each other and are so identified with the dominant cultural values that they do not challenge culture except on occasions when their national governing body issues a proclamation about some social issue. These proclamations are to be taken seriously, for they are often all we have to remind us of our role as social critic. But such pronouncements do not always represent the views of the majority of people in the pew's, so we must return to the congregation as the place where we interpret and live the Christian life.

How can Christians and lay leaders in a congregation help members understand their beliefs as the foundation of their community and as the basis on which they are different from the world? Is it possible for mainstream congregations to become conscious of themselves as a community oriented to ways in which they can understand and help bring about the reign (kingdom) of God in their time and place? The answer to the second question is "Yes"; the means follow.

Worship

Worship is the first and most fundamental act of a congregation, an act that separates it from all other human groups. Other organizations may open meetings with a prayer or conduct some brief worship program, but the church is the only community that by its nature is gathered to worship God. This uniqueness is recognized in law and custom and is protected by the national government. The assumption behind worship is the reality of God as described in the Bible—a God who is concerned about and who influences human affairs.

Every part of the public worship of God goes counter to the prevailing culture. Take the confession of sin, for example. In formal patterns of worship it is positioned near the opening of the worship and is repeated by all worshipers; or a confession may be contained in the pastoral prayer. Where else do we regularly inventory our failures? Moreover, the confession of sin is an indirect declaration that we know of a more desirable way of life and have gathered publicly to express both our sorrow over our shortcomings and our dependence on God for forgiveness. This portion of worship usually ends with a declaration of pardon and implies, or may even state, that we are to rededicate ourselves to the things in which God has a special interest. This identification of the resolve of believers to live a different life is extremely important in forming a counterculture.

Other parts of worship assume that God is present and is available to all who trust in God. This is particularly true of prayers of petition in which we ask God to protect, to guide, to comfort, or to change conditions that are damaging human life. Music and hymns similarly lift us out of this worldly haze into a clearer atmosphere, where we get a sense of the past as we express our hope for the future. Worship includes sacraments, scripture, and sermon. The Lord's Supper, the central act of worship, contains the irreducible fundamentals of faith; in that sacrament we have a celebration of all that is important in our relation with God. Baptism, another central act of the congregation, incorporates people into the fellowship of believers and marks them as God's own. These sacraments are distinctive characteristics of the Christian religion and should be sufficient to make a congregation different from any other human group in the community.

Scripture, used throughout prayers, hymns, sacraments, and sermon, has a message according to the passage used. Regardless of our setting, the words of the Bible turn our minds back to former times and describe how God responded to those life situations. The description of what God said and did under the circumstances produces a mental image of what God is, an image that can become our guide in the present. Probably no aspect of worship—with the possible exception of the sermon—has such power to produce a perspective on our lives as does a reading of scripture. This perspective is necessary if we are going to be serious about our differences from the world.[21]

Sermon

The sermon is such an important part of worship that it deserves special mention. Its possibilities are endless for interpreting the past, for describing a vision of what ought to be, for encouraging people to mold their lives by the example of Christian saints, for illustrating how people have been led by the Spirit of God, for guidance in ethical decision making, and for building morale within a congregation. If the preacher considers the congregation to be in accord with American values, he or she will use all these possibilities to proclaim and explain that continuity. If he or she understands the congregation to be a gathering of believers who are seeking the will of God for their lives, the preacher will use the sermon to explore and support that mission of the congregation.

Preachers who see congregations as communities that are unique by reason of their beliefs and practices will use life situations in the congregation and conditions in the community as material for their sermons. If they do so, they will relate to the experiences that members are having and will provide guidance for events as they take place. Some ministers do not understand the congregation as a community with needs of its own. These ministers are the ones who seek elsewhere for sermon topics—such as in lectionaries prepared for general use throughout the nation or in special interests the preacher has acquired. In chapter 11, I will say more about sermon topics and how congregation-based sermons may enhance learning.

Prayer and Planning

Mainstream congregations have a variety of committees making plans for almost every aspect of congregational life. Most of the time these committees function efficiently because members are schooled in committee work, especially in the role of planning in voluntary organizations. But the goal of efficiency (which comes from participation in committees related to other community organizations) may not be the most important element in congregational committee work.

Mary Elizabeth Moore has written a fine essay on the role of meditation in the administration of a congregation. It is her conviction that much church work is done in an "uproar." By that she means the planning committees are too task-oriented; they forget they are to be a caring community. In their haste to accomplish something they tend to bring into church committees the values they have acquired from society. As a result they make the church like society, forget the people who have little power or visibility, and shape the church's program to support their personal interests or concerns.[22]

Although Moore does not use the idea of the congregation as a counterculture, she has put her finger on the exact spot where the church should be radically different from the world. She urges congregations to make prayer, meditation, and contemplation the center of their life. Prayer she considers communication with God, meditation is deep reflection on the truths of the faith, and contemplation is a concentrated focus on God and God's will for the world. These disciplines need to be cultivated. To do so church leaders, especially educators, must plan time when people can receive—from the Bible and tradition—an image of what these matters are, a place to practice, and opportunities to share their experiences as they become more consciously aware of God's presence.

What impresses me about Moore's suggestion that congregations deliberately turn attention to God is her linkage of this emphasis with planning. She is absolutely correct. The reason mainstream denominations become similar to society is that their members bring values and procedures from business, the professions, and government into the congregation as their guide to planning. Unless church leaders challenge those values and procedures by using the methods indigenous to the Christian faith—prayer, meditation, and contemplation—congregations will slowly secularize religion, as described in chapter 2.

Moore uses the rebuilding of the cathedral at Coventry, England, to illustrate the practicality of prayer for planning. The city of Coventry was just about leveled by German bombing in World War II, and the old cathedral was destroyed by fire. In the late 1950s the diocese began plans for a new cathedral and a reconstruction of its work in the center of the city. Stephen Verney, as diocesan missioner, met with the clergy in small groups simply to listen for an answer to the question "What is the Spirit saying to the churches?" This led the clergy to whole days of silence, to Bible study, and to a new appreciation of one another. Verney relates that people learned how to organize their time to include prayer as well as work. They also learned that they could relate to non-Christians by sharing their search for truth. This kind of learning can come about only as people experience the presence of God. Although such experience cannot be scheduled, it can be described and encouraged. Out of the atmosphere in Coventry came the decision to leave the ruins of the old cathedral as a symbol of war's destruction. On the altar the clergy placed a cross made out of charred wood, and on the front of the altar are engraved the words, "Father forgive." The cathedral staff, through their meditation, found the special mission they were seeking—a mission of reconciliation. It developed into a program of inviting youths from Germany to visit and work in Coventry, while English youths went to Germany to express Christian reconciliation.

Linking prayer with planning will not be easy in mainstream congregations, because planning is considered to be a rational process that sets goals after a consideration of facts, trends, and available resources. It focuses attention on the human situation and on our ability to change that situation by the procedures we employ. Moreover, we expect to evaluate our success on the basis of predetermined goals. A certain amount of planning must be done by this rational model, because the congregation as an institution must meet a payroll, pay for utilities, and be responsible for the people involved. The issue, however, is the extent to which the congregation operates by the rational model or whether there is a deliberate effort on the part of the leaders to turn members' attention to what God desires for the world.

Spiritual formation is a lifetime task that cannot be speeded up. But there are ways that the spiritual life can be cultivated. Congregations can provide places and times when people can meditate or contemplate. Leaders can learn to rely more on prayer as a part of planning. Almost all church committees, for example, begin their meetings with a prayer, which often includes a request for God's guidance in the decisions to be made. The agenda is then distributed and the meeting gets under way. This process does not really link prayer and planning, because the members often see the agenda items for the first time at that meeting. One way to relate prayer and agenda is for the committee chairperson and other leaders to post agenda items a month or more in advance. That way, at the end of the committee meeting the group could agree on the items about which they will have to make a decision at the next meeting, and the closing prayer would be the beginning of a season of prayer for the decisions lying ahead. Committee members would then have time to contemplate a specific issue in silence and in the mood of prayer before being required to speak or vote on that issue at the next meeting.

How to Change

The stated purpose of this chapter was to show how life together in a congregation is educational. Teaching and learning are going on whenever members meet for worship, planning, programs, service projects, or recreation. There is nothing unusual about this situation, for the same educational dynamic takes place in business organizations and social clubs. But the church, because of its beliefs, should be different from other human associations; what people learn in a congregation should be unique. The problem with mainstream congregations is their similarity to society. This condition is extremely difficult to change because church members are so attuned to culture that they have difficulty understanding the congregation as a community with different goals, values, and customs.

The differences cause conflict, but these conflicts can be of use in helping the congregation become more attuned to the concerns of God. Church members can learn deep truths about religion when they begin to distinguish themselves from the world, to deal with challenges from outside the congregation and differences from within. Out of all this will come a community with a culture counter to the surrounding society.[23]

How does a mainstream congregation become more of a counterculture? Who takes the initiative? How do leaders proceed?

A Gradual Process

What we know about changing a congregation comes from church history, from social scientists, and from ministers and lay leaders who have tried to heighten members' awareness of the presence of God in their lives.[24] These sources agree that human institutions change when a few people get a vision of what ought to be and then, through discussion and testing of ideas, influence others until a sizable group is committed to the new policy or viewpoint. This is similar to the method suggested by Jesus in regard to the coming reign of God. He thought of God's developing kingdom as a tiny seed that would grow into a large tree, or as yeast that would slowly permeate the dough so as to make bread (Matt. 13:31–33).

I do not want to lay the responsibility for congregational change on the minister alone. Mainstream denominations, regardless of polity, have considerable participation of lay people in the management of the congregation, and almost all teaching is done by members. What happens in the congregation is everyone's responsibility. However, ministers are the designated leaders—trained for and experienced in that role. Under normal circumstances, the way for a church to change its self-understanding would be for the minister to have a vision of the congregation as a community seeking to understand and do God's will in its time and place. This vision would be sketched out in general terms through worship, sermons, planning committees, and conversations during pastoral visits. Thus a mental vision would be created of what a congregation could and should be. Meanwhile, individuals would be attracted to the vision; they would enter into dialogue with one another and with the minister so that the mental image would be the product of a partnership in a common venture. An informal association would form—an inner circle of people increasingly guided by the vision. This would not be an elitist group, "running" the church in a political way because it had power to influence policy making. Rather, it would be a group of people (not a committee or elected council) who as individuals served on various committees and taught in the church school. Their purpose would be not political power but a sharing of their vision in order to enlarge the circle of God-oriented church members. Although the vision in concrete terms would vary from place to place according to the conditions in the neighborhood, it would be evident in the church's administrative policies, sponsored activities and service projects, educational program, and allocation of money.

There are many variations of this scenario. Ministers who are good at projecting the vision may then depend on lay people to translate it into programs. Some congregations contain lay people who because of their religious experience and background have developed a dedication to one another and to the church. Such a group of lay people may already have a strong momentum going when a new minister is installed; the new minister, inspired by the group, then learns from them what is good and appropriate in that congregation. Occasionally, the initiative is taken by lay people, like those in the Ohio congregation that voted to become a sanctuary church (see chapter 1). The women who raised the sanctuary issue in that congregation planned a year-long series of events that led to the congregational decision. However, if a church's ministers are not interested in change or are preoccupied with other matters, the prospect of moving a congregation to more of a counterculture position is rather poor.

A Warning

This book, addressed to mainstream congregations, deals with the need for congregations to distinguish themselves in the world on the basis of their belief in God. I have not considered it necessary to issue a warning about the dangers of a congregation's becoming so separate from the world that it develops a fortress mentality. But there are

Christian congregations with a rigid belief system that separates members from the world and expects them to let the world go its own way. Such congregations have enormous power over individual members; their life together constantly reinforces their beliefs and the truth of those beliefs in relation to conditions outside the congregation. Dogmatic doctrines that treat the world as something we must endure or escape from, however, are not in harmony with the theology of mainstream denominations and are not going to affect the "outside" lifestyle of their members.

If readers of this book are skeptical about its thesis—that the way a congregation worships and works and the way members relate to each other form a dynamic teaching and learning situation—then I propose that such readers put the thesis to a test. Find a fundamentalist congregation or a sect group in the community; go to that group for a while and participate in as much of its life as possible. I am confident that anyone who does this will see a community governed by a vision, a clearcut value system, and a certain life-style. All these things are communicated (and learned) so consistently and constantly that there is hardly any need for separate classes for the young. There will probably be such classes, taught by one of the more zealous members, but what happens in class will be only a formal explanation of what the children have already accepted in the depths of their being.

We mainstreamers need an understanding of the educational power of life together. Then we will be more deliberate in our efforts to create the kind of congregation which, through its natural associations, will teach the meaning of Christian faith to every member.

10

Strategy for Faith Maturation

Chapter 9 was devoted to the proposition that the congregation is a unique social institution by reason of its purpose and mission. This uniqueness creates conflict, but such dissonance has enormous educational value in helping a congregation develop itself into a countercultural community. Congregational change will emerge gradually if the minister and a group of members generate a vision of what the congregation ought to be.

In this chapter I want to discuss in some detail one major reason why congregations have difficulty functioning as a community with a center of energy and vision. The reason concerns the educational strategy we inherited for interpreting and communicating the Christian faith; since our social situation now is different, this former strategy is no longer appropriate.

Educational Strategy

Educational strategy is the way adults expect to get their ideas and values embedded in the rising generation. Strategy, however, is different from method. *Strategy* has to do with the agencies of education, such as family or school, whereas *method* has to do with the way education is carried on by an agency. Strategy is directly related to one's philosophy of education. For example, if one thinks of religion as something that is "caught" from adults and peers rather than "learned" in a schoolroom, the strategy would arrange for an informal relation with adults and peers who hold a common religious faith. If one thinks of religion as being correct doctrine, the strategy would be to use catechisms in the home plus Sunday school or day school to present and explain the doctrines.

Strategy is also related to the social situation of the geographic area in which the church is located. If the church is on a mission field where the people live in a traditional tribal culture with a religion of animism, Christian missionaries will use many entry points into that society to show their concern for the total well-being of the people, including schools with daily worship, courses in religion, and counseling within a religious perspective.

Historically, biblical religion has used different strategies, depending on the social situation of believers. In the tribal societies of the Old Testament there is little reference to educational strategy because education was not a specialized activity assigned to a class of people called "teachers." Since education about all of life's activities—including the nature of God and one's response to God—was the responsibility of all adults, we have only reminders that parents and adults are to attend to that task. For example, God tells Joshua to select a man from each tribe to take a stone from the Jordan River and make a memorial. "When your children ask in time to come, 'What do these stones mean to you?' Then you shall tell them . . ." (Josh. 4:1–7; see Ex. 13:14 and Deut. 6:20 for similar instructions about adults' responsibility to explain the meaning of God's presence to children). The fact that these learning events were unscheduled does not mean that children's religious education was casual or inadequate. On the contrary, for a child to ask a question at a point of need or interest and have the answer immediately given by an adult is a powerful form of education. In fact, the problem with this strategy is its very power: tribal beliefs and customs communicated deliberately but informally through stories, rituals, and person-to-person conversation by parents and other adults are extremely difficult to change later.

When the Hebrew people became a nation and lived in a more settled way among people who worshiped other gods, it became necessary for them to identify how their religion was to be communicated to their children and to fix responsibility for doing so. The strategy was rooted in the family, with strong support from the community that shared their faith. Described in the Shema (Deut. 6:4–9), this strategy was so important that the Hebrews were expected to recite it twice a day. The first part—love of God—summarizes the first two commandments in positive form. Jesus also used this as a summary of the law, and he added that one should also love one's neighbor, thus capturing the major idea underlying the rest of the Ten Commandments (Matt. 22:36–40; Mark 12:28–34; Luke 10:25–37). The rest of the Shema is about one's responsibility. Because of a sincere belief in God (v. 6), adults are deliberately to teach God's word to their children (v. 7a), explain the beliefs to children in all the ordinary circumstances of life (v. 7b), and make a public declaration that their primary allegiance is to God (vs. 8–9).

When the Hebrew people were allowed to return to Jerusalem from exile in Babylon, they rebuilt the city. But they were now a people with a tragic history. Why had they lost their kingdom? Would they ever be in full command of their life again? Would Hebrew people who were in the Northern Kingdom vanish forever into the general population? What had they done wrong, that God had punished them with such humiliation? These and other questions haunted their lives. They could rebuild the temple, but they could not restore the glory of Solomon's reign; they could live in dignity, but they could not shape their destiny. Now their problem was how to endure as a religious ethnic minority within a larger culture that barely tolerated their presence. The Hebrews addressed this problem by developing new educational agencies to interpret and communicate their faith in God. Probably the most important educational agency was the development of the synagogue as a regular worship and instructional event for adults. In time the Hebrews also developed an elementary school (Beth Hassepher) to teach children to read Hebrew and to know the written Torah, a secondary school (Beth Hammidrash) for the study of the oral tradition (Mishnah) and the commentaries (Gemara), and a class of scholar-teachers known as scribes.[1]

The scribes proved to be so important as an educational strategy that they became the primary agent for interpretation and communication of Israel's faith. Originally, the scribes were probably official secretaries who were in charge of legal documents. As such they functioned as lawyers for the kings of Israel. During the Exile, while the Hebrews were without a central governmental authority, the scribes continued to keep the sacred record; they also became teachers and interpreters of the law, and the law of Moses became the center of Jewish life. The scribes probably had a major role in helping to edit and shape what was later to be approved as the official canon of the Old Testament. Ezra, a scribe, was described as a person who "had set his heart to study the law of the LORD, and to do it, and to teach his statutes and ordinances in Israel" (Ezra 7:10).

Kings respected scribes (Ezra 7:11–12), and whole towns gathered to hear scribes read and explain the law of Moses (Neh. 8:1–7). In Ezra the role of priest was commingled with that of scribe (Neh. 12:26). The most complete and perhaps the most idealistic description of scribes as a group was written later, about 180 B.C., by Ecclesiasticus (38:24–39:15), who placed their vocation at the top of all others because they were wise and gave meaning to life.

In terms of educational strategy, there are no new agencies of education in the New Testament. This is probably because the newly formed Christian church was patterned on the synagogue, out of which many early converts came. Moreover, the new Christian congregations found themselves in the same social situation as the synagogue. They were a small minority within an alien culture desperately trying to understand the new revelation of God in Jesus, relate this event to Jewish traditions, and establish congregations with worship and customs in harmony with their beliefs. They used the educational strategy they knew: (1) a community of believers sharing their life while searching for God's will, (2) parents instructing children, and (3) all adults seeking to lead a life worthy of the Lord (Gal. 5:16–25) or "walk in newness of life" (Rom. 6:4).[2]

The history of the church shows many variations in educational strategy, depending on the interpretation of the faith and the social situation in which the church was located. It is unfortunate that church historians usually have been so concerned with leaders, doctrines, church-state relations, wars, movements, and other documented events that they have seldom written about the strategies the churches have used to interpret and communicate the faith in different historical eras. John H. Westerhoff and O. C. Edwards, Jr., have helped to overcome this deficiency in the book they edited about catechesis, defined as "the process by which persons are initiated into the Christian community and its faith, revelation, and vocation; the process by which persons throughout their lifetimes are continually converted and nurtured, transformed and formed, by and in its living tradition."[3]

The book deals with particular historical epochs and thus illustrates my contention that we must assay educational strategy in terms of social conditions. The essay by Westerhoff at the beginning of the book explains why catechesis is central to the life of the church. His chapter at the end sketches a future for church education based on the catechesis concept rather than on a schooling model. In general terms I affirm Westerhoff's view that a congregation through its worship, pastoral care, sacraments, and concern for the world has the means for transmitting the Christian faith to the next generation. There is no reason to rework what he and others have written about catechesis.[4]

There is, however, a possible weakness in the socialization model of Christian education that I proposed in *Where Faith Begins* (1967) and the catechesis model that has recently been revived for Protestants— the natural drift toward conserving, rather than living out, religious beliefs. Describing this natural process in chapter 4 under the rubrics of sin, secularism, and sectarianism, I used the words "possible weakness" because the model of a community of believers communicating its faith to the next generation and to the surrounding society does not necessarily contain this weakness. The weakness discussed in chapter 4 is a human proclivity to which we must be alert in any model of faith transmission: somehow we must combine people's current experiences with the image of God from our tradition to help congregations learn the contemporary meaning of the Christian faith. Where in the life of a congregation can this be done? Individuals can do it to some extent as they participate in worship and resonate with the sermon; yet this kind of activity has little influence because it is not shared with other believers often enough to be used, as the apostle Paul said, for "the edification of the church." Edification can come about only when people who are in charge of and responsible for congregational life discuss their religious experiences and test their conclusions over a period of time. Corporate critical thinking is essential for creating the contemporary meaning of faith. This kind of education is seldom planned for our congregations, because we consider education a matter for children and youth and merely an elective for adults.

Problem: The Sunday School

Since the Sunday school is considered by mainstream denominations to be the agency for education, we must be careful in appraising its significance and its potential for the future. When the Sunday school began, it was not a problem but the solution to a problem. The reason it is a problem today is that, although times have changed, the Sunday school as an *agency* of education has not. Educational strategy, we have said, is a product of a people's understanding of faith and the social situation in which they are located. We will use these two facts to understand how the Sunday school began and why it became the principal agency of church education.

The Sunday school movement was started in 1780 in Gloucester, England, by Robert Raikes, a printer and newspaper publisher. Established for poor children in Sooty Alley near the city jail, it was called a Sunday school because it met all day on Sunday. Its aim was to help educate socially disadvantaged children, many of whom worked six days a week in the nearby pin factory. The teachers were paid; instruction was given in reading, writing, and religion; and a great deal of attention was devoted to developing proper manners, moral behavior, and good citizenship. Given the problems brought on by the industrial revolution, the crowded conditions of cities, the lack of schooling for poor children, and Raikes's concern for Christian citizenship, school on Sunday was an innovative idea. As such it spread rapidly through England, but when it came to America the Sunday school changed to fit the social situation of a new nation founded on democratic principles.

With a successful revolution behind it, a settled plan of government, a judicial system in place, inexhaustible natural resources all around, and a whole continent to the west just waiting to be explored and exploited, the United States entered the nineteenth century with enormous confidence. Martin Marty considers this a time when religious leaders attempted to build a "righteous empire,"[5] and Robert T. Handy quotes Horace Bushnell to capture the spirit and intention of church leaders during this era:

The wilderness shall bud and blossom as the rose before us; and we will not cease, till a christian nation throws up its temples of worship on every hill and plain; till knowledge, virtue and religion, blending their dignity and their healthful power, have filled our great country with a manly and happy race of people, and the bands of a complete christian commonwealth are seen to span the continent.[6]

With such an emphasis on the building of a complete Christian commonwealth, it seems strange that the churches turned to the Sunday school as their agency of education. There were two reasons for this move. First, the new nation had committed itself to the separation of church and state, and that doctrine was applied to the emerging state-supported common school during this time. Second, the churches, basking in the confidence of a strong Protestant ethos and morality, accepted the Sunday school as an agency to supplement what was already being done by the churches, ministers, homes, and schools.

Separation of the Church from State Schools

In the early part of the 1800s the United States was just emerging from the Colonial period, in which many states had an established religion integrated into school worship and instruction. Although the first article of the Bill of Rights (1791) separated church from state, it took a long time to remove religion from the schools. This was due, in part, to the slow development of free common schools throughout the United States. New York State is credited with the formation of the first state school system in 1812, but Massachusetts is usually cited as the leader, because of Horace Mann, who was president of the state senate when the Massachusetts State Board of Education was established, in 1837, and became its first executive secretary. From that position and from editorship of *Common School Journal* he improved curriculum, helped establish the first normal school for the training of teachers (1839), consolidated small local schools, and in many other ways shaped an excellent school system. He also had to contend with church leaders who wanted religion taught in the schools. Mann was sympathetic to religion; but, given the First Amendment to the Constitution and the fierce struggle between denominations (each of which wanted its particular doctrine taught statewide), he could do no more than support a general Protestant piety with strong emphasis on moral conduct. As a result, religion as a subject for study gradually dropped out of the curriculum, although it was present especially in terms of moral conduct in McGuffey's *Eclectic Readers* all through the nineteenth century.

During the same period of time that the public school movement was being established (about 1800–1860), the Sunday school movement was adjusting to and being shaped by the social situation in the United States. In the early 1800s the Sunday school movement was non-denominational and very evangelistic; managed by lay people, it moved westward with the pioneers. Henry Barnard, the first U.S. Commissioner of Education, observed that on the western frontier the Sunday school was "the precursor and pioneer both of the district school and of the church."[7] But as William B. Kennedy indicates in his history of this period, the denominations, seeing themselves squeezed out of public schools, took over the Sunday school as a department within their organization so they would have a place to teach their beliefs and practices. Thus in a subtle way over half a century, the Sunday school became the chief agency of education in Protestant denominations because they needed a place to teach their doctrines when public schools, by reason of the Constitution, became secular. Two American historians looking back on this arrangement, James Hastings Nichols and Sidney Mead, judged it to be a decisive turning point in American religion. It compartmentalized religion in the church and made it unrelated to the affairs of life taught in public schools.[8]

Church leaders who made the decision to rely on the Sunday school as their agency for Christian education were mindful of other options. Roman Catholics, for example, were emigrating to the United States in large numbers before the Civil War; when they realized they could not change the schools' Protestant atmosphere, they began to establish parochial schools. Some Protestant denominations—such as some Lutherans—also decided on church-sponsored day schools. Presbyterians and other Protestants reacted to the secularization of the public schools by founding parochial schools about 1846, but the disruption of the Civil War and lack of funds caused them to abandon the effort about 1870.[9]

Why the Sunday School Succeeded

The Sunday school as a supplement to other means of communication of the Christian faith in the nineteenth century was successful for a number of reasons.

1. The ethos of the first half of the nineteenth century was Protestant. Alexis de Tocqueville, visiting the United States in the 1830s, judged that "there is no country in the world in which the Christian religion retains a greater influence over the souls of men than in America."[10] When religion permeates almost all aspects of common life, the common life transmits that religion in a powerful way. Just in going on a daily round of conversation, reading newspapers, hearing public officials speak, or attending public schools, Americans effectively learned the prevailing Protestant views. Nowhere was this better

illustrated than in the newly developed public school system. Although the public schools were separated from the control of the church, they reflected the Protestant ethos of the times. For example, the first edition of McGuffey's *Readers* (1836–37), widely used throughout the nation, was written from the perspective of Calvinist theology, with over half of the lessons designed to cultivate the virtues of honesty, obedience, kindness, thrift, industry, patriotism, cleanliness, and curiosity. After William H. McGuffey's death in 1873, his books were revised (1879) to eliminate much of the theology; their values were adjusted to affirm "the morality and life-styles of the emerging middle class and those cultured beliefs, attitudes, and values that undergird American civil religion."[11]

Robert W. Lynn is of the opinion that in the 1830s McGuffey was part of a small but influential group of Cincinnati intellectuals who were concerned about the future of the western part of the nation just opening up. They saw the problem as one of absorbing immigrants or, in more positive terms, as needing to develop a distinctive American character or civic personality. Lynn believes that the McGuffey *Readers* accomplished this goal by providing a common historical story that nourished civic piety, especially through the use of the legends surrounding George Washington; a cultivation of declamatory literature of a patriotic and civic nature to be used on national holidays, festive occasions, school commencements, and various public meetings; and a well-defined moral code of conduct.[12]

Kennedy believes that one of the major reasons Protestants continued to support public schools—even though religion as a subject of study was slowly being eliminated—was that Protestants were primarily interested in moral education or Protestant civic religion. Therefore, to separate the church from the state schools was not too much of a loss, for Protestants thought they could continue to influence the character of the schools through Bible readings, prayer, religiously oriented teachers, and a curriculum emphasizing such works as McGuffey's *Readers*.[13] We should not fault the judgment of nineteenth-century Protestants, for when we realize that four out of every five school children from 1836 until 1900 used the McGuffey *Readers* during the elementary school years, we can understand how influential these books were in forming a distinctively religious civic mentality.[14]

2. Protestant churches had great influence in society. Although this influence produced the ethos referred to above, I mention ethos first because the national agenda for developing a secular common-school movement, motivated in part by economic and political forces, happened to take place during a time of Protestant hegemony.

This hegemony was achieved because Protestants were the dominant religious groups in the early nineteenth century. Roman Catholics had not yet arrived in large numbers, and there were very few Jews

in the United States at that time. The power of the Protestants came
not so much from their numbers—only a small percentage of the
population held church membership in the early 1800s—but from the
Second Great Awakening, which dominated the nation up to the time
of the Civil War. Revivals emerged almost simultaneously in New
England, in Virginia and states to the south, and in Kentucky and states
to the west of the Ohio River. Moreover, the revivals were not limited
to the poorly educated or to camp meetings in remote settlements of
the West; they also took place among college students and professionals. When Timothy Dwight, president of Yale College, preached a
series of sermons in 1802, one third of the student body responded
by making a confession of faith.[15] From Yale and other colleges animated by the revival spirit of the Great Awakening came the leaders
who created an expanding evangelical Protestantism along with the
expanding frontier and the enlarging population. The most notable of
such leaders were Lyman Beecher (1775–1863), a great organizer, and
Nathaniel Taylor (1786–1858), the principal theologian of the revival
movement.

For business and professional classes, the representative figure of
the Second Great Awakening was Charles G. Finney (1792–1875).
Finney, a lawyer, attended a Presbyterian church and sang in the choir;
but by his own account, he was a worldly man. One day he had a
conversion experience while walking to his office. Afterward he studied theology under his pastor's supervision for a few years, then began
to preach with great success, mainly in New York and other cities of
the Northeast. The close relationship between evangelical religion and
higher education is also evident in Finney's life, for he ended his career
as a professor and president of Oberlin College.

To document the rapid expansion of churches during this period is
difficult, because church membership records were not always preserved and because membership had a serious meaning in those days.
It was fairly normal among some denominations to examine members
in a formal way before communion; if deviant moral behavior could be
proved, the member was disciplined. Even with these stringent requirements, Hudson estimates that one out of every fifteen persons
was a church member in 1800, and one out of eight was a member by
1835. However, membership does not tell the whole story, for in the
1830s about three times as many people attended church as were
members.[16] The United States census for 1860 shows a total of 54,745
churches with a seating capacity of about 19 million people, at a time
when the nation had a population of just slightly more than 31 million
persons.[17]

The rapid expansion of denominations (such as the Methodists
through their circuit-rider method) and the founding of new denomi-

nations related to the needs of the western frontier (such as the Cumberland Presbyterians and the Disciples of Christ) were supported by a wide range of societies for special missions. The idea of "voluntary societies" came from England, where the technique of gathering people to promote common interests had developed. The modern missionary movement, for example, is usually traced to the Baptist Missionary Society in England (1792), which collected funds to send William Carey to India. Using that method, people formed societies in the United States to promote missionary work among Indians and to establish churches in the west. The American Bible Society was founded in 1816 to distribute Bibles, and the Sunday School Union was founded in 1824 to establish new Sunday schools and to strengthen the educational work of existing ones. In 1830 the Sunday School Union launched a drive to "establish a Sunday-School in every destitute place where it is practicable, throughout the Valley of the Mississippi."[18]

3. Ministers were leaders of church and society. From the early Colonial period until well up into the 1800s ministers were among the best-educated people in the community, and they most often came from the elite segment of society. Harvard, for example, was established in 1636 in order to "advance learning and perpetuate it to Posterity, dreading to leave an illiterate ministry to the churches when our present ministers shall lie in the Dust."[19] Most of the colleges in the nineteenth century were founded by denominations to supply ministers for the rapidly growing churches and to influence society by providing a Christian higher education for lawyers, doctors, business people, teachers, and other leaders. In 1855 it was estimated that one fourth of the 40,000 graduates of American colleges had become ministers. The ministry had a strong appeal for young men, as Donald Tewksbury observed, because "the church in that day was an active force in society, and under the leadership of able men it took a prominent part in the social, political, and intellectual interests of the day."[20]

Ministers in this period of American life held high social status, partially because of their educational attainments. Since the number of college graduates was small in proportion to the population, ministers with a degree had the distinctiveness of other community leaders. Moreover, education at that time provided general knowledge shared by all professional people. The physical sciences were not advanced beyond the level of college subjects and the social sciences were not yet separated from philosophy. Many college professors were ministers because they had command of this general knowledge.

The prestige of ministers in the community was also due in part to the high social status ministers had enjoyed since Colonial days. During the Second Great Awakening, when evangelical Christianity was the dominant form of religion, ministers reflected the power and confidence that were characteristic of religion at that time. Sydney Mead attributes the relatively high social status of ministers to the widely accepted reverence for the Bible. Mead also judges that "it would be difficult to find any genuinely secular anticlericalism or antiecclesiasticism anywhere during our whole period."[21]

4. The home was an agency of Christian character. America was predominantly a rural society until the Civil War, but after the war, the country rapidly became industrialized and urbanized. Although in 1850 only 15 percent of the population lived in urban areas, by 1860 that percentage had increased to 20 percent. In 1860 about 60 percent of the labor force was farm labor; by 1910 only 31 percent were classified as farmers.[22] This does not mean, however, that the underlying structure of the family underwent a dramatic change. A careful examination of census data indicates that the nuclear family—father, mother, and children in one household—was remarkably stable, though the number of children decreased with the increase of industrialization.[23]

Victorian ideas controlled family life during this period. The maintenance of family morals and morale was the role of the mother: she looked after the physical and character developments of children, and on the frontier she was sometimes their teacher. The father in this rural society was the head of the family—in and out of the house during the day but normally home at night. Children, according to their ability, helped with household chores and with work that had an immediate relevance to their life, such as cooking, washing clothes, or bringing in firewood. Rural families were often isolated from one another, for Americans developed the pattern of living on their farms rather than following the European custom of living in small villages and then going to the outlying fields to work. This isolation was broken when children went to small neighborhood schools and the families attended church. Because of its relative isolation, however, the family was the primary social group—that is, the group on which all members relied for guidance and support. Thus children during their formative years had time to absorb deeply the values that were lived and taught in the home. Moreover, society offered almost no competition for the children's affection.

We should not put too much reliance on one mental image, but the picture of Abraham Lincoln as a boy, lying on his stomach and reading the Bible by candlelight, illustrates our point. Lincoln grew up in Illinois during this period. There was time to read, but little reading material other than the Bible or school readers (such as McGuffey's), which contained Bible stories and lessons on moral behavior. Although Lincoln did not attend church, he was greatly influenced by the

Bible; Christian beliefs of forgiveness and mercy informed some of his major decisions during the Civil War. Thus Lincoln, a representative figure from this era, learned a religious outlook on life from his home situation and from the general religious ethos of society.

Bushnell's Strategy

From the standpoint of Protestant educational strategy, the most important person in this period was Horace Bushnell. Born in 1802, educated at Yale College and Divinity School, and pastor of the North Congregational Church of Hartford, Connecticut, from 1833 to 1859, Bushnell spanned the era under discussion. He opposed the intellectualized and dogmatic interpretation of Christianity behind the Second Great Awakening, although he affirmed basic evangelical doctrines such as the sinfulness of human nature and the need for salvation by the grace of God. Bushnell wanted to emphasize the love of God and also God's use of natural Christian education, such as the nurture of the children in the home. To this end he wrote two "Discourses on Christian Nurture," which he delivered in 1846 to the Massachusetts Sabbath School Society. The published discourses caused so much opposition that they were withdrawn, yet Bushnell continued his work on the idea that children should be raised as Christians without the jolt of a conversion. He published his views on this subject in 1861 under the title *Christian Nurture*. [24]

Bushnell's book is properly regarded as the beginning of the Christian education movement in America. When we read *Christian Nurture* today, we are so overwhelmed by its insight and the way it speaks to our present situation that we forget Bushnell was formulating a strategy for Christian education. Education was to take place in the home because children, properly raised, will have the Christian faith deeply embedded in their whole being. When Bushnell discussed the methods of such education, he was extremely practical; he considered the qualifications of the parents, the way the body—especially during a child's feeding —is a means of grace, the use of holidays and Sundays, the importance of play and of family prayers. The clear implication of this book is that Christian education is accomplished in the family, and the family is nurtured in the congregation. Bushnell, for example, in his discussion on what to do with children on Sunday, criticized the two extremes of his day: the "soundly orthodox" way of keeping the children indoors most of the day (memorizing the catechism or scripture), and the liberal way of simply sending them off to Sunday school. Bushnell advised that parents plan Sunday as a special day for children by having special toys for that day, books and pictures about scripture, practice in singing hymns, and, above all, conversations initiated by parents about events of the day, including church attendance. Such conversations would include the sermon, about which parents were to make "a good and lively children's version," the sacraments, what the church is, and so on. Sunday was to be a pleasant day, oriented to God and to the church, for which the parents were responsible.[25]

Bushnell rejected the Sunday school as an agency of education partly because it was under the influence of a revival theology and partly because he saw great possibilities for the family to be the church's chief agency of nurture. He recognized these possibilities because the family in the first half of the nineteenth century was a stable social unit in which children learned religion, a moral code, and a predisposition to participate in the life of a congregation.

Search for a Modern Strategy

Robert W. Lynn is the person in modern times who has best explained the critical importance of educational strategy. In his book *Protestant Strategies in Education* (1964), he reviews briefly the ambivalence and hesitation that characterized the church's incorporation of the Sunday school as its agency of instruction. Lynn then turns to the twentieth century and identifies various efforts to change the strategy. Early in this century a group of liberal religious educators, influenced by progressive education, sought to improve the effectiveness of the Sunday school by making it a "sound" educational institution. To do this they prepared a child-centered curriculum according to progressive educational ideas, developed a remarkable nationwide interdenominational leadership training program, and in some places, such as Union Theological Seminary in New York, conducted a model school on Sunday. This effort to revitalize Sunday church schools was so tied to liberal theology that it played out as that philosophy waned in the 1930s, although some of the educational ideas expressed in curriculum reform still continue today.

Seeing the declining influence of the Sunday school, some church educators sought additional times for instruction. Youth groups, separate from the Sunday school and with a somewhat different type of Christian education, began in Boston (1881) and grew rapidly under the name Christian Endeavor. Denominations soon developed their own versions of youth activity groups. These groups still exist today, but now they reach only a small percentage of the young people who belong to a congregation. Summer camps and conferences for youth were also developed in the early 1900s. This outdoor setting for Christian education has now expanded to include family camping, training events for lay leaders, marriage seminars, and retreats for spiritual life development. Although these intensive programs aimed at a particular age or interest group have special value for the people involved, the number of people attending such events is not large. Vacation Bible schools began in various places at the turn of the century. If a church sponsors such a school today, however, it reaches only a small percentage of the children enrolled in its Sunday school.

Some church educators continued to be attentive to the possibility of an alliance with public schools, because all children of the community are there. These efforts have taken three forms. One plan was for the church to have a period during the public school schedule when children could attend classes in religion on a voluntary basis. The "released time" plan as devised in 1914 in Gary, Indiana, became the pattern. This plan spread rapidly, but it was declared unconstitutional by the Supreme Court in 1948. Later, in 1952, the Supreme Court ruled that teaching religion was constitutional as long as it took place off school property, but the obstacles to such a plan are so great that it has not become a viable option for the churches.

Another plan was for church weekday schools to share time with the public school. In this "shared time" plan, church weekday schools would teach religion and other "value-oriented" subjects, and the public schools would teach the rest of the curriculum.[26] An early version of this plan was prepared by Walter Scott Athearn in 1917 for the town of Walden, Massachusetts. Athearn's plan did not succeed, and more recent versions have not been acceptable. Athearn is to be commended, however, for seeing so clearly that, "utilize it and standardize it as you may, the Sunday session of the church school will not furnish an adequate religious education for our people."[27]

The third effort to use the public schools to support religion can hardly be called a plan, but it had symbolic value and contained some religious substance. This effort was to continue the religious influence in public schools that had not been eliminated by Supreme Court action, specifically the devotional reading of the Bible and the opening of the school day with prayer. Other religious influences from the past, such as observing Christmas and Easter with school-sponsored programs, including Christian songs or the display of a nativity scene, were evidence of a lingering religious influence. But in 1962 the Supreme Court ruled that prayer in public school was unconstitutional; and in 1963, in the *Abington* v. *Schempp* case, the Supreme Court also declared unconstitutional a devotional reading of the Bible. The Schempp case is important, for Justice Clark in the majority opinion made it clear that public schools could teach religion only "when presented objectively as part of the secular program of education." This principle gave the final definition of public schools as secular institutions: if they treat religion and religious practices at all, they must do so as items to be studied "objectively."

The Strategy Issue Today

The Sunday school as the principal agency of instruction thus became the church's strategy in the early part of the nineteenth century. It was a success at that time because it fitted into a social situation characterized by a Protestant ethos, a time when churches had great influence over individuals and communities, ministers were among the best-educated leaders, and home was the place where Christian character was formed. As the state schools became secularized and the nation became industrialized and urbanized, church leaders in the twentieth century saw the inadequacies of the Sunday school as a weekly instructional period. Many efforts have been made since the early 1900s to supplement or enhance the effectiveness of the Sunday school or to create a dual system of instruction by some kind of alliance with public schools. Lynn, however, reviewing this effort to find a usable strategy, labels it "a history of failure."[28]

The Sunday school itself is not a failure. The failure is the idea that the Sunday school alone—with little help from parents, church, or community—can be an effective agent of Christian education. What is lacking are the other parts of the nineteenth-century strategy. Churches in some rural areas or small towns may still influence community mores, but in the large towns and urban areas where most of the population is now located, the churches today have so little influence that they can barely prevent public school events, footraces, athletic contests, and community picnics from being scheduled on Sunday morning. Although ministers of mainstream denominations are still well educated, the education of doctors, lawyers, business people, and various technicians has increased and has become so specialized that the minister is no longer a natural leader of the community by virtue of his educational attainment. Nor is the home today the most decisive influence in the nurturing of children. On the contrary, the home is the target of TV programs and consumer advertising. It is the sleeping place of children and adults, who spend most of their time elsewhere surrounded by the ethos of secular individualism. In a secular society, the Sunday school is not capable of being the principal educational agency of the church.

The school as a place for communicating the Christian faith requires some additional comments. In the early nineteenth century the Sunday school was more a school of the heart than of the head, so it was conducted almost anywhere by anyone who felt called of God to do so.[29] By the twentieth century, however, the churches had accepted the schooling concept, which emphasized instruction in schoolrooms by trained teachers. The place was usually a separate educational building, symbolizing that what went on in that building was different from what took place in the church itself. Teachers, although lay volunteers, were given as much training as possible in short courses or through instruction in teacher manuals. Therefore church education became institutionalized in the Sunday school and took on the characteristics of a special area. Larger churches employed directors of Christian education who had special training for this work—thus professionalizing the leadership and holding up the ideals of professional educators.

This movement toward shaping the Sunday school along the lines of professional public school education is not necessarily undesirable. The good points are rather clear: education is taken seriously; curriculum is better related to the needs, interests, and abilities of an age group; teachers receive some training; better equipment, including audiovisual aids, is available; and often some good reading material is provided for home use. But problems have emerged that are seldom identified or properly assessed. One problem is the notion that schools can "teach" faith. Pupils can learn something about the Bible, theology, and religious practices in a classroom setting, but they have little chance of developing proper piety if they are cut off from congregational life and worship. Moreover, the Sunday school class, meeting for only thirty to forty minutes a week, tends to be focused on acquiring knowledge. With such a short time for a lesson, teachers cannot use the life experiences of the pupils in a meaningful way unless the class is very small. Faith as the "set of one's heart" or trust in God comes to individuals as they participate (or participate through their parents, in the case of small children) in a community of believers where such faith is assumed and practiced. Unless we are very careful about the limitations of the schooling model, we will give parents the impression that if they drop off their children in Sunday school we can teach them Christian faith, just as swimming classes can teach children to swim.

A more serious problem is leadership. As long as the Sunday school was an instructional agency within a broad evangelical context, teachers and ministers shared the same orientation to scripture and life. However, as Janet Fishburn pointed out, since the 1950s it has become obvious that lay people who teach in the Sunday school are often not in tune with the ministers' theology or method of Bible interpretation. Fishburn believes this has come about because church educators took over leadership training as an educational specialty, and thus it became separate from the theology of the church. As a result some of the best curriculum material prepared by Protestant denominations in recent decades has been rejected or abandoned by many Sunday school teachers because it was difficult to understand or did not fit their religious views or moral code.[30]

The important issue here is the difference between the training of our ministers and the interests of the lay people who teach in our Sunday schools. Ministers in our mainstream denominations have three years of graduate theological education and some supervised practice of ministry before they are ordained. After ordination they attend continuing education events, read current studies in theology, and associate with other ministers where biblical interpretation is frequently discussed. Lay teachers, on the other hand, have little formal training; they depend on their own personal experience, observation of morality in the marketplace, and whatever church-sponsored teacher training they may have time to take. The issue is not so much that ministers have more theological and biblical training as it is that lay people have a different perspective. Thus in many congregations there may be two theologies functioning side by side, and the resulting confusion is often suppressed or glossed over in the interests of harmony. The tragedy in this condition is that although ministers use their theology in preaching and as a background for whatever teaching they may do in the Sunday school, they do not see themselves as educating the Sunday school teachers; in their minds such training is about "methods" or "the psychology of children"—subjects about which they often feel inadequate. Sunday school teachers, on the other hand, are having face-to-face relationships with children and teenagers. They know a lot about the experiences these immature young people are having, but they often lack the ability to relate life experiences to beliefs. As a result Sunday school teaching can become dreary, because it is presented as something pupils must believe, or it can become superficial, because it caters to experience without seriously relating that experience to what we know about God.

Options

Since the matter of educational strategy has been a concern of Protestants since the early 1800s, the options are well known. In terms of broad design there are three.

As a first option, Protestants can continue their present strategy and attempt to improve all of its parts. This would mean trying to make congregational life more meaningful, home experience more stable and informed by the faith and morals of the church, Sunday school and the age group organizations more significant, and so forth. Although this is not a bad scenario, mainstream Protestants have been doing these things to revitalize the existing agencies of education without much success. As indicated earlier in this chapter, there are limitations to this school-centered design because our social situation has changed.

The second option is for Protestants to develop parochial schools. The idea of having their own day schools is an ancient one that reasserts itself among certain Christians when there are no schools at all; when the existing schools are of poor quality, are infused with other religions, or are so secular that parents refuse to use them; or when the Christian group has particular doctrines it wants to protect from criticism. Some Lutheran denominations, the Christian Reformed Church, and some sect groups have established and maintained day schools for a long time because of the distinctiveness of their beliefs. Since the 1960s conservative and fundamental churches have increasingly established day schools because they believe that the public school curriculum is too secular or the moral conditions within the student body too permissive.

Mainstream Protestants, however, will not embark on a system of parochial schools unless social conditions become much worse. Here and there, Episcopal churches in large urban areas may start a day school with support from wealthy individuals from other denominations; such schools, however, represent more a desire for high-quality education than a desire for a particular theology. Mainstream denominations have a long history of supporting public schools, and they have neither the motivation nor the money to develop an alternate school system any time in the near future.

The third option is for mainstream Protestants to consider the *congregation* as the agency of education. This requires a shift in perspective. First, we must recognize that the congregation is a dynamic interaction of people that through worship (including sermon), program of activities, use of money, and allocation of leadership is an interpretation of Christianity (chapter 9). Second, we must realize that the congregational interpretation of faith permeates the membership through natural channels of influence. These channels are through adults, who make decisions for the congregation; who, as parents, select moral values and model a religious faith for their children; who exhibit to their friends and colleagues the meaning of faith for practical situations in which they must speak and act; and who teach church school classes or lead youth groups. Third, we must acknowledge that, because the congregation is a community, teaching and learning are going on incessantly. This means we must constantly remind ourselves of the educational opportunities in all aspects of congregational life. For example, if lay people are to help with public worship, someone should go over the service with them in order that they understand *why* they are to do certain things as well as *how* they are to do them. Or if lay people are asked to visit the sick in hospitals, they should have some coaching on how to conduct such visits.

This third option means that the minister and lay leaders of a congregation must resolve to develop the congregation as a community of believers who are seeking God's will for their lives. This places the nature and mission of the congregation first, so that preaching and teaching are subordinated to that goal. Additionally, this option requires adults to take responsibility for the interpretation and communication of the faith. Adults cannot sidestep this responsibility by saying that ministers are to do this for the adults and Sunday school teachers are to do it for children. This third option will continue the Sunday school or some form of instruction for children, but the purpose of that instruction will change. Rather than being *the* place where children are expected to learn the Christian faith, it will become *a* place where they learn something about the faith, to *supplement* what they get in the home and through participation in other aspects of the congregational life and work.

Chapter 11 will describe a practical plan for considering the congregation as the agency of education. But before I move on, I would like to give two reasons why Protestants should change their educational strategy.

First, the social situation has changed. Now and in the foreseeable future we must deal with secular culture that is and will be communicated to children and youth through television, peer groups, public schools, and governmental programs related to health, such as abortion and birth control. In this social situation the church must see itself as a religious subculture that goes counter to the dominant culture of America. This will be difficult, because mainstream Protestants still consider themselves custodians of American values. But our secular society, with its neutrality toward any religion, no longer provides an informal environment that will communicate faith in God.

Recent studies from a historical perspective identify a progressive disestablishment of religion in America. The first disestablishment occurred in 1791 when the First Amendment separated church from state, thus ending the long Colonial period during which states formally or informally supported a certain religion. The second disestablishment took place, according to Robert Handy, about 1920 to 1935.[31] During this time the nineteenth-century influence of mainstream Protestantism began to wane as the nation became conscious that it was made up of many religions. The third disestablishment, according to Wade C. Roof and William McKinney, is occurring now. The place of religion in American society has been altered. Religion has been privatized; although it may be important for an individual, persons have difficulty extending their religious beliefs to the public realm.[32] Phillip E. Hammond uses an illustration of Hindu parents insisting on vegetarian meals for their children in public schools. Christians may object to such a request, but finally one side will prevail; either the students will be removed from school or some kind of accommodation will be worked out. In the public area, religion is more and more being held in abeyance in order for our country to maintain a democratic society.[33]

I believe that the recent studies of mainstream Protestant denominations, based on long-term trends, are probably correct. However, we must be careful about predicting the future of Christianity, for the

Holy Spirit has on many occasions brought about unexpected changes. We could have another Great Awakening; the younger generation may turn their backs on secularism; moribund denominations may develop a vigorous spiritual life. But none of these possibilities will come about until Protestants begin to disassociate their well-being from American secularism and begin to "hunger and thirst for righteousness" (Matt. 5·6)

Second, when society is secular, only a community of believers can provide a place where the practical significance of faith in God can be discussed and tested and where believers can support one another in their effort to live by the Christian faith. Centering the religious life in a community of believers is the normal expression of both Judaism and Christianity. In the Jewish religion it came about after the Exile when the Hebrews were living under the control of a foreign power in a land with many other religions. The synagogue emerged as a place where they could worship and probe for meaning in their condition of political powerlessness. The first Christians, converts from Judaism, reflected the synagogue pattern of assembly because they needed to separate themselves from the Jews, Romans, and others who did not hold to their beliefs about Jesus Christ. The point I want to emphasize is not so much the natural affinity that draws people together when they have a common belief separating them from culture, but the power a community can develop in individuals and in a group to influence society. Established religious sects are a case in point. (I do not mean cult groups led by a charismatic person who makes a sharp break from society; cults seldom outlast their leaders, because there is little if any effort to establish their movement as a historical reality.) Established sects are like denominations, except that they use their beliefs as a basis for joining and maintaining fellowship with the congregation. As settled organizations, sects have rules for dealing with conflict, procedures for selecting leaders, a high level of adult participation, and ways for members to support one another as they express their differences with the world. The community of kindred minds in a sect congregation gives members power to affirm their beliefs and to ignore or reject certain parts of society. Seventh Day Adventists, for example, can generate enough power in congregations to support any members having trouble with employers who will not respect Saturday as their sabbath. Or consider the courage Jehovah's Witnesses showed during World War II when they refused to salute the American flag on the grounds that it violated their conscience. Children of Jehovah's Witnesses were ostracized in school and society for such lack of patriotism, but the sect community explained to them why such conduct was correct and supported them personally and legally all the way to the Supreme Court, where the protest was sustained (see *West Virginia State Board of Education* v *Burnette,* 1943)

Denominations cannot become sects, because they are in the mainstream of society and have a proprietary relationship to it. Moreover, the national or regional organization of a denomination is so involved in maintenance and meets so infrequently that it can function only as a legislature. Yet congregations within denominations can be *communities,* for they meet regularly to worship God and to work for God's rule in life. Congregations within mainstream denominations can deliberately set themselves to become sectlike by engaging in serious and sustained reflection on what the Christian faith means in their time and place, by developing loyalty to each other in this enterprise, and by assuming a responsibility for the welfare of all people in their community.

11

Congregational Edification

Chapter 9 presented the congregation as the place where theology and life experiences are blended. Although this blending process creates a certain amount of conflict, it can have positive value in helping a congregation become more attuned to God's will and therefore more able to run counter to the surrounding culture.

One of the major reasons why American Protestant congregations do not live up to their potential as communities governed by their beliefs is that we continue to use an educational strategy that is no longer appropriate. Chapter 10 explained in some detail how our present social situation differs from that of the early nineteenth century, when congregations adopted the Sunday school as their educational strategy. Because today's secular society offers no support for the Sunday school and because the congregation often considers it merely an auxiliary enterprise, we must devise a different strategy with contemporary conditions in mind.

The strategy outlined in this final chapter is not really new. It is inspired by recent studies in what the first urban Christian assemblies were like and by my observation of some Protestant congregations that have found a way to influence their members and help them become more mature in their faith.

Goal and Strategy

The goal is a congregation seriously seeking to bring about the reign or kingdom of God in their lives. A secondary goal is the maturation of the individuals' faith as they participate with others in seeking to understand and do the will of God in their community. This goal is in sharp contrast to Christian education or faith development goals, which are stated in terms of individual growth or achievement and are unrelated to congregations or to the responsibility of congregations for the welfare of the community.[1]

The strategy is a process of edification or upbuilding of the congregation by means of a sustained study of the Christian tradition (Bible and theology) in relation to the events that are taking place in the lives of members. This strategy is based on the work of a central study group A center of energy vision and spiritual discipline, this group shapes the congregation's purpose and mission, inspires and encourages adults to use their faith in their vocation, provides help for parents and guardians of children, and supplies leaders for whatever classes and groups are needed in the congregation.

Central Study Group

Congregational edification will come about when a group of adult members develop spiritual power by relating Christian beliefs to their life situations and sharing their understanding and convictions with the whole congregation. This group consists of ministers, officers, and interested adults. Some name should be selected to describe what the group is about—perhaps something like "Theological Workshop"—but here I will use the general title Central Study Group, or CSG. Names that imply organizational authority, such as "Senate," should be avoided because this study group has no administrative or legislative responsibility. If ideas emerge in the CSG that suggest congregational action, they should be referred to the appropriate committee.

The general purpose of the CSG is congregational edification—a purpose of critical importance, because it provides the basis for study and evaluation. This is not a conventional adult Sunday school class, which aims at individual understanding and exists to enrich the lives of persons who want to know more about the Bible and theology. The CSG is consciously aware of its role as the place where a practical theology is being developed for use by the whole congregation. In turn, this practical theology should help produce a Christian mentality in the congregation. "Mentality" here means a Christian basis for decision making and a desire to use that basis in daily living. Practical theology is neither speculative nor systematic; it is theology to be used in real-life situations when people have to decide on some course of action.

A major feature of congregationally generated practical theology is integration of beliefs and experience. Ministers, with their more extensive study of Bible and theology, meet lay people, who have a more thorough knowledge of the business world and professional practices Integrating these two forms of knowledge and experience is difficult. In fact, under ordinary circumstances little effort is made in a congregation to bring about such reconciliation. The worst-case scenario is the one found in congregations where the ministers with their life-styles and beliefs are set apart—like the Sunday worship—as objects of respect or holiness, to be contaminated as little as possible with the realities of the world. A more moderate case is that of most mainstream congregations, where the ministers and lay leaders want to provide guidance for Christian life-style, but the Sunday school classes do not foster the integration of faith with life.

The leadership of a CSG will ordinarily be assumed by the ministers, since they are the designated leaders recognized by church and society. Moreover, this study group will be generating ideas that will be lodged in various committees and officer groups, so the ministers need to be at the center of this enterprise. It will require a major commitment of ministers' time and effort, yet in the long run it may coordinate the many disparate tasks required of them. Certainly, some kinds of pastoral work—such as acute illness, death, and crisis situations—always receive immediate attention, but when scheduling tasks, ministers should give first priority to their leadership of the CSG, because this group is generating the theology by which the congregation lives. Since worship, including the sermon, will flow from and enhance the general line of thought going on in the CSG, ministers will have considerable help in their preparation for congregational worship on Sunday mornings. Moreover the CSG, by its composition of officers and lay leaders, cannot help but be an informal clearing house of information about members and the status of various activities conducted by the congregation. The ministers, being at the center of this exchange, may find they can give direction to various enterprises through conversations with lay leaders and perhaps reduce their schedule of committee meetings.

I have been careful to use the word "leadership" to characterize ministers' relation to the CSG. In most cases ministers will teach the group, but because the word "teach" stereotypically means standing up before people and telling them what they should know, I have avoided it. At times, however, certain themes under discussion might suggest that the minister would preside and respond, but another member of the group would present ideas for the group to work on.

Initiative

The initiative for starting a CSG rests with the ministers. If ministers are unwilling to take leadership in this strategy, it has little possibility of success. A practical way to begin would be for ministers to select a few of the most interested adults and engage them in an informal discussion of the nature of congregational life. The first two parts of this book may be helpful in presenting issues such as the secular nature of our social environment and the nature of religious experience. A review of chapter 9 about the uniqueness of the congregation may help the group realize the power and potential of the congregation as a community. Chapter 10 on strategy will help the group understand why a different strategy of congregational education is necessary. Another recent book that may open up the issues is entitled *Congregations: Their Power to Form and Transform.* [2] A discussion of all ten chapters of that book would provide a solid base for further planning, but the group might want to select only the chapters that fit their special needs. There are other books about congregations that might better fit some churches' situations. [3]

I believe this congregational strategy has a biblical warrant that should also be examined. Later in this chapter, I will use the church at Corinth as an illustration. The small informal group could also study some of the New Testament churches by means of Paul's letters, in order to see how Paul related beliefs to the life situations of people in particular congregations.

Planning Committee

If the small informal group of interested adults decides to try this edification model of congregational life, they should formalize it according to their congregational situation. Since congregations differ so much even within the same denomination, I cannot give an exact set of suggestions to follow. In some situations the informal group that discussed the nature of congregational life could go forward with plans for a CSG without official approval. In others, the informal group would need to write a proposal and have it approved by an official board. But in every situation it is of critical importance to inform the officers about the plan in some detail and explain the matter in general terms to the whole congregation. Everyone involved needs to understand that no sudden changes are to be expected or made. Whatever happens as the result of having a CSG will take place slowly, for its purpose is spiritual growth.

The CSG will need a planning committee. It might be the same informal group, or it could be that group enlarged somewhat in order to better represent the congregation. In any case it needs to be recognized as the committee responsible for the CSG. Ordinarily the chairperson would be the minister, but something can be said for the chairperson's being a lay person as long as it is understood that the minister is the leader.

The planning committee should consist of not fewer than four or more than ten people, appointed by the minister. It might be a good idea to have everyone understand that each year the composition of the planning committee would be reviewed, so that those who serve would have a chance to renew their commitment and so that some new persons might be added. I think it would be in keeping with the idea of edification if the planning committee reported regularly to the CSG and made clear to everyone that their meetings were open. This planning committee should meet about once a month, more often if necessary. Its general purpose is to help the minister manage the CSG, which will involve two important tasks.

The first task is the selection of topics or themes for the CSG to study. Since the CSG is not an ordinary adult class, the ordinary criteria for selecting themes do not apply. The planning committee will *not* select themes because they are fashionable, have been used successfully in a church somewhere else, are of "interest" to some adults, are available because there is a teacher interested in the topic, are considered to be what well-informed adults should know, are easy to plan because there is a new book on the subject, or are handed down from national denominational headquarters.

Ordinary adult classes use such criteria because they consider themselves auxiliary to the congregational life. But the CSG does not use these criteria to select themes or topics. Since the CSG is working on matters for the whole congregation, two criteria emerge by which topics are selected for reflective thinking: (1) Topics must be for the edification of the congregation, which will require judgment about the needs of the particular church, and (2) they must be about something that requires decision. In some cases the decision will be made by the congregation in one of its official groups, and in other cases by members themselves, in the areas in their lives over which they have some control; but in any case the matter selected for study will have some connection with the lives of people in the congregation. With these two criteria in mind, the planning committee should start with the spiritual needs of the congregation and then select the biblical or theological material needed to open up that area to the Christian tradition. In some congregations the overriding need might be prayer, for which a three- or four-month study of the Lord's Prayer would be proper. For another congregation the major need might be distinctive Christian beliefs, for which the Apostles' Creed or some other statement of faith is appropriate study material.

If the planning committee has decided on a topic or issue that happens to coincide with a study paper or pronouncement of its national denomination, that denominational position should be given careful attention. The CSG should arrive at its own beliefs about the matter under consideration, but denominational position papers are often well thought out and have the advantage of bringing a cross-section of denominational views. In some ways the process of arriving at denominational position papers is the process I am advocating for the congregational CSG. First, there is an issue about which a decision should be made. Next comes careful systematic study of every aspect of the issue, including biblical and theological beliefs. Finally, discussion leads to modifications of the statement, until the denomination has arrived at a position appropriate to both the issue and its own beliefs.

Denominations also offer curriculum material for adult classes. These materials are often well prepared and have guides for the leader. When suitable, some of these materials could be used with the same appreciation and critical analysis the congregation uses when it considers denominational pronouncements.

In some congregations the best way to start a CSG would be to study a book of the Bible. The book should be selected because it has some special relevance to the spiritual needs of the congregation, and the method of study should allow plenty of time for people to raise questions about the meaning of the text and its value for their lives.

If the planning committee is carefully selected, its members should have no problem identifying themes to be studied, for they know the spiritual needs of the congregation. If, however, committee members are uncertain, they could distribute to the CSG a simple questionnaire asking for suggestions. The responses would guide the planning committee in their selection of themes.

The second task of the planning committee is to monitor the ongoing educational process of the CSG. I do not mean that its members assign to CSG activities ratings of "excellent, good, fair, or poor," as so many evaluations require. Although this type of evaluation has its place at the end of a course, the CSG is different in that it is an ongoing group of people with a purpose that can never be completely achieved. What the committee needs to do is to constantly monitor the educational process and make changes or corrections as needed. Most of the time, members of the planning committee will be able to suggest revisions simply by listening to what people around them are saying as they participate in the CSG. For example, ministers tend to think that church members understand the vocabulary of religion. They use common religious words such as "amen," "righteousness," "grace," "sin," and "kingdom of God" and assume that adults have the correct meanings in mind. Although that may have been true twenty or thirty years ago, it is not true of young and middle-aged adults today. Planning committee members may advise the minister to explain the background, significance, and meaning of the words commonly used in worship and in biblical passages. Furthermore, ministers leading the CSG may be proceeding rapidly through a theme on the assumption that the lack of response means the group is familiar with the ideas. The opposite may be true. Members of the group may be slow in responding because they do not understand very well, or they may be having trouble relating their experiences to what the Bible or theology is affirming. If that is the case, the planning committee will suggest a slowdown or a different way to help members bring their experience into the discussion.

CSG Members

The CSG should consist of the ministers, officers, and some of the most interested adults in the congregation. Ideally all the adults in the church would be directly involved, but this is seldom possible even in small congregations. Some adults are not ready to relate to others in a task of this nature.

Officers of the congregation are a special concern. Next to the leadership of the ministers, they are of critical importance for the success of this strategy. If they understand this edification model, they will be a support group for the ministers. They will see their work as decision making based on the beliefs of their Christian faith rather than as administration based on efficiency, which they learn in the marketplace. I think such a conception of their work will transform the tedium of policy making into the excitement of discovery as these members seek the faith basis for planning and administration of congregational affairs. But this reorientation to creative work will not take place unless church officers are involved in the CSG. How to do this will depend on the congregational situation. In many congregations it would not be wise to require that all officers participate in the CSG, even if the officers approve this model of learning together. In such cases the CSG would start with as many officers as possible; however, in time the congregation would understand that its officers were to be selected from the people involved in the CSG.

The selection and number of interested adults for the CSG will have to be decided on the basis of congregational conditions. The size and history of the congregation are important considerations, as is the organizational pattern already in place. I will discuss some of the options later, when I make practical suggestions about congregations. At this point I will comment only on selection and number.

Probably the planning committee should select the interested adults, for that group will know the church members well enough to choose adults who have a serious interest in the Christian faith and want to learn how to interpret the faith for the events taking place in their lives. There may be a problem with how the CSG is perceived by the congregation. It must be constantly emphasized that the CSG is a study group and has no administrative or governing functions. Disharmony could arise from the idea that it is a high-prestige class because the ministers are the leaders and because most—if not all—of the officers attend. If this happens, the planning committee should give the matter careful thought. One solution would be to set up the CSG for a two-year sequence and start a new CSG class each year. Although there are liabilities to this solution, it has the advantage of keeping the CSG open and of reaching more members. Another solution would be to review the CSG membership each year and expect some members to drop out. New members would be added to keep the number at a constant level.

The number of people in the CSG also needs careful thought. There should be no problem with low numbers, because any congregation with a minister would have at least ten to twelve eligible people. The difficulty is with higher numbers. A group of thirty to forty people is ideal for this purpose; if the CSG gets much beyond fifty in number, it will tend to rely too much on the lecture method, with questions and answers at the end of each class period. I will suggest options for larger churches later on.

Educational Process

The CSG should meet weekly at the church—and not on Sunday morning, because at that time the ministers are too occupied with worship and with maintaining pastoral relations. Its study sessions should last about one hour, but no longer than an hour and fifteen minutes without a break. Although singing a hymn or having a prayer to provide a devotional setting is desirable for the CSG's study, a longer period of worship would change the nature of the meeting.

It is extremely important to remember that the educational process envisioned for the CSG must involve the life situations of the members, and also the mind-set or interests they bring to the group.

1. The study session is not a lecture with questions from the audience for clarification; rather, it is a place to generate practical theology. This means scheduling times and planning methods that move the members to participate.[4] The leaders can involve people's life experience in two ways. One is to start with the Bible or theological statements and then set up ways the group members can respond out of their own experience. Although this takes time, it builds the right structure for a living faith. The other method is to take some kind of human situation about which people need to have a Christian belief— perhaps the presence of evil in the world, accidents or disease that cuts people off from a normal life, or the constant urge to do things about which we feel guilty or ashamed. These situations then need to be related to the Bible and theology. In both methods the elements of faith and experience as discussed in Part Two of this book are to be brought to the group for discussion. Thus a person's experience with faith is taken out of the realm of the purely personal and made available for correction by and edification of others.[5]

2. How to deal with the mind-set or preconceptions that members bring to the study group is an ongoing problem. Many people are only

dimly aware of their preconceptions; when they do realize their bias, they may become defensive or abusive because they have such an emotional investment in their position. These unargued assumptions are difficult to isolate objectively from our mind and view. When we attempt to do so, our mind flinches just as our body does when threatened with pain. However, until we can to some extent transcend our socially produced mentality, we cannot be open to the meaning of the text.

Mainstream Protestants are middle-class people who place a high value on education, professional competence, success, competition, personal worth, financial security, rational planning, health, patriotism, and similar assumptions, which they bring to any text they read or to any life situation they face. These values are not good or bad in themselves; in moderate form and with proper interpretation, all of them could be considered appropriate to the gospel and of little hindrance to adults' interpretation of Christian beliefs. But some of these values, in certain forms, could distort judgment about interpretation. For example, when a group of adults assumes that everyone can be a success—as measured in terms of money or status—if they will just work hard enough, we have a serious problem. Is measurement of money or status appropriate? From a Christian point of view, success could be living a good life with low income and a simple job.

A more complex illustration is that of rational planning. Congregations by their very nature are communities of people—organized for various functions—that own property and have relationships with the business community. None of this system for supporting congregational life would be possible without insurance, bank accounts, employees, and other forms of rational planning. Yet if the mentality expressed in rational planning becomes the basis for judging religious situations, we have allowed this socially determined value to define the gospel. From a rational point of view, church officers may need to curtail some of the congregation's work for lack of funds, but the curtailment may not happen if the faithful people understand the problem and are led by the Spirit to increase their giving.

Other common predispositions are the condescending attitudes some men hold toward women; the belief that poor people must somehow have failed to take hold of their opportunities; the feeling that there must be something good or right in anything that is successful; the idea that misfortune is punishment for misdeeds and goodness is always rewarded; the belief that God has planned all aspects of our lives and we have only to be compliant. There may be some truth in all these assumptions, but because they are predispositions by which some people make decisions, we need to examine them carefully.

Examining these and other assumptions formed by personal experience is threatening to our well-being. Occasionally people have an experience that jolts a prejudice out of their unconsciousness into the light of day where they can examine it and change it if necessary. But ordinarily the only practical way to work on this aspect of our lives is through group discussion of specific topics. If the CSG allows time for small-group discussion and encourages people to say *why* they hold the positions they do, gradually their assumptions will get out into the open where they can be discussed with the same seriousness as other ideas under consideration. This process is natural and nonthreatening and can help people become more objective about themselves and therefore more open to other views. However, if more aggressive means are judged desirable, the consciousness-raising methods used by women's groups to help women see themselves more objectively may be used. Or if a group wants a more militant model of consciousness-raising, examples can be obtained from South American educators who have helped peasants become aware of their human dignity in spite of oppressive economic conditions.[6] Regardless of methods, though, we will never be completely objective about our own religious beliefs. The goals of this process are only an examination of our assumptions and an openness to the leading of the Holy Spirit.

Summary

At this point, the strategy of this edification model of congregational life should be clear, but I would like to summarize it in linear form.

1. The strategy starts with a CSG of adults who are officers, leaders, and teachers of the congregation. The officers will interpret the purpose and mission of the congregation through the way they receive members, raise money and allocate its use, select ministers, set and administer policies for employed personnel and use of property, decide the relationship of the congregation to other religious groups in the community, and in other ways create the corporate personality of the congregation.

2. The leaders and teachers, through church school classes, youth groups, and other activity groups, will influence other segments of the congregation.

3. The adults in the CSG will have some influence with the adult members of the congregation who are not very active in the congregation or who need spiritual guidance from a friend they trust and with whom they feel free to discuss matters of faith.

4. The adults in the CSG, and other adults in the congregation who have come under its influence, will have some effect on the community. This effect will range from one person's influence on another at the workplace to owners' and managers' policies that affect hundreds of people. Such individual influence is different from the role of the congregation in community affairs. Although Christian groups may be

neither large nor traditionally powerful, we must constantly point out that Christians have an effect on and responsibility for the community's general welfare. This includes efforts that individual Christians can make to improve public schools, provide affordable housing, and in other ways create a better community.

5. The adults who are in the CSG and those who are influenced by the congregation's worship and work are also the parents and guardians of children and youth. Although the home is not now as influential in the lives of children as it was in the nineteenth century, it is still the strongest influence on the religious and moral development of children.

Some church leaders in recent decades have almost given up on the home as a place where children learn a religious life-style and social values. They usually cite as evidence a lack of supervision because both parents work, the secular view of life portrayed by most TV programs, and the corroding effect of peer groups. Although the evidence cited is true, this analysis wrongly assumes that children are learning about life in a new and different way.

The way children learn religion and morals has not changed since the Shema was written three thousand years ago. What has changed is the parents' and guardians' values; many of these adults rate high income above child care, unregulated use of TV as a pacifier above personal time with their children, and convenient neighborhood groups above a careful selection of playmates. Things will not change until parents and guardians reorder their values and give their children the attention they need and deserve. The congregation is the place where parents can sort out these values and receive support as they reorder them to develop the proper environment for their children.

Illustrations: The Congregation at Corinth

The notion of the congregation—rather than the Sunday school—as the agency for communicating the meaning of faith is relatively easy to see in the small congregation of a sect where only worship and a few congregational activities take place. There the interaction of adults formulates the meaning of their faith and transmits it dynamically to both children and converts. Our problem in mainstream Protestant congregations is to establish a center where we can generate a practical theology for our situation and in that process influence the mentality of members devoted to seeking and doing God's will.[7]

Before I make some practical suggestions about how modern American congregations can change their strategy and help members mature in their faith, I would like to compare the main arguments of this book with the first written record of a Christian congregation. We cannot move with precision from the church at Corinth to a congregation in the United States, but we can identify the principles Paul used and apply them to our situation.

Paul's earliest letter, to the church at Thessalonica about A.D. 52, mainly answers theological questions; it does not tell us very much about congregational life. However, Paul's first letter to the Corinthians gives us a better glimpse of what went on in a congregation. About 50 A.D. Paul founded the church in Corinth, where he lived for about eighteen months—longer than with any other church he founded except the one in Ephesus, from which he wrote this first letter to the Corinthians about A.D. 54. Reading First Corinthians will show us Paul's strategy for communicating Christian beliefs and for helping people become more mature in their faith.

1. Paul considered the congregation to be a place where individuals learned to practice their faith. When he pointed out sinful behavior in an individual, he looked to the congregation to mourn for this person and to discipline him or her (1 Cor. 5:1–2). If there was controversy between members, they were to resolve the matter in the church (1 Cor. 6:1–6). Paul reported that he spoke in tongues more than the Corinthians did; but the implication is that he did so in private, whereas in a congregation he would rather speak five intelligible words than thousands of words without meaning (1 Cor. 14:18–19). In the congregation one should be concerned for the nurturing of other believers rather than for showing off one's private religious life.

2. Paul respected the culturally formed mind-set of the Greeks and interpreted the gospel within those assumptions. This task must have challenged all his resources, for he had no training for this complex endeavor. Paul was a Pharisee, the son of Pharisees (Acts 23:6), educated to be a rabbi under one of the most famous teachers of his day (Acts 22:3), and extremely zealous in the Jewish tradition (Gal. 1:14). But here he was in Corinth, an important Greek city and capital of the Roman province of Achaia. His Jewish background was of little help in understanding the mind of the Greeks. These people came to the Christian congregation with assorted Greek ideas of gods, philosophy, and mystery religions in which ecstatic speaking was given special preference.

One illustration concerns the Corinthian understanding of religion. Paul's instructions about baptism and the Lord's Supper corrected the Greek ideas that these sacraments were magic (1 Cor. 10:1–13). And the Corinthians' behavior at the Lord's Supper was so boisterous that Paul had to remind them of the reasons for this sacrament, the way to administer it, and the proper attitude toward it (1 Cor. 11:17–34). Paul's discussion of conscience shows how he had to deal with Greek mentality in relation to the Gospel. "Conscience" is not a biblical word. It is not in the Old Testament, and it was not in the New Testament until the Greeks in Corinth reported that they felt guilty about eating meat offered to idols (1 Cor. 8:1–13).[8] The biblical word that relates to the same human experience is "heart," but the biblical idea of heart is much more profound, for it is the center of a person's affections and is related to God.[9] The Greeks came to church feeling uneasy, because in Greek society one sensed a prick of conscience when one failed to do what was commonly accepted.[10] Thus some newly converted Greeks thought that as Christians they should not eat meat that had been sacrificed in pagan temples or their conscience would hurt. Other Greek converts—knowing that idols were nothing—had no scruples about eating such meat. Paul's response to this situation is brilliant. While respecting the workings of conscience in these Greek Christians' minds, at the same time he shows the people that freedom in Christ means responsibility for helping fellow Christians in the congregation become more mature in their faith. Paul's brilliance is not restricted to his theological maneuvering—it appears also in the way this life situation was to become the curriculum that would mature the faith of the whole congregation.

3. Within a congregational context, Paul unified experience with tradition. He claimed his Jewish tradition as "a Hebrew born of Hebrews" (Phil. 3:4–7), and he used his extensive knowledge of Hebrew scripture to the last day of his career (Acts 28:23–31) Paul's conversion experience affirmed the necessity of an experience of God's grace in one's life. In Paul's case the experience was a theophany that had all the characteristics of religious experience discussed in Part Two of this book (Acts 9:1–22). The unification is summarized in Paul's conclusion to his Corinthian letter, where he proclaims the terms on which he preached and ministered and on which the people were saved: "that Christ died for our sins in accordance with the scriptures" (1 Cor. 15:3). The first part of that phrase insists that a person must have experience with Christ to be a Christian; the second part affirms the role of tradition in validating experience.

The unity Paul exhibits is of critical importance for a perennial problem—the relation of reason to faith, law to grace, or tradition to experience. In each pair one element is primarily of the mind: reason, law, tradition. We treat these elements with a certain amount of objectivity. The other elements—faith, grace, experience—are primarily of the sentiments. We realize, at least dimly, that these elements are the result of relationships we have with our parents, peers, relatives, and other significant persons in our past. Trying to put the two elements in a workable harmony is very difficult. So we often allow our faith to exist in a childlike, immature state, while our reason is being trained and stimulated to make us productive, competitive individuals in business or professional life. We accept law in the sense of a "right" moral code to be used in dealing with people in general, and we restrict grace to our family or small-group relations. Perhaps, like Paul before his conversion, we vigorously object when anyone does not interpret religious tradition exactly as we do without trying to understand the experience they claim to have had with God (Acts 7:54—8:1). There is no solution to this problem·as long as the elements are separate; it cannot be solved by thinking or acting alone. To the extent that the problem can be solved, it must be done as Paul told the Corinthians: individual Christians gathered in the congregation must help each other subordinate themselves to God as revealed in Jesus Christ. The whole letter is written from this point of view. For example, in chapter 1 where Paul is dealing with the quarreling going on among members because some preferred Apollos while others preferred Cephas, Paul reminds the Corinthians that because of their baptism their first loyalty is now to Christ. In chapter 12 he uses the body as an illustration of how the parts work harmoniously under the direction of the head, with no part of the body being superior to another part simply because it has a special function. What is important is the proper functioning of the entire body under the head—which is Christ.

4. Paul expected the congregation to generate practical theology about its life situations. The issue of ecstatic speaking in Corinth is a good illustration, for it combines many of the other points and shows how an issue in a particular congregation has to be dealt with. Paul first addresses this issue in chapter 12, where he differentiates the work of the Holy Spirit from the ecstatic speaking that the Greeks brought with them from their "heathen" past (1 Cor. 12:2). In the famous chapter 13 he singles out love as the greatest gift of the Spirit. Then in chapter 14 he becomes more specific, giving the criteria by which the congregation is to make judgments. He uses the word "prophecies" in chapter 14 to mean sermons, explanations, or teaching. Spoken prophecies in the congregation are for (1) edification, (2) encouragement, and (3) consolation. The idea that the group should work to build up the congregation, mentioned earlier in Paul's discussion about food offered to idols (1 Cor. 8:1 and 10:23), is repeated in this chapter both as the major goal for members (1 Cor. 14:12) and as a summary of everything a congregation should do (1 Cor. 14:26).

Wayne Meeks, in his recent study of the earliest Christian assemblies, pays special attention to Paul's concern for "building up" the proper ethos by "teaching and admonition" in Corinth and in other churches he established. This formation of Christian ethos, or way of life, was the function of the whole congregation by means of all of the things the members did—singing, reading psalms, using special theological language, discussing issues, and interacting with one another in their assembly. The by-product of such activity was cohesion, but the congregation's goal was to build itself up as a community of believers.[11] Meeks also points out that Paul's letter revealed the assembly as an informal meeting. There was oral give-and-take on topics about which members had to make decisions. Strangers came in off the street to see what was going on in those meetings, and Christians had a responsibility to discuss sensibly with them the meaning of faith in Christ (1 Cor. 14:23–25).[12]

These meetings were designed to be educational. Speaking in tongues was permitted if what was said was intelligible (1 Cor. 14:6–9); if it was not intelligible, an interpreter was required. Otherwise, such people must keep silence in the church (1 Cor. 14:26–28). Members were not to separate faith from reason. Prayer, for example, was to be of the spirit and mind, and singing was to be done with the mind as well as the voice (1 Cor. 14:15). Paul made a strong appeal to the Christians in Corinth to work on the issue of speaking in tongues during their congregational meetings. He challenged them to abandon childish reactions, "but in thinking be mature" (1 Cor. 14:20) about this matter. He then suggested ideas for congregational discussion that would help members mature in this aspect of their faith.

These four principles were Paul's way of helping a group of Christians become a community in, but not of, the world. There are some parallels with our situation today, as mainstream Protestants come to realize that the period of a "Christian" America is over. For the foreseeable future we must learn both to define ourselves as Christians and to critique the secular culture in which we live. Moreover, the Corinthian church is an excellent illustration of the role of conflict in this enterprise as described in chapter 9. Because of the conflicts in that congregation we have the words instituting the Lord's Supper, the discussion of church administration, the famous chapter on love, and the mental image of how a congregation is to generate practical theology.

New Beginnings

This congregational strategy will be most easily planned for congregations where a new beginning is possible. This would include both new congregations and small congregations where the members know each other so well they can keep their fellowship intact while they reformulate the work of the congregation. The following practical suggestions for using the congregation as the agency of education may help stimulate such congregations to make plans that fit their special needs.

First, the minister with a small planning group will arrange for all the officers and interested adults to meet weekly for prayer and study. The topic or themes will be selected to fit the situation of the congregation, and a devotional booklet based on the topic may be prepared for home use. The minister will then plan Sunday worship, including the sermon, on the weekly topic. In a newly beginning church the group members may be uncertain about how much time to allow for work on different facets of a topic. These congregations should probably plan a year in advance in outline form, and the next three months in detail. When the planning committee members gain experience, they will project the study and reflection schedule with greater confidence.

The congregation's responsibility for those not in the CSG includes (1) adults who cannot attend or who do not want to be so deeply involved, (2) children, and (3) youth. One or more classes can be scheduled for the adults, and these should be led by an adult who participates in the CSG. But those classes are not to be a place where the leader just repeats the CSG's ideas or conclusions; the leader should conduct these adult classes just as the minister or leader conducts the CSG—that is, as an open inquiry into the topic. It is possible—and highly desirable—that the adult classes may arrive at different conclusions or bring up points that should be reported to the CSG, for edification is a process in which all people have a part.

Concerning the Christian nurture of children, two problems need special attention. One is children's vast difference in stages of mental and emotional development, a situation that requires some grouping by ages. The other problem follows from the first: the material for children needs to be suitable to their developmental level. We cannot easily adapt for the children what the adults are discussing. The best solution to both of these problems would be for a small group of adults from the CSG to prepare lesson guides on some part of the CSG theme for the children's groups. This would create a situation in which every planned aspect of the congregational educational work was supporting and enhancing the other.

However, since creating curriculum week by week for children is beyond the ability of most congregations, some compromise must be worked out. One way would be to use the denominational curriculum for children up to about ten or twelve years of age; some plan should then be proposed to involve the parents so they will understand and reinforce the ideas discussed in the children's classes. The parents, for example, could have monthly meetings and go over the children's lessons for the next month. Alternatively, each Sunday the children could take home leaflets about things that could be done in the home—stories, prayers, or projects—about which they report the following Sunday.

The best thing the church can offer young people is a chance to be together in a group with some friendly, interested, Christian adults. Most beginning churches are in the 100- to 300-member range, so the number of teenagers will not be large. Decisions regarding whether there should be a younger teenage group and an older one, what day of the week they should meet, and so forth are all subject to community conditions.

According to the thesis of this book, these youngsters should be an organic part of the congregation. They should be treated as young members and given leadership positions in worship and administration in line with their abilities and interests. With a CSG adult as their study leader, they too can become involved in the reflective thinking going on at the center of the congregation's life. Being involved does not mean merely receiving from the CSG stimulation and material for thought; the youth group should respond to topics from their own perspective, and those responses should be given to the CSG as part of their ongoing consideration. On some topics the CSG may ask the young people to study a specific issue and then come to the CSG as a group to share their ideas and participate in a discussion. The purpose is to demonstrate the value of each part of the body of Christ as long as each part is seeking to follow Christ as head. Other ways for teenagers to relate to the CSG and yet have opportunity to test their ideas among themselves will emerge as congregations gain experience in using education to further the church's mission rather than as an end in itself.

The youth group should not, however, consider its role in the congregation as limited to its association with the CSG. During the teen years, individuals slowly develop an image of who they are and what they want to be. To do this extremely important psychological work they have to evaluate all they have learned in the home, and from their parents, and test themselves as they try out new or somewhat different self-images. This places them in tension with their families. Needing support and assistance, they turn to one another and form small groups in which they talk and act their way through various possibilities. Life is complex nowadays, and many life-styles are paraded before the teenagers. As a result, few adolescents come through their teenage years with a clearcut image of who they are and what they want to be. This process of forming a conscious selfhood with which one is pleased is now extending well into the third decade of a person's life. Thus young people have special needs for belonging to a group in which they can work on themselves as well as on the meaning of the Christian faith.

Conventional Congregations

Because most congregations of mainstream denominations are conventional, they develop a suitable program that they continue from year to year. The program does not necessarily remain the same, but changes usually evolve slowly from previous experience. If a church has a record of a good vacation Bible school, the odds are high that the school will be continued. If there is an adult Bible class Sunday morning for women and another for men, this pattern will most likely endure. And if the congregation has regular church suppers, probably the members who attend will keep coming even if the program is not always to their liking.

Conventional congregations also develop a way of being together as a community. Certain people are expected to take the lead in new or different ventures; others routinely make or clear decisions, even if they do not hold official status. Some people who make substantial contributions of money will give little time to the work of the church, and there are always those who contribute little time or money but nevertheless complain about almost everything that happens. Members learn to understand and accept these human situations and relationships as they constantly adjust to one another.

Conventional congregations, furthermore, are not dead churches. The Christian faith is likely to be alive and well in many members and in some of the church groups. The institutional nature of adult Bible classes just referred to is well known, but why are the classes like this? Probably it is because adults in those classes have over a period of years shared a great deal of their life with one another and have learned mutual trust. If this is the case, we have much to learn from such classes in how Christians can care for one another. In worship— through music, scripture, prayers, or sermon—people may gain a perspective on their life that they do not find anywhere else. Moreover, the sacraments communicate the meaning of life and death in ways so profound that we are unable adequately to describe them. If we characterize the congregation as a place where people can find a sense of community not available elsewhere and as an institution that stands for the higher qualities of life, the congregation has an impressive set of experiences to offer its members.

The question is not whether conventional congregations provide the gospel and a program for communicating their beliefs, but how they are responding to God, the source and object of faith. Responding to the living God means that conventional congregational ways will be subject to critical analysis and the members will be open to the leading of the Holy Spirit. Both matters are difficult for a conventional congregation. If the congregation is getting along rather well, why should members question what they are doing? And the idea of being open to new ways of being Christ's body in the community is surrounded with anxiety. As a result, the momentum of tradition makes it easier to continue conventional programs than to change.

Changing Conventional Congregations

Conventional congregations can be led to a new understanding of themselves as agencies by which the Christian faith is interpreted and lived. The first requirement is a small group with a vision of what the congregation can be and do. The ministers must be involved in this small group, or the efforts to change will be thwarted at every turn. Normally the movement to change would be a matter of conversation between ministers and some officers and lay leaders on topics (such as those treated in this book) related to the circumstances of the particular church. If this small group envisions its congregation's becoming a more counterculture community working out a practical theology, then there will be a base from which changes can be made.

The second requirement is the establishment of a CSG. Although the exact nature of this group will vary widely, its role in upbuilding the congregation is essential. Here are several suggestions for starting a CSG in a conventional congregation.

1. The ministers could start a Bible study class to which officers and certain lay leaders were invited. In time it would be informally understood that officers and teachers normally were selected from this pool of adults.

2. A Bible study or practical theology class could be established for officers. This has the advantage of dealing directly with the elected leaders, but it excludes other leaders and teachers.

3. In some congregations with few adult classes, or where the custom is to rearrange the classes annually, the ministers might set up a CSG and other adult groups for special concerns. For example, in most conventional congregations there are older adults who want to study the Bible their own way. This desire should be met. In some fast-growing urban areas there may be young adults who are so preoccupied with their personal or family situation that they need a support group where they can get a foundation of basic Christian beliefs. If so, then such a group should be provided, perhaps connected with the CSG through leaders.

The third requirement is for changes to be introduced gradually. Proposals for quick change or for a thorough reorganization of a conventional congregation seldom succeed. After the initial enthusiasm wears off, people most often go back to their old way of doing things. Unfortunately, such an experience lingers in the minds of members, and they become more resistant to change; thus it is important to introduce changes gradually and absorb their repercussions before going on to further change.

I do not want to give the impression that congregations are unusual in this regard. It is difficult to make significant changes in any social institution because we do not know exactly how intended changes will work out. Those who have studied the process of decision making in institutions have concluded that the more the managers know about the desired changes, the goal to be achieved, ways to achieve it, and the side effects, the smaller the change will be. For example, if officers want to change the start of Sunday worship from 10:45 A.M. to 11:00 A.M., they know how to do it and what most of the repercussions will be. But that change is small. The greater the change that managers want to make in a social institution, the less clear their understanding about the procedure for doing so. If the ministers and officers want to start a CSG with the implications described in this book, the results are going to be uncertain. Setting up a CSG would not be difficult, but will the members who do not attend the CSG understand its purpose? Will some members leave the congregation because the congregation is getting too serious about religion? Some Sunday school classes and groups in the congregation are accustomed to doing what they want to do—how will they respond to this effort to focus attention on life situation themes? There is no way to answer these and other questions except as such a decision is played out in the life of a congregation.

Because efforts to make significant changes in social institutions are so fraught with uncertainty, David Braybrooke and Charles E. Lindblom came to the conclusion that progress in human affairs should be made by "disjointed incrementalism." That is, decision makers should take small steps toward a goal; then they should stop and consider where they are before they take the next step. The process is disjointed because managers often have to make changes in a section of a social institution when there is an opportunity, rather than when they think it should be done.[13]

The idea of change by disjointed incrementalism fits the conventional congregation. If some form of a CSG is established and is reasonably successfull in generating a practical theology in the congregation, opportunities will emerge for taking small steps toward the goal of church edification. Progress will be slow, for this is a conservative method of making change. But what progress is made will be secure.[14]

Modifying Conventional Congregations

This section is for ministers and lay leaders in conventional congregations where it is not possible to establish a CSG, yet the leaders want to move toward the congregation edification model. It is possible in such congregations to bring about some connections between life situations and Christian beliefs and to relate the results to the congregation so that everyone's life is enriched and confirmed in the faith. The following illustration and suggestions come from a variety of situations. The events described fall short of the edification model because they do not connect to a center that is constantly generating practical theology, but they do represent an effort to take the congregation seriously as the place where we must make meaning out of our faith.

1. Some congregations during Advent or Lent plan a total congregational effort to focus attention on the theme of the season. These programs may coordinate the most obvious elements of congregational life: worship, preaching, and teaching youth and adult classes around weekly topics supported by scripture. The strength of these efforts lies in the way one element enhances and elaborates the others. The study programs provide intellectual exploration; the worship and preaching provide engagement of heart, mind, and will. Since these elements take place over time and in different settings, the effect accumulates.

I have seen some of these seasonal efforts at thematic focus attempt an even further coordination of congregational life. In one congregation a family devotional guide was supplied and promoted throughout the Sunday school. Because Sunday school classes were related to the devotional booklet, everybody was involved with the theme of the week. Another congregation selected prints of classic Christian art that illustrated the weekly topic and displayed them throughout the building. References were made to the paintings in the Sunday school classes. This congregation, during the Lenten season, also had a local drama group perform a play appropriate for the theme, and a discussion of the play was scheduled for the following Sunday by each class except that of the youngest children. Thus a congregation—over a period of time, through various ways of experiencing truth, and in different settings—can intensify learning opportunities.

2. Ministers in conventional congregations are allowed to take initiative within their role as designated leader. One minister of a church of about fifteen hundred members has developed a system for relating to parts of the congregation through a set of Bible classes. He projects a study of a book of the Bible about six to eight months in advance. On Tuesday noon he meets in a midtown hotel for lunch with business and professional people, and within the confines of an hour he discusses the book bit by bit, leaving some time for questions and comments. This class has the outward appearance of a Bible study; but it also plays an evangelistic role, for members can bring their friends from work. On Wednesday afternoons, this minister uses the same biblical passage with the youth group. In the light of his study and of the responses from the adult and youth groups, he prepares his sermon for Sunday on this same passage. The people involved in these groups look forward to the sermon because they are already mentally and emotionally involved in the text.

Another minister offered to preach one Sunday each month on any topic the young people suggested, if on Sunday evening he could meet with them and discuss the topic and the sermon in more detail. This simple device illustrates the latent power in edification-type education. The youngsters were reminded from week to week to think about what they wanted the minister to discuss; two weeks in advance they spent a whole meeting sharing ideas and coming to a consensus on the topic they wanted to propose to the minister. On the Sunday when the sermon was to address their topic, they all sat in the front row and took notes, thus learning how to listen to a sermon. Then on Sunday evening when the minister and the young people engaged in serious conversation about the Christian faith, the minister was able to be both a friend and a teacher. An unexpected side effect was the interest of parents, for most of them had not previously known what kinds of religious questions were uppermost in the minds of their teenagers.

3. Throughout this book I have considered educational activity as a function not to be separated from the congregation's purpose and mission. Because worship is the center of congregational life and is its most unifying act, I would like to indicate how education can serve in the worship service.

Many congregations have a time in Sunday worship for children, but far too often the minister uses this time to elicit "cute" comments from children to amuse the adults. Such efforts show that the minister thinks of the congregation more as an audience than as a community. Other ministers, viewing worship as a gathering of people before God, a time when all segments of the congregation have a chance to help according to their ability, see the children differently. They may arrange with leaders of a children's class to write a prayer or litany for use in the worship. This will require two or three weeks' work in their Sunday school class. When the litany is used in worship the children will lead it, and their names will be in the bulletin as the writers. Written in simple words and from children's experience, the litany is the children's honest offering to God—something they do in and for the congregation. Although they are functioning at their developmental level, what they are doing is a contribution to the ongoing worship service. Thus the worship service is not compromised.

Other groups in the congregation can from time to time prepare prayers, music, or even sermons for the upbuilding of the community. Such activities keep before our minds the whole body of Christ and help us learn from one another.

Eight Questions and Answers

1. Does this emphasis on the congregation as the agency of education downplay the role of teaching?

No The congregation as agency is a strategy in which teaching is central. The strategy requires a CSG. By its makeup and method the CSG can be a way to generate practical theology for a congregation. Since the work of the CSG is study focused on topics that matter to the congregation, teaching and learning are more important in a congregation using this edification model than in a congregation where teaching is not coordinated with congregational needs.

2. This idea of faith maturing through edification requires that ministers teach. If ministers believe they are not good at teaching, what can be done?

This question opens up such an important area that I would like to divide the answer into two parts.

First, if ministers believe they are not good at teaching because of inexperience or poor results from previous attempts, remedial action is appropriate. It may be of some help to ministers' self-understanding to recall that Jesus was always referred to by friends, enemies, and disciples as "teacher." Paul's work is constantly described as teaching, especially when he stayed in a town for any length of time. Teaching is not something added to preaching but is, rather, a somewhat different way to communicate the gospel. With that understanding, ministers who feel uneasy about teaching should regard the matter just as they would any other area of ministerial competence—such as counseling or fund-raising—in which they need practice or advice. Some help can be found in seminary-sponsored continuing education events; however, the best help at the least cost is usually close at hand. Inquiry among nearby ministers can net a list of those who enjoy teaching adults and are so engaged, and consultation with those ministers will provide the help and encouragement necessary to start regular teaching. If ministers initially feel inadequate, they should remember that they had those same feelings when they first started preaching, but they kept preaching until they had those feelings under control.

Second, if ministers believe they are not good at teaching because teaching is a specialty, a reinterpretation is necessary. Teaching adults is an activity that can be greatly improved if one understands the learning situation of adults and knows how to arrange a presentation in an interesting way. But teaching adults, like preaching, can be learned from experience because it involves skills that are already a part of what a minister does. Moreover, adults come to a Bible or theology class looking for truth about life and death, so they are not overly concerned with carefully programmed presentations. Adults are more interested in substance than in style. They are more concerned with participation in a serious discussion than with overhead projectors outlining a logical progression of ideas. Ministers can do good teaching if they keep in mind that they are holding a conversation with adults in which they are engaging life situations with the Christian faith.

Some ministers may think there is a certain "right" way to teach and they will be open to criticism if they do not do it accordingly. Those who have made a careful study of teaching do not hold such a view, for they know there is no single "right" way to teach.[15] Rather, there are models of teaching, each of which has methods and a goal. Teaching is so closely associated with the personality, interest, and enthusiasm of the teacher that it can more properly be described as a form of art than as a set procedure. Moreover, few teachers are good at all models. Teachers of teachers usually advise persons to try out various ways and find the way they enjoy. Then teachers can refine their skills—as lecturers, discussion leaders, or whatever style they prefer.[16] Ministers should realize that there are styles of teaching just as there are styles of preaching. The "right" style is the one a minister can do well.

3. Can someone other than the minister lead the CSG?

The key word in the question is "lead." If the question assumes the CSG to be an adult class that any qualified person can lead, the answer is "no." If the question means that the ministers are deeply involved in every aspect of the CSG and preside at the study sessions, it is possible that for *some* segments of study someone else could be the teacher. Ministers, however, must feel that the CSG is as much their responsibility as are leading worship and preaching.

4. Ministers are already overworked; how can they add a regular teaching responsibility to their schedule?

Ministers are often overworked, but they complain more about being improperly employed than about long hours. The issue here is what is important for the spiritual leadership of a congregation. Teaching the CSG takes little more planning or study time because the sermon and suggestions for worship all come from the same preparation: ministers are simply sharing their study time with a group of adults. This type of planning and study is what ministers are trained to do, so they should get a sense of satisfaction out of a wider use of the time they are already spending in study. The composition of the CSG is such that ministers will have regular contact with the most interested members of the congregation. As these lay people mature in their faith, they will become increasingly well equipped to minister to others in the congregation (Eph. 4:11–16).

5. How does the edification model work if a congregation has several ministers, one of whom is an educational specialist?

If a congregation has more than one minister, it is fairly common for one to have educational responsibility. The critical factor is the job description. If one of the ministers has general duties and specific responsibility for the youth, there is no special problem fitting into this model. But if one of the ministers gives full time to the educational program, or if a church has a trained lay person as "Director of Christian Education," an understanding must be worked out. *The important thing is not to split the educational work from the ministerial leadership.* This means that the educational specialist must be involved with the other ministers in planning and managing the CSG. The exact role for the educator in the conduct of the CSG will depend on his or her abilities and interest. Since the CSG is a pool of the most interested adults, it will be a natural place for the minister of education to find and inspire teachers and group leaders.

6. Can this plan be used by a large church?

This plan as described is for churches of up to about a thousand members. If the congregation is much larger than that, the number of officers and interested adults becomes so large it is difficult to have a good educational exchange in the CSG. Some large churches have had success in building and maintaining a dynamic spiritual center, which accounts, I think, for their growth and vitality. Usually these large churches have a senior minister who has been the leader for a long time. Through teaching and preaching these senior ministers have been able to shape the spiritual outlook of an inner corps of members. That is, an informal kind of CSG has developed over the years to provide the congregation with stability and direction. So, large size itself is not necessarily a problem, but it is a condition that would have to be taken into consideration. If a church, for example, had six thousand members and five ministers, it might be possible for the ministers and a few members to plan the themes for a set of CSGs, each taught by one minister. This requires more coordination and planning, but churches of this size are accustomed to such organizations.

7. Since the CSG is required to deal with the mind-set or preconceptions that members bring to the study group, is the CSG designed to be a therapeutic experience?

No. Groups of people brought together for psychotherapy have a special goal; they focus on the needs of individuals. Such groups are formed and disbanded as needed. In contrast, the CSG is made up of the most active and interested people in a congregation. The CSG is rooted in the Christian tradition and dedicated to the task of making meaning out of events that are taking place. Members of the CSG are committed to create a community where faith in God is nurtured and to help each other throughout their life span.[17]

Individuals who participate in the CSG will probably experience some healing of psychological wounds as they become more mature in their faith. But such achievements are by-products of the interaction of people in the group, not its primary purpose. Even so, I am not sure we ought to label this experience "therapeutic," for that term connotes the healing of an individual—as a person might be cured of a disease. The CSG is one of the few places—if not the only place—in American life where people can discuss the meaning of faith in God and get a response from people they respect. Something profound happens when one compares one's self with the way one is perceived by others. Moreover, the way people relate to one another after they have struggled for ultimate meaning out of common experience is different from ordinary business, professional, or social relations. Under these conditions problems or issues become more "our" concerns, which require corporate understanding and cooperative action, than matters about which we take sides. These human responses can be given a psychological explanation, but they are not fostered for psychological reasons.

8. Congregational edification appears to depreciate the role of proclaiming the truth about Christ *(kerygma)*. Do not the New Testament sermons show that preaching is first and that teaching *(didache)* comes along in second place to explain the preaching and elaborate the practical aspects of faith?

Nc. There is no clear separation of kerygma and didache in the New Testament. James I. H. McDonald has reviewed all the studies of this matter since 1892 and has come to the conclusion that the New Testament does not separate these two modes of communication as we do. Kerygma and didache were actually joined or looked on as complementary ways of communicating the meaning of Jesus Christ. In fact, it is difficult to separate kerygma and didache material, for a statement can at the same time be intended to proclaim and to teach. McDonald identifies and traces the historical background of four types of preaching in the New Testament, and teaching is a normal part of each.[18]

McDonald concludes his study with a reminder that it was the congregation *(koinonia)* where the Christian message was received, believed, and tested in practical life situations. It was the congregation that had to translate the message "into intelligible terms for the purposes of edification (cf. 1 Cor. 14:1–19), evangelism and apologetic exposition (cf. Acts 2:14ff.)."[19]

Congregations have the same responsibility today. The issue is not whether preaching *or* teaching is the preferred means of communication of the gospel, but how congregations can become aware of the presence of Christ and become more dedicated to being the body of Christ in our secular society. A central study group formed for this purpose may be the way to turn our attention to the message and probe its meaning for the situations in which we have to make major decisions

A New Era

Our social situation in the last half of this century is vastly different from that in the first half of the nineteenth century, when the educational strategy of Protestant churches evolved, yet we continue to use that strategy as if little had changed.

Throughout the nineteenth century the established denominations grew in size and influence. Endowed with an evangelistic spirit from the Second Great Awakening, they educated their children and others in Sunday schools, held revivals for youth and adults, established schools if no public schools were available, and founded colleges and seminaries to train leaders for church and society. The evangelistic spirit with its underlying theism motivated denominations to found new congregations as people moved west to establish a "righteous empire." Congregations helped settle people into communities, provided meaning for their venture of faith, and contributed to the development of social institutions needed for an ordered life. The influence of these denominations extended well into the twentieth century, as congregations helped many millions of immigrants to secure a place for themselves in American society.

Today our social situation is different in almost every respect. The land is settled. Slavery has been abolished, and civil rights for all people are a matter of law. The pattern of life is urban rather than rural. The economic order is now a government-regulated form of capitalism, and the United States has become a world power with all the resulting political and psychological problems. Science and technology dominate our national agenda for both economic and defense purposes. State universities and well-endowed private universities so influence higher education that most church-related colleges offer an education almost indistinguishable from that of secular schools. Media communication, especially television, is profit-oriented and therefore either entertains or mirrors back to the consumer the values it finds to be commercially viable.

A student of history—I think it was Wilhelm Dilthey—said that to understand a historical era one needed to identify the "spell" under which it unfolded. The early nineteenth century was under the spell of evangelical Christianity. But the spiritual momentum from that era has almost played out, and the late twentieth century has increasingly come under the spell of secularism. This secularism is expressed in the schools by their deliberate avoidance of religion, in government through its neutrality toward religion, in higher education by its dedication to rational inquiry, and in popular culture by its appeal to the senses. Even religion has felt its influence.

Can this spell be broken? Yes, it can be broken when people learn to examine their experiences critically in the light of the Bible and

Christian tradition. This kind of learning is extremely subtle, because it involves adults as they relate to a community of believers, and it subordinates individuals to the task of building up the congregation so that it more adequately represents Christ's ministry in the world. Such learning is also slow and difficult, because it requires individuals to change their life-style toward a greater harmony with the values of the faith to which the congregation is dedicated. This "congregational edification" strategy, with all its problems, responds to the present social situation. It focuses attention on the community of believers so that children, youth, and converts will have a fellowship from which they can draw the spiritual guidance they need.

Notes

Chapter 1: Introduction

1. Don S. Browning, *Practical Theology* (San Francisco: Harper & Row, 1983). For a different perspective see Johannes A. Van Der Ven, "Practical Theology: From Applied to Empirical Theology," *Journal of Empirical Theology* 1(1):7–29 (1988).

2. In an earlier book I discussed how the social situation forms a person and how a congregation can use that process to shape the faith of its members. See C. Ellis Nelson, *Where Faith Begins* (Richmond: John Knox Press, 1967).

3. Nelle G. Slater, ed., *Tensions Between Citizenship and Discipleship: A Case Study* (New York: Pilgrim Press, 1989).

Chapter 2: Our Age of Secular Individualism

1. This was written in June 1987, when the Supreme Court handed down its ruling in the Ardith McPherson case. Ms. McPherson was an employee in the constable's office in Houston, Texas. On March 30, 1981 (the day President Reagan was shot), she said to a co-worker, "I hope if they go for him again, they get him." For this she was fired. The Supreme Court ruled she had a "free-speech right" to make that statement and ordered a lower court to provide "an appropriate remedy."

2. *The World Almanac and Book of Facts* (New York: Newspaper Enterprise Association, 1985), p. 610.

3. Walter Prescott Webb, *The Great Frontier* (London: Secker & Warburg, 1953).

4. *Webster's Third New International Dictionary* (Springfield, Mass.: G. & C. Merriam Co., 1961), paraphrased.

5. Sigmund Freud, *The Future of an Illusion* (New York: W. W. Norton & Co., 1975). For a general overview of Freud's writings about religion see Ernest Jones, *The Life and Work of Sigmund Freud*, Vol. 3 (New York: Basic Books, 1957), pp. 349–375.

6. Karl Marx and Friedrich Engels, *On Religion* (New York: Schocken Books, 1964).

7. Bryan Wilson, *Contemporary Transformations of Religion* (Oxford: Oxford University Press, 1976).

8. John A. Coleman, "The Situation for Modern Faith," *Theological Studies* 39: 601–632 (Dec. 1978). For an overview of secularization from a somewhat different point of view see Meredith B. McGuire, *Religion: The Social Context* (Belmont, Calif.: Wadsworth Press, 1981), ch. 8.

9. Evangelical groups make this point. See the Lausanne Occasional Papers No. 8, *Christian Witness to Secularized People* (Wheaton, Ill.: Lausanne Committee for World Evangelization, 1980), pp. 6–7.

10. Talcott Parsons, "Christianity and Modern Industrial Society," in James F. Childress and David B. Harned, *Secularization and the Protestant Prospect* (Philadelphia: Westminster Press, 1970).

11. Andrew M. Greeley, *Unsecular Man* (New York: Dell Publishing Co., 1974).

12. Robert N. Bellah, *Beyond Belief* (New York: Harper & Row, 1970), p. 246. See also p. 227 for his reason why religion will continue to be of major interest for humankind.

13. Mary Douglas, "The Effects of Modernization on Religious Change," in *Religion and America*, ed. Mary Douglas and Steven Tipton (Boston: Beacon Press, 1983), pp. 26–27, 32.

14. Peter L. Berger, *A Rumor of Angels* (Garden City, N.Y.: Doubleday & Co., 1969), pp. 49–75. Compare his essay "A Sociological View of the Secularization of Theology" in his *Facing Up to Modernity* (New York: Basic Books, 1977), pp. 162–182.

15. Thomas Luckmann, *The Invisible Religion* (New York: Macmillan Co., 1967), pp. 36–49, 69–76, 90–91.

16. Alasdair MacIntyre, *Secularization and Moral Change* (London: Oxford University Press, 1967), p. 32.

17. Gerhard Ebeling, *Word and Faith* (Philadelphia: Fortress Press, 1963), p. 364.

18. Harry Emerson Fosdick, *A Guide to Understanding the Bible* (New York: Harper & Brothers, 1938).

19. Norman Karol Gottwald, *The Tribes of Yahweh* (Maryknoll, N.Y.: Orbis Books, 1979).

20. Thomas H. Olbricht, "Intellectual Ferment and Instruction in the Scripture: The Bible in Higher Education," in *The Bible in American Education*, ed. David L. Barr and Nicholas Piediscalzi (Philadelphia: Fortress Press, 1982), p. 108.

21. The trial was a series of events beginning in 1890 with an attack on Briggs's theology in a church paper. The matter became a case before the 1891 General Assembly and was concluded when the 1893 General Assembly suspended Briggs from the office of minister. See Robert T. Handy, *A History of Union Theological Seminary in New York 1836–1986* (New York: Columbia University Press, 1987), pp. 69–93. The substance of the charges and Briggs's defense will be found in Charles A. Briggs, *Inaugural Address and Defense* (New York: Arno Press, 1972).

22. So that this chapter not be too long, I have restricted my comments to the effect of reason on our understanding of history. A more comprehensive review of the ideas that form the mentality of twentieth-century Americans

would include the theory of evolution (Charles Darwin), the origin and power of the unconscious mind (Sigmund Freud), the central role of economics in society (Karl Marx), and the social source of mind and self (George H. Mead). These theories provide a secular answer to some of our most important questions. This does not mean that such theories are necessarily opposed to Christianity just because their authors were atheists. It does mean, however, that Christians are required to do their thinking about God in an intellectual environment in which God has become more remote, more elusive, and less important for practical decisions. I have examined this matter in more detail in the essay, "Religious Education? Yes, Indeed!" in *Does the Church Really Want Religious Education?*, ed. Marlene Mayr (Birmingham, Ala.: Religious Education Press, 1987).

23. Thomas Jefferson, *The Life and Morals of Jesus of Nazareth* (New York: N. D. Thompson Publishing Co., 1902).

24. John H. Westerhoff III, *McGuffey and His Readers* (Nashville: Abingdon Press, 1978), p. 13.

25. Paul C. Vitz, *Censorship: Evidence of Bias in Our Children's Textbooks* (Ann Arbor, Mich.: Servant Books, 1986).

26. Douglas and Tipton, *Religion and America*, p. ix.

27. Ibid., p. 3.

28. Don S. Browning, *Religious Ethics and Pastoral Care* (Philadelphia: Fortress Press, 1983), pp. 31–41.

29. Douglas and Tipton, *Religion and America*, p. 5.

30. Robert N. Bellah et al., *Habits of the Heart* (Berkeley, Calif.: University of California Press, 1985), p. 29.

31. Ibid., p. viii.

32. Ibid., p. 221.

33. Robert Wuthnow, *The Restructuring of American Religion* (Princeton, N.J.: Princeton University Press, 1988), pp. 55–57.

34. Robert T. Handy describes Protestant religion of 1860–1890 as "The Religion of Civilization," which in the 1890–1920 era led to "The Christian Conquest of the World." However, the 1890–1920 era overlapped with "The New Christianity" of the social gospel. See his *A Christian America* (New York: Oxford University Press, 1971), chapters 4, 5, and 6. For a favorable account of American liberal theology of the early twentieth century see Henry P. Van Dusen, *The Vindication of Liberal Theology* (New York: Charles Scribner's Sons, 1963).

35. "The Fundamentals" were a series of articles published in twelve booklets from 1910–1915. In 1917 they were published in four volumes now available under the title *The Fundamentals: A Testimony to the Truth*, ed. R. A. Torrey, A. D. Dixon, et al. (Grand Rapids: Baker Book House, 1973).

Chapter 3: Our Religious Experience

1. W. Allison Davis and Robert J. Havighurst, *Father of the Man* (Boston: Houghton Mifflin Co., 1947). A more recent study dealing with adults is Robert Kegan, *The Evolving Self* (Cambridge, Mass.: Harvard University Press, 1982).

2. Mary Douglas, ed., *Essays in the Sociology of Perception* (London: Routledge & Kegan Paul, 1982), p. 1.

3. C. Ellis Nelson, *Where Faith Begins* (Richmond: John Knox Press, 1967), pp. 35–66.

4. George DeVos, "Dimensions of the Self in Japanese Culture," in *Culture and Self,* ed. Anthony J. Marsella, George DeVos, and Francis L. K. Hsu (New York: Tavistock Publications, 1985), p. 149.

5. Ibid., p. 163.

6. Ibid., pp. 149–150. In addition to the chapter on the Japanese to which I referred there is a chapter on the Hindu self, the Western self, and the changing self-conception in China. For help on the cultural background of the American self see Sacvan Bercovitch, *The Puritan Origins of the American Self* (New Haven, Conn.: Yale University Press, 1975), and Robert N. Bellah et al., *Habits of the Heart* (Berkeley, Calif.: University of California Press, 1985).

7. DeVos, "Dimensions of the Self," p. 179.

8. Mary Douglas, *Natural Symbols* (New York: Pantheon Books, 1970), p. x.

9. Nancy Tatom Ammerman, *Bible Believers: Fundamentalists in the Modern World* (New Brunswick, N.J.: Rutgers University Press, 1987).

10. Mary Newgeon Hawkes, *The Church as Nurturing Faith Community: A Study in One Congregation* (Ed.D. diss., Columbia University, 1983), pp. 173–174.

11. Ibid., pp. 159–168.

12. Alan Richardson, *History Sacred and Profane* (London: SCM Press, 1964), pp. 20–24.

13. Ibid., p. 26.

14. Abraham H. Maslow, *Religions, Values, and Peak-Experiences* (Columbus, Ohio: Ohio State University Press, 1964), pp. 59–68.

15. Bercovitch, *Puritan Origins,* p. 57.

16. Ibid., p. 93.

17. "Infiltration Case Heard by Appeals Court," *Presbyterian Outlook,* August 17–31, 1987, p. 3.

18. Nelson, *Where Faith Begins,* pp. 33–34. See also Paul D. Hanson, *The People Called: The Growth of Community in the Bible* (San Francisco: Harper & Row, 1986), pp. 1–5, 537–539.

19. James A. Sanders, "The Bible as Canon," *Christian Century,* December 2, 1981, p. 1252.

20. James A. Sanders, *Canon and Community* (Philadelphia: Fortress Press, 1984), p. 33.

21. Walter Brueggemann, *The Creative Word* (Philadelphia: Fortress Press, 1982). See p. 3 where he affirms, "Canon is a clue to education, both as substance and as a process."

22. Sanders, "The Bible as Canon," p. 1252.

23. Hanson, *The People Called,* pp. 467–518.

24. Ibid., p. 252.

25. James T. Borhek and Richard F. Curtis, *A Sociology of Belief* (New York: John Wiley & Sons, 1975), pp. 111–156.

26. James M. Gustafson, after an interpretation of our modern situation, has come to the conclusion that we must develop an ethic from God's perspective. See his *Ethics from a Theocentric Perspective* (Chicago: University of Chicago Press,

1981), vol. 1, pp. 87–113. However, as Gustafson starts his analysis from God's perspective, he gives human experience first priority. See pp. 115–129.

27. Although these three points are written from my own viewpoint I was encouraged by reading Sanders, *Canon and Community*, pp. 53–56. See also his *God Has a Story Too* (Philadelphia: Fortress Press, 1979), pp. 1–27.

Readers interested in a detailed analysis of how Hebrew writers used but greatly changed the myths that were common knowledge in their day should consult Foster R. McCurley, *Ancient Myths and Biblical Faith* (Philadelphia: Fortress Press, 1983).

Chapter 4: Why Is Experience Necessary?

1. H. H. Gerth and C. Wright Mills, eds., *From Max Weber: Essays in Sociology* (New York: Oxford University Press, 1958), p. 250.

2. Thomas F. O'Dea, *The Sociology of Religion* (Englewood Cliffs, N.J.: Prentice-Hall, 1966), pp. 90–97.

3. Robert M. Grant, *The Apostolic Fathers*, vol. 4 (Camden, N.J.: Thomas Nelson & Sons, 1966), pp. 72–73.

4. Mircea Eliade, *Patterns in Comparative Religion* (New York: Sheed & Ward, 1958), pp. 444–445.

5. Raimundo Panikkar, "Preface," in Teresa of Avila, *The Interior Castle*, trans. Kieran Kavanaugh and Otilio Rodriguez (New York: Paulist Press, 1979), p. xvii.

6. C. Ellis Nelson, "Theological Foundations for Religious Nurture," in *Changing Patterns of Religious Education*, ed. Marvin J. Taylor (Nashville: Abingdon Press, 1984), pp. 10–22.

7. George Tyrrell, *Through Scylla and Charybdis* (London: Longmans, Green & Co., 1907), p. 105.

8. J. Kenneth Kuntz, *The Self-Revelation of God* (Philadelphia: Westminster Press, 1967), p. 17.

9. Abraham H. Maslow, "Some Educational Implications of the Humanistic Psychologies," *Harvard Educational Review* 38(4):685 (Fall 1968). See also *Toward a Psychology of Being*, 2nd ed. (New York: Van Nostrand Reinhold Co., 1982).

10. Kuntz, *Self-Revelation of God*, pp. 44–45.

Chapter 5: The Situation

1. C. Ellis Nelson, "Toward Better Methods of Communicating the Christian Faith," in *The Future Course of Christian Adult Education*, ed. Lawrence C. Little (Pittsburgh: University of Pittsburgh Press, 1959), pp. 202–218.

2. J. Kenneth Kuntz, *The Self-Revelation of God* (Philadelphia: Westminster Press, 1967), pp. 138–154.

3. Ibid., pp. 149–152.

4. Dietmar Mieth, "What Is Experience?" in *Revelation and Experience*, ed. Edward Schillebeeckx and Bas van Iersel (New York: Seabury Press, 1979), p. 40. This is an excellent treatment of experience. I have used ideas from it in several places in this chapter.

5. George H. Mead, *On Social Psychology*, ed. Anselm Strauss, rev. ed. (Chicago: University of Chicago Press, 1956), pp. 209–228. A good overview of perception as it relates to maturity will be found in Charles C. L. Kao, *Psychological and Religious Development: Maturity and Maturation* (Washington, D.C.: University Press of America, 1981), pp. 261–292.

6. Search Institute, *Early Adolescents and Their Parents* (Minneapolis: Search Institute, 1984), pp. 20, 43.

7. T. W. Adorno, *The Authoritarian Personality* (New York: Harper & Brothers, 1950).

8. Paulo Freire, *Pedagogy of the Oppressed*, trans. Myra Bergman Ramos (New York: Herder & Herder, 1970), pp. 75–118.

9. William H. Willimon, "Growing Up Christian in Greenville," *Christian Century*, June 4–11, 1980, pp. 638–639.

10. James E. Loder, *The Transforming Moment* (San Francisco: Harper & Row, 1981), pp. 1–27.

11. Jürgen Moltmann, *Experiences of God* (Philadelphia: Fortress Press, 1980), p. 7.

12. Ibid., pp. 7–9.

13. Ibid., p. 55.

14. Hugh T. Kerr and John M. Mulder, eds., *Conversions* (Grand Rapids: Wm. B. Eerdmans Publishing Co., 1983), p. 208.

Chapter 6: The Person

1. Edward Robinson, *The Original Vision* (New York: Seabury Press, 1983).

2. Paul Minear, *Eyes of Faith* (Philadelphia: Westminster Press, 1946), p. 19. See also Karl Barth, "The Word of God and Experience," in *Church Dogmatics* (Edinburgh: T. & T. Clark, 1936) I/1 226–260. For example, on p. 227: "Experience of the Word of God, of course, takes place always in an act of human self-determination."

3. This view and the basic idea that follows are from the research of Ana-Maria Rizzuto, M.D. She originally became interested in this matter during her psychiatric treatment of a priest who had been unable to resolve the conflict between his infantile images of God and the God of his mature mind. After fifteen years of study and research at Boston State Hospital she published her findings in *The Birth of the Living God* (Chicago: University of Chicago Press, 1979). Rizzuto summarized her work in "The Psychological Foundations of Belief in God," in *Toward Moral and Religious Maturity*, ed. James W. Fowler and Antoine Vergote (Morristown, N.J.: Silver Burdett Co., 1980), pp. 115–135.

4. I have provided a rather commonsense description of the process of shaping an image of God. If the reader is interested in a theory that unites psychological and social data from a human perspective, I suggest Erik H. Erikson's essay reviewing his life work. See his "Elements of a Psychoanalytic Theory of Psychosocial Development" in *The Course of Life: Psychoanalytic Contributions Toward Understanding Personality Development*, ed. S. I. Greenspan and G. H. Pollock (Adelphi, Md.: Mental Health Study Center, Division of Mental Health Service Programs, National Institute of Mental Health, U.S. Government Printing Office, 1980–1981), vol. 1: *Infancy and Early Childhood*, pp. 11–59.

Chapter 7: The Mission

1. Coretta Scott King, *My Life with Martin Luther King, Jr.* (New York: Avon Books, 1969), p. 123.
2. Quoted in Thomas Lickona, "Critical Issues in the Study of Moral Development and Behavior," in *Moral Development and Behavior*, ed. Thomas Lickona (New York: Holt, Rinehart & Winston, 1976), p. 12.
3. John Bright, *The Kingdom of God* (Nashville: Abingdon Press, 1953).
4. Richard R. Niebuhr, *Experiential Religion* (New York: Harper & Row, 1972), pp. 119–124.
5. Teresa of Avila, *The Interior Castle*, trans. Kieran Kavanaugh and Otilio Rodriguez (New York: Paulist Press, 1979), p. 61.
6. Ibid., p. 70.
7. Ibid., pp. 109–111.
8. Ibid., p. 83.
9. Ibid., p. 84.
10. Ibid., p. 190.
11. Ibid., p. 70.
12. Ibid., p. 155.
13. Ibid., p. 165.
14. Ibid., p. 189.

Chapter 8: The Residue of Experience

1. James E. Loder, *The Transforming Moment* (San Francisco: Harper & Row, 1981), pp. 1–6.
2. James M. Gustafson, *Ethics from a Theocentric Perspective* (Chicago: University of Chicago Press, 1981), pp. 19–20.
3. Paul Tillich, *Systematic Theology* (Chicago: University of Chicago Press, 1963), vol. 3, pp. 130–131, 134.
4. Erik H. Erikson, "Identity and the Life Cycle," *Psychological Issues*, vol. 1, no. 1 (New York: International Universities Press, 1959), pp. 55–61. See also his *Identity: Youth and Crisis* (New York: W. W. Norton & Co., 1968), p. 97.
5. Erikson, *Identity: Youth and Crisis*, p. 106.
6. Wilfred Cantwell Smith, *Faith and Belief* (Princeton, N.J.: Princeton University Press, 1979), p. 6.
7. There are few, if any, careful studies of how faith operates in a person's life over a period of years. However, there are some studies of "ordinary people" facing ordinary life situations over a long time span; see Robert W. White, *Lives in Progress* (New York: Dryden Press, 1952). For an intense study of a small group of adolescents at two different time periods, see Percival M. Symonds's *Adolescent Fantasy* (New York: Columbia University Press, 1949) and his *From Adolescent to Adult* (New York: Columbia University Press, 1961).

There are many accounts of experiences that resulted in faith on the part of individuals. For conversion experiences see Hugh T. Kerr and John M. Mulder, eds., *Conversions* (Grand Rapids: Wm. B. Eerdmans Publishing Co., 1983). For examples of how faith functions in the personal life of theologians see Jürgen Moltmann, *Experiences of God* (Philadelphia: Fortress Press, 1980) and Dorothee Sölle, *Death by Bread Alone* (Philadelphia: Fortress Press, 1978).

8. James Barr, *The Semantics of Biblical Language* (London: Oxford University Press, 1961), pp. 161–205.

9. E. C. Blackman, "Faith, Faithfulness," in *The Interpreter's Dictionary of the Bible*, vol. 2 (New York: Abingdon Press, 1962), p. 227.

10. E. A. Speiser, *Genesis* (Garden City, N.Y.: Doubleday & Co., 1964), p. 112.

11. Rudolf Bultmann and Artur Weiser, *Faith*, trans. Dorothea M. Barton (London: Adam & Charles Black, 1961), p. 2.

12. Walther Eichrodt, *Theology of the Old Testament*, vol. 2 (Philadelphia: Westminster Press, 1967), pp. 268–315. See also Gerhard von Rad, *Wisdom in Israel* (Nashville: Abingdon Press, 1972), p. 66.

13. The theme of faith-doubt-disobedience in the Abraham/Sarah story is repeated in a special way in the Zechariah/Elizabeth story, which Luke used to begin his account of Jesus. There are many parallels and also some differences in these stories. Abraham was the one who believed in the promise of a son, while Sarah laughed. In contrast, Elizabeth believed her prayer for a son would be answered, but Zechariah did not. Their son John ("God is gracious") baptized Jesus and later certified him as the Messiah (see Luke 1; 3:2–21; 7:18–23).

14. R. B. Y. Scott, "Isaiah," *The Interpreter's Bible*, vol. 5 (New York: Abingdon Press, 1956), p. 216.

15. Ibid., p. 226.

16. Hans-Jürgen Hermisson and Eduard Lohse, *Faith*, trans. Douglas Stott (Nashville: Abingdon Press, 1981). This section and the interpretation of the Abraham story reflect my reading of this book. The entire book is helpful and should be carefully studied by anyone interested in this topic.

17. Gerhard Ebeling, *Word and Faith* (Philadelphia: Fortress Press, 1960), pp. 208–209.

18. Hermisson and Lohse, *Faith*, p. 123.

19. Blackman, "Faith, Faithfulness," pp. 233–234.

20. James W. Fowler's *Stages of Faith* (San Francisco: Harper & Row, 1981), gives a developmental view of faith. Soon after his book was published, I was asked to write a critique to use in a consultation with Fowler. It was later published under the title "Does Faith Develop?" in *The Living Light* 19(2):162–173 (Summer 1982). Since then, Gabriel Moran has published *Religious Education Development* (Minneapolis: Winston Press, 1983). Moran deals with the idea of development as well as with Fowler's use of that notion.

A good critique of the idea of faith development was edited by Craig Dykstra and Sharon Parks, *Faith Development and Fowler* (Birmingham, Ala.: Religious Education Press, 1986).

There are difficulties with structural developmental psychology as applied to the moral realm by Lawrence Kohlberg. Since Fowler patterned his system on Kohlberg's, evaluations of Kohlberg's writings will help a person understand the issues. From a Christian perspective, see Craig Dykstra, *Vision and Character* (New York: Paulist Press, 1981). From a psychological and social perspective, see C. M. Beck, B. S. Crittenden, and E. V. Sullivan, eds., *Moral Education* (Toronto: University of Toronto Press, 1971), and Brenda Munsey, ed., *Moral Development, Moral Education, and Kohlberg* (Birmingham, Ala.: Religious Education Press, 1980). See also Donald M. Joy, ed., *Moral Development Foundations* (Nashville: Abingdon Press, 1983). Barry Chazan, in his book *Contemporary Approaches to Moral Education* (New York: Teachers College Press, 1985), provides an excellent overview of five major theories of moral education, including Kohlberg's cognitive-developmental.

Chapter 9: Life Together

1. Dorothy C. Bass, Benton Johnson, and Wade Clark Roof, *Mainstream Protestantism in the Twentieth Century: Its Problems and Prospects* (Louisville, Ky.: Council on Theological Education, 1987). See also Robert S. Michaelsen and Wade Clark Roof, *Liberal Protestantism* (New York: Pilgrim Press, 1986).

2. Wayne A. Meeks, *The Moral World of the First Christians* (Philadelphia: Westminster Press, 1986), pp. 12, 130. In *The First Urban Christians* (New Haven, Conn.: Yale University Press, 1983), Meeks gives a detailed description of the factors that influenced the formulation of the first congregations and the necessity of congregations as the place where converts learned to live their faith in Jesus Christ (see pp. 74–110).

3. Don S. Browning, in *The Moral Context of Pastoral Care* (Philadelphia: Westminster Press, 1976), discusses the role of context in pastoral care. Although his interest in this book is in the moral aspect of care, he notes that "pastoral care is a subsystem of the church" (p. 19).

William H. Willimon, in *Worship as Pastoral Care* (Nashville: Abingdon Press, 1979), shows how the congregation heals as it worships; and Donald Capps, in *Pastoral Counseling and Preaching: A Quest for an Integrated Ministry* (Philadelphia: Westminster Press, 1980), describes the way people may be helped by the sermon in the context of congregational life.

4. Jackson W. Carroll, "The Congregation as Chameleon: How the Present Interprets the Past," in *Congregations: Their Power to Form and Transform*, ed. C. Ellis Nelson (Atlanta: John Knox Press, 1988), pp. 43–69. Denham Grierson, in his *Transforming a People of God* (Melbourne: Joint Board of Christian Education of Australia and New Zealand, 1984), proposes a practical way to judge the needs and interests of a congregation.

5. See the case study edited by Nelle Slater and referred to in note 3, chapter 1, and the study by Nancy Ammerman and Mary Hawkes referred to in notes 9 and 10–11, chapter 3. A brief case is presented in *Building Effective Ministry*, ed. Carl S. Dudley (San Francisco: Harper & Row, 1983). One of the most helpful studies of how people interact in a congregation is Samuel Heilmann's *Synagogue Life* (Chicago: University of Chicago Press, 1976). M. D. Williams's *Community in a Black Pentecostal Church* (Pittsburgh: University of Pittsburgh Press, 1974) is an excellent study of that congregation. For a study of how congregations change under different pastors see R. Stephen Warner, *New Wine, Old Wineskins* (Berkeley, Calif.: University of California Press, 1988).

6. Lyle Schaller reflects the wisdom of ministers and careful observers of congregations in his *Looking in the Mirror* (Nashville: Abingdon Press, 1984).

7. David A. Roozen, William McKinney, and Jackson W. Carroll, *Varieties of Religious Presence* (New York: Pilgrim Press, 1984), pp. 32–36.

8. Readers interested in helping a congregation identify itself or shape its mission should consult Jackson W. Carroll, Carl S. Dudley, and William McKinney, *Handbook for Congregational Studies* (Nashville: Abingdon Press, 1986).

9. Carl S. Dudley, "Using Church Images for Commitment, Conflict, and Renewal," in *Congregations*, ed. Nelson, pp. 89–114.

10. James F. Hopewell, *Congregation: Stories and Structures*, ed. Barbara G. Wheeler (Philadelphia: Fortress Press, 1987).

11. Carl S. Dudley and Earle Hilgert have written an excellent treatment of conflict: *New Testament Tensions and the Contemporary Church* (Philadelphia: Fortress Press, 1987). Chapter 4, "Using Conflict Constructively," explores the theme of this section in detail, whereas I have limited this discussion to education.

Donald E. Bossart's *Creative Conflict in Religious Education and Church Administration* (Birmingham, Ala.: Religious Education Press, 1980) considers the sociology, psychology, and theology of conflict. Bossart then discusses the creative role of conflict in church education and administration. This is a very good treatment of conflict in all aspects of congregational life.

12. Lewis A. Coser, *The Functions of Social Conflict* (Glencoe, Ill.: Free Press, 1956), p. 74.

13. Ibid., p. 87.

14. Ibid., p. 111.

15. John H. Leith, ed., *Creeds of the Churches* (Richmond: John Knox Press, 1973), p. 2.

16. Ibid., p. 3.

17. Coser, *Functions*, p. 114.

18. Ibid., pp. 39–48.

19. Ibid., pp. 133–137, 139–149.

20. H. Richard Niebuhr, *Christ and Culture* (New York: Harper & Brothers, 1951), pp. 1–44.

21. Robert L. Browning, "Belonging: A Sacramental Approach to Inclusion and Depth of Commitment," in *Congregations*, ed. Nelson, pp. 166–192.

22. Mary Elizabeth Moore, "Meeting in the Silence: Meditation as the Center of Congregational Life," in *Congregations*, ed. Nelson, pp. 141–165.

23. This is a good place to pay tribute to my friend and colleague John H. Westerhoff. With Gwen Kennedy Neville he wrote an important book on religious education in which the cultural setting is taken seriously: *Generation to Generation* (Philadelphia: Pilgrim Press, 1974). This was followed by a number of books in which the "socialization model" of Christian nurture was explored in terms of the nurture of children and the importance of worship for faith development. More recently, in *Building God's People in a Materialistic Society* (New York: Seabury Press, 1983) and *Living the Faith Community* (Minneapolis: Winston Press, 1985), Westerhoff has been concerned to show how the community of faith should develop a distinct form of life and mediate that life-style through "catechesis."

24. Robert A. Dahl, *A Preface to Democratic Theory* (Chicago: University of Chicago Press, 1956), p. 132.

Chapter 10: Strategy for Faith Maturation

1. Lewis J. Sherrill, *The Rise of Christian Education* (New York: Macmillan Co., 1944), pp. 52–64.

2. Ian A. Muirhead, *Education in the New Testament* (New York: Association Press, 1965), pp. 49–64.

3. John H. Westerhoff III and O. C. Edwards, Jr., *A Faithful Church* (Wilton, Conn.: Morehouse-Barlow Co., 1981), p. 1.

4. See Michael Warren, *Sourcebook for Modern Catechetics* (Winona, Minn.: Saint Mary's Press, 1983), for a Catholic conception of catechesis in different historical periods and various countries. Protestants would be greatly enriched if they would study this book and absorb the wisdom the Roman Catholic Church has accumulated through the centuries about receiving and nurturing people in the faith.

5. Martin E. Marty, *Righteous Empire* (New York: Dial Press, 1970).

6. Quoted in Robert T. Handy, *A Christian America* (New York: Oxford University Press, 1971), p. 27.

7. Quoted in William Bean Kennedy, *The Shaping of Protestant Education* (New York: Association Press, 1966), p. 21.

8. Ibid., pp. 71–72.

9. Lewis J. Sherrill, *Presbyterian Parochial Schools, 1846–1870* (New Haven, Conn.: Yale University Press, 1932).

10. Quoted in Winthrop S. Hudson, *Religion in America*, 2nd ed. (New York: Charles Scribner's Sons, 1965), p. 130.

11. John H. Westerhoff, *McGuffey and His Readers* (Nashville: Abingdon Press, 1978), p. 19.

12. Robert Wood Lynn, "Civil Catechetics in Mid-Victorian America: Some Notes About American Civil Religion, Past and Present," *Religious Education*, Jan.–Feb. 1973, pp. 5–27.

13. Kennedy, *The Shaping of Protestant Education*, p. 30.

14. Westerhoff, *McGuffey and His Readers*, p. 15.

15. Hudson, *Religion in America*, p. 135.

16. Ibid., pp. 129–130.

17. Donald G. Tewksbury, *The Founding of American Colleges and Universities Before the Civil War* (New York: Teachers College, Columbia University, 1932), p. 69.

18. Kennedy, *The Shaping of Protestant Education*, p. 15.

19. Tewksbury, *Founding*, p. 81.

20. Ibid., p. 85.

21. Sidney E. Mead, "The Rise of the Evangelical Conception of the Ministry in America: 1607–1850," in *The Ministry in Historical Perspectives*, ed. H. Richard Niebuhr and Daniel D. Williams (New York: Harper & Brothers, 1956), pp. 234–235.

22. Rudy Ray Seward, *The American Family* (Beverly Hills, Calif.: Sage Publications, 1978), p. 119.

23. Ibid., pp. 176–177.

24. Horace Bushnell, *Christian Nurture* (New Haven, Conn.: Yale University Press, 1947).

25. Ibid., pp. 301–314.

26. Robert W. Lynn, "The Public Schools and the Study of Religion," in *An Introduction to Christian Education*, ed. Marvin J. Taylor (Nashville: Abingdon Press, 1966), pp. 336–339.

27. Walter Scott Athearn, *Religious Education and American Democracy* (Boston: Pilgrim Press, 1917), p. 113.

28. Robert W. Lynn, *Protestant Strategies in Education* (New York: Association Press, 1964), p. 49.

29. Robert W. Lynn and Elliott Wright, *The Big Little School* (New York: Harper & Row, 1971), pp. 45–47.

30. Janet F. Fishburn, "Leading: Paideia in a New Key," in *Congregations: Their Power to Form and Transform*, ed. C. Ellis Nelson (Atlanta: John Knox Press, 1988), pp. 197–204.

31. Handy, *A Christian America*, pp. 184–225.

32. Wade Clark Roof and William McKinney, *American Mainline Religion* (New Brunswick, N.J.: Rutgers University Press, 1986), pp. 33–39.

33. Phillip E. Hammond, "The Extravasation of the Sacred and the Crisis in Liberal Protestantism," in *Liberal Protestantism*, ed. Robert S. Michaelsen and Wade Clark Roof (New York: Pilgrim Press, 1986), p. 56.

Chapter 11: Congregational Edification

1. The most influential set of Christian education goals in the twentieth century was formulated by Paul H. Vieth in *Objectives in Religious Education* (New York: Harper & Brothers, 1930). His work in codifying the objectives of religious education became the standard for most mainstream denominations. The individualism of these goals is shown in the wording. Each objective and subobjective is aimed at "growing persons." Objective Number 6, "To develop in growing persons the ability and disposition to participate in the organized society of Christians—the church," implies that the individual rather than the congregation is the goal of education (see pp. 80–88).

D. Campbell Wyckoff has an excellent critique of objectives in *Theory and Design of the Christian Education Curriculum* (Philadelphia: Westminster Press, 1961), pp. 56–79. Wyckoff sorts out the differences between goals for instruction of individuals and the purpose of the church.

The best-known recent effort to describe faith development in stages is James W. Fowler's *Stages of Faith* (San Francisco: Harper & Row, 1981). Since his study was based on individuals, Fowler had no reason to include the role of congregations in faith development.

2. C. Ellis Nelson, ed., *Congregations: Their Power to Form and Transform* (Atlanta: John Knox Press, 1988).

3. Probably the best recent book to help a congregation understand itself is *Handbook for Congregational Studies*, ed. Jackson W. Carroll, Carl S. Dudley, and William McKinney (Nashville: Abingdon Press, 1986). This is not a simple how-to-do-it book. Designed to help congregations understand styles of life together, it suggests ways leaders may encourage congregations to live up to their potential.

4. Sara Little, *Learning Together in the Christian Fellowship* (Richmond: John Knox Press, 1956).

5. Teaching religion within a congregation rather than a secular school requires a special understanding of the teaching task. Here are some excellent books to help ministers and others explore the possibilities: Sara Little, *To Set One's Heart* (Atlanta: John Knox Press, 1983); Charles Foster, *Teaching in the Community of Faith* (Nashville: Abingdon Press, 1982); and Maria Harris, *Teaching and Religious Imagination* (San Francisco: Harper & Row, 1987).

6. Paulo Freire, *Pedagogy of the Oppressed* (New York: Herder & Herder, 1970), pp. 85–118.

7. George A. Lindbeck, in *The Nature of Doctrine* (Philadelphia: Westminster Press, 1984), is concerned about the place of theology in a postliberal age. According to Lindbeck, religion is like a language, and theology is the set of rules by which a religious social group lives. This position, absolutizing the life-style or culture of a community of believers, is more than I am willing to accept. I see the congregation as a place where two processes are going on simultaneously: one process is a critique of the beliefs that members bring to the congregation; the other is the development and testing of beliefs in the light of what we know about God from the Bible and theology.

Lindbeck's judgment, that local communities of believers are the places where religion is made meaningful, is similar to what I am proposing in this chapter. Lindbeck uses the term "sociological sectarianism" to describe religious groups that have drawn aside from culture to form a counterculture (pp. 78, 127). This is necessary because "Western culture is now at an intermediate stage . . . where socialization is ineffective, catechesis impossible, and translation a tempting alternative" (p. 133).

Lindbeck's "inconclusive" conclusion is that theology should resist the temptation to make faith intelligible: "It should instead prepare for a future when continuing dechristianization will make greater Christian authenticity communally possible" (p. 134). I accept this statement more as a critical comment on our superficial Christianity or civic religion than as advice for ministers. The practical suggestions in this chapter are for ministers and serious-minded lay leaders who want to counteract "the acids of modernity" by building a faithful congregation.

8. C. A. Pierce, *Conscience in the New Testament* (Chicago: Alec R. Allenson, 1955), pp. 55, 60–65.

9. Paul Lehmann, *Ethics in a Christian Context* (New York: Harper & Row, 1963), p. 353.

10. C. Ellis Nelson, *Don't Let Your Conscience Be Your Guide* (New York: Paulist Press, 1978), pp. 29–51.

11. Wayne A. Meeks, *The First Urban Christians* (New Haven, Conn.: Yale University Press, 1983), p. 145.

12. Ibid., p. 147.

13. David Braybrooke and Charles E. Lindblom, *A Strategy of Decision* (New York: Free Press, 1963), pp. 61–79.

14. Theological seminaries are more difficult to change than are congregations, but I think the method is the same. See C. Ellis Nelson, *Using Evaluation in Theological Education* (Nashville: Discipleship Resources, 1975), pp. 43–71.

15. Bruce Joyce and Marsha Weill, *Models of Teaching* (Englewood Cliffs, N.J.: Prentice-Hall, 1972), pp. 3–5.

16. Ibid., pp. 5–26.

17. E. Mansell Pattison, a minister and professor of psychiatry, in his *Pastor and Parish: A Systems Approach* (Philadelphia: Fortress Press, 1977), describes the difference between psychotherapy groups and what he calls "natural community groups," of which congregations are an example (see pp. 15–16). This book will be helpful to anyone who wants to understand how a congregation is an agency of education.

18. James I. H. McDonald, *Kerygma and Didache* (Cambridge: Cambridge University Press, 1980), pp. 4–7

19. Ibid., p. 126.

Index
of Names and Topics

Index
of Scripture Passages